THE ALMS TRADE

Charities, Past, Present and Future

Ian Williams

UNWIN

HYMAN

LONDON SYDNEY WELLINGTON

First published in Great Britain by the Trade Division of
Unwin Hyman Limited, 1989

UNWIN HYMAN LIMITED
15–17 Broadwick Street
London W1V 1FP

Allen & Unwin Australia Pty Ltd
8 Napier Street, North Sydney, NSW 2060, Australia

Allen & Unwin New Zealand Pty Ltd with the Port Nicholson Press
Compusales Building, 75 Ghuznee Street, Wellington, New Zealand.

British Library Cataloguing in Publication Data
Williams, Ian
   The alms trade: Charities, Past, Present
and Future
1. Great Britain. Society. Role of charities
I. Title
361.7′632′0941
ISBN 0–04–440435–2

Typeset in 10 on 12 point Garamond by Columns of Reading
and printed in Great Britain by Billing & Sons Ltd, Worcester

Contents

To the Poor
who always deserve more

Acknowledgements

My thanks go first to Nadia Hijab without whom it would have been impossible, instead of just very difficult, to complete the work in time. I should like to thank the following people who are some of the many who have given their time and energy to assist me, even when they knew they were unlikely to agree with the conclusions: John Rentoul, Edward Murphy, Ushar Prasha, Richard Perceval, Perri 6, Marilyn Turner, Peter Hildrew, Luke FitzHerbert, Caroline Barker, David Wickert, Sheila McKechnie, Robin Guthrie, Sheena Smith, Paddy Feeny, Alan Martin, Fiona MacFarlane, David Fishel, John Posnett, Ben Whitaker, Roger Smith, Paul Anderson, Barbara Smoker, Nicholas Walter, Derrick Knight, Hugh Sampson, Alison Whyte, Chris Mowles, Margaret Simey, Frs John Methuen and Philip Sumner, Mike McCrink, Bob Russell, Nick Warren, Bert Clough, Peter Archer MP, Nick Baring and Barry Till. Special thanks are due to Vice-Chancellor Graeme Davies of Liverpool University for his determined but unavailing attempts to secure cooperation from the university library's hierarchy.

I should also like to acknowledge the following organisations which have assisted with information and advice: the Charity Commission; the press offices of the Inland Revenue; the Home Office; the DoH and DSS; Adam Smith Institute; ISIS; LCVS; NCVO; NACAB; Labour Party; BUPA; Nuffield Hospitals; Christian Aid; Oxfam; War on Want; Western Goals; SHELTER; CPAG; Rationalist Press Association; CAF; Directory for Social Change; the Thomas Coram Foundation; the Baring Foundation; the Wellcome Trust; the Nuffield Foundation; and the staff of Liverpool University Law Library and Liverpool Central Library.

How Long Is a Tangle of String?

In 1988, Charities had a turnover of around £15 billion and employed some 200,000 people. They took the time and money of millions more on a voluntary basis. The charitable sector formed and still affects our education, health and social services, and permeates much of the structure of our society. Charities operate schools educating half a million children. They run hospitals here and aid missions abroad. They put roofs over the heads of thousands. As theatres, art galleries and orchestras, they put sublime (and, legally, educational) thoughts into the heads of millions more. They have campaigned on behalf of slaves, children and animals, and also to keep the Sabbath holy. In short, the charitable sector has a vast social and financial significance which is often ignored by politicians and social scientists. Even social historians who have dwelt at length on the Poor Law have tended to ignore the charity law which paralleled it.

Perhaps one explanation for this reticence is that statistics for what is called the voluntary sector are mostly questionable guestimates; all that can be said with accuracy is that numbers involved are large. Over 160,000 charities are registered with the Charity Commission but many of them are defunct, their only existence a terse entry in a Civil Service ring-binder. On the other hand, many more are not registered because they are too small or because they are legally exempted, like Eton, the universities and churches.

The statistics are not the only questionable aspect of charities. Lawyers and the public have widely differing views of charity. The legal definition has been built up by almost four centuries of judicial decisions which have often been tendentious and confused. Some modern jurists now claim to be able to perceive guiding principles. Those less committed to the principle of judicial omniscience admit that the law is a tangled web of *ad hoc* precedents. That is why the Royal Society for the Prevention of

1

Cruelty to Animals is a charity but Amnesty International is not; why Eton College is charitable and the National Council for Civil Liberties is not.

The lay use of the word also has an ambivalence of its own. In the *Oxford English Dictionary*, the Victorian entries under 'charity' roll in a sanctimonious tide of good will and good works. 'God's love to man', is followed by man's love of God and his neighbour, and the Christian love of our fellow men. Towards the end, in the list of phrases using the word, is just one little hint of dissent, a look at the concept from the viewpoint of the recipient: *'cold as charity*, referring to the perfunctory unfeeling manner in which acts of charity are often done, and the public charities administered'.

That Victorian ambiguity survives. Most people would think that charity is a 'Good Thing'. Against that general approval is a residual worry, almost a folk memory, of the times when it implied humiliation and disenfranchisement, a surrender of privacy to social superiors to check on behaviour and moral probity.

Epitomising those Victorian values when

> The organised charity, scrimped and iced
> In the name of a cautious statistical Christ
> > > John Boyle O'Reilly

was the Charity Organisation Society whose Pharisaical approach proved with maps and diagrams that giving money to the poor was the *cause* of pauperism.

The Poor Law Lives

Such attitudes were not confined to Victorian days, nor to charities. It often seems that the State's welfare services have retained a whiff of the workhouse in the way they are delivered. Successive governments have striven to make welfare benefits less eligible than any other form of existence, while the years since the establishment of the Welfare State have seen a steady erosion of National Insurance entitlements in favour of more discretionary supplementary forms of benefit. The consistent leniency shown to tax evasion in comparison with social security fraud demonstrates that the issue is *moral* rather than financial.

However, the Victorians saw the birth of a new concept, combining the intelligence of the scientist with the humanity of the

Samaritan; charity to change the world. In 1904, Joseph Rowntree summarised his experience of the old and the new trends: 'I feel that much of current philanthropic effort is directed to remedying the more superficial manifestations of weakness or evil, while little thought or effort is directed to search out their underlying causes' (quoted Waddilove, 1983).

Let alone, it might be added, to remedy those underlying causes. Rowntree wrote from a dissenting Quaker background at the turn of the century when the Sea of Faith was receding from its Victorian high tide. In earlier days, social and moral failure were easily and evangelically equated. The roots of poverty for them were in the moral depravity of the poor rather than in the inequalities of the economic system. For many charities, redemption of the soul brought along the body as an eleemosynary hitch-hiker.

Although that attitude is still audible in speeches by Cabinet ministers, many modern charities have tried to redeem their beneficiaries in a social and political rather than a theological sense. They have tried not to inflict a preconceived view on passive, or even resisting, beneficiaries, but rather to enable clients to make their own wishes known. Robin Guthrie, the Chief Charity Commissioner, has pointed out that to brandish dependence in front of donors can 'easily become negative, a condescension, a means of keeping suffering, and the sufferers, in their place, which is not in our lives, and of salving conscience without understanding or commitment. There have been programmes which the disabled in this country have found degrading, and unhelpful to their cause; frankly not worth any money' (Wynford Vaughan Thomas Memorial Lecture, 5 December 1989).

Guthrie's client-centred approach has been in the ascendant, even though very recently a writer could reprimand a social worker for 'forgetting that charity had benefits for the benevolent, as well as the beneficiary' (Prochaska, 1988, p. 81). This indicates the atavistic appeal of the Lady Bountiful syndrome which is reflected in the legal principle that charity depends upon bounty, not bargain; that is, that beneficiaries must depend on the caprice of the donor, not on contractual arrangements over which they might have some power.

In this brief overview of a wide and complex subject, I hope to demonstrate that the legal precedents and social attitudes surrounding charity are more than just eccentric historical accretions; that the seeming randomness does have a pattern. The shape which emerges is of a humane concept consistently distorted to fit particular social needs as perceived from time to time by Britain's remarkably tenacious Establishment. Legal fossilisation embalmed Victorian values in charity law when the rest of society had thought them deservedly buried.

The policies of Margaret Thatcher's government, far from sweeping away that vestigial Victorianism, now seem set to revive it, and because of the consensual approach to charity law, the revival is unlikely to be vigorously challenged. Charities themselves are precluded by law from serious political activity, and by expediency from challenging legal restrictions on charitable activity.

As for the Labour Party, it is only now recovering from post-war decades of identification with state-based solutions which saw volunteers as premature conscripts. It still neglects the voluntary sector, although the 1989 policy reviews showed promising signs of a change of direction.

This book is intentionally critical and provocative, in a manner which may appear negative to some readers. However, although it looks closely at the unsatisfactory aspects, its main purpose is to focus attention on the neglected voluntary sector and to awaken interest in the opportunities presented by the better models within it.

It should be remembered that the law dealt with here applies in England and Wales, not in Scotland or Northern Ireland. However, it does apply for tax purposes across the United Kingdom, as do the social relations which gave rise to the law. Those relations are often steeped in history, and no more so than in relation to charity where century-old statutes and precedents still hold force (readers who agree with Henry Ford that history is bunk had better stop here). However, this book looks at history in order to understand the present, in the hope that history will not repeat itself as the tragicomedy threatened by some politicians' nostalgia for past Golden Ages. Historical assay reveals their gilding to be fool's gold. Present social practice shows their creations to be base metal.

1

Piety and Poverty

The present legal position of charities depends on one of the most obscure disciplines of English law, with concepts and precedents rooted in feudal and ecclesiastical customs and practices. In this chapter, we shall examine the historical development of charities and demonstrate the extent to which the modern concept carries within it relics of earlier social philosophy.

Just how early, is shown by the references in William Langland's *Piers Plowman* which, written in the fourteenth century, appears to have echoed already well-established precepts of philanthropic behaviour. These anticipate the list of good causes in the preamble to the 1601 Statute of Uses by which charities are still defined. Langland's poem has Truth enjoining rich merchants to obtain remission of sins and a happy death by giving their wealth,

> And therewith repair hospitals
> help sick people
> mend bad roads
> build up bridges that had been broken down
> help maidens to marry or make them nuns
> find food for prisoners and poor people
> put scholars to school or to some other craft
> help religious orders and
> ameliorate rents or taxes

In medieval times, charity was generally administered by the Church. As such it was not, as it is sometimes regarded now, part of the private sector but an integral part of the overall public apparatus of the State.

Church as State

One of the oldest surviving charities (Whitaker, 1979) is Week's charity, originally set up in the fifteenth century to provide faggots for burning heretics. It exemplifies the, for some, uncomfortably close relationship between Church and State. In a more humanitarian mode, medieval wills contained bequests to the poor, to the maimed and the suffering; and for the upkeep and renewal of hospitals, bridges, roads and dykes. Not surprisingly, since the ecclesiastical courts had control over wills and testaments, such benefactions *ad pias causas* were made to include the Church's own financial needs. But they were all, even the secular purposes, 'pious causes'. The Church was, and had been since late Roman times, the arm of the State as far as social welfare was concerned.

If someone died without a will, the Church could administer the estate to ensure that provision was made for pious causes. This proto-death duty was levied in an official spirit of helpfulness, since the Church was concerned to avoid the soul of the intestate deceased suffering through his oversight. Anyone who had the temerity to make a will omitting pious bequests could be refused final rites before, and burial in consecrated ground after, death. The Reformation gained support because of resentment at such exactions which detracted from the voluntary element associated with charity.

The Church administered many of the pious causes and adjudicated in disputes over wills. Many of the present privileges of charities were established in this period. They were enforced when private bequests would have been ruled 'void for uncertainty' – i.e. charitable bequests would not be overruled simply because of imprecise wording. If the object was unclear, or not feasible, the bequest to charity stood but would be applied, according to the 'cy prés' rule, to the nearest object possible. So, for example, if a testator left money to found a hospital, but there was not enough to do so, the judge could order it to be applied to an existing hospital. Additionally, if there were insufficient resources to meet the terms of the will, debts were to be settled out of the private bequests before the pious ones were touched. Charitable trusts were also allowed to use the Church's time-scale of eternity since they were the only trusts allowed in perpetuity.

As the Middle Ages came to an end, the ecclesiastical courts lost some of their power. Excommunication was the penalty for being uncharitable and those impious enough to be so were unabashed by the threat. Executors valued the actual enjoyment of their property in this world more highly than the promises of rewards for piety in the next.

It was in this period of transition that there developed the legal concept of the Trust, or the Use as it was then known. Those who uphold the continuity of our island's story will be pleased to know that it began as a form of feudal tax evasion, thereby establishing a tradition which has remained to this day a source both of imaginative jurisprudence and continuing employment for the legal profession. A testator could 'enfeoff' land when he was still alive to a third party for a particular purpose or use enjoined in the final will, and the transaction would be free from the feudal levies usually consequent upon death.

The drawback was the lack of a mechanism to enforce the trustee's charitable duty. There were many petitions to the Chancellor seeking to enforce the pious conditions on negligent feoffees or trustees. One method used, which combined an element of worldliness with spiritual concern, was to leave money to a charity on condition that it maintained a chantry – regular masses said for the soul of the deceased. To that would be added a clause transferring the gift to another charity if the first failed to pay due attention to the soul of the benefactor. This created an interested party with a motivation to oversee the first.

Chantries, however, rarely lasted a century before they disappeared, while the specific rituals rarely lasted a generation (see Jordan, 1959) which was as long as anyone who cared about enforcement happened to be about to supervise the trust. Perhaps some of the support for the chantries' abolition came from a common-sense recognition of their futility.

First, Henry VIII and then Edward VI had, in effect, nationalised the chantry bequests, converting them to 'good and godlie uses, as in erecting of Gramer Scoles to the educacion of Youthe in virtewe and godlinesse, the further augmenting of the Universities and better provision of the poore and nedye' (preamble to the Act of Edward VI in 1545). There developed the doctrine of 'Superstitious Uses' which outlawed bequests to forms of religious activity – like masses for the dead – that ran counter to sanctioned religious observances.

The expropriation of the chantries helped to separate the concepts of piety and of charity. This effectively secularised charity and may well have paved the way for the Poor Laws of Queen Elizabeth I, as the secular authorities were forced to take up the burden of social welfare previously borne by the Church.

It was not only the Tudor State which was diverting resources to charity. The 'New Men', the *nouveaux riches* who took over the property of the monasteries, gave to charity on an increasingly lavish scale (see Jordan, ibid.). By Elizabeth's time, charitable bequests were estimated to amount to a quarter of London merchants' estates. This has been ascribed to a desire to 'buy' social stability (Kamen, 1976, p. 456), but it may well have been a manifestation of the same desire for immortality previously manifested in now outlawed chantries. The bequests, like modern foundations, could perpetuate the name and memory of the testator. Had the main motivation been social stability through buying off the poor, then the rich would have given while they were still alive to enjoy the balance in peace.

Meanwhile, ordinary grievances over private wills were directed to the ecclesiastical courts even as late as Elizabeth's reign, but petitions to enforce charitable bequests were admitted straight to the Chancellor's office to avoid their expense and alleged corruption. The Court of Chancery had begun as an informal, speedy and cheap method of securing equity and justice. Obviously, this must have been an intolerable challenge to the legal profession and they rose to it with all the ingenuity one would expect. By the time Dickens wrote *Bleak House*, the court was epitomised by the case of Jarndyce and Jarndyce which consumed the lives and fortunes of litigants. Even earlier, Sir Thomas More's feat in clearing the backlog of cases left by his predecessor was remembered by the legal fraternity (possibly with some acerbity) generations later (see Jones, 1969).

The 'New Poor'

The 'poor' to whom money may have been left were in no legal or financial position to bring action on their own account if trustees did not fulfil their obligations. If the petitioner was worth less than £5, he could bring a case *in forma pauperis* and did not have to pay costs if he lost – but he could be whipped for impertinence (Jones, ibid.).

In fact, the Elizabethan State was desperately concerned at the threat which unrelieved poverty posed to a society which was not as stable as it looks when seen through the eyes of later loyal historians. The wars with Spain were fought with money as much as men; there had been disastrous harvests; and land enclosures were still proceeding as old feudal relations broke down. The end of the sixteenth century saw a European-wide economic crisis which posed new threats to the social order. The new poor were often not just impoverished but masterless. Owing no social obligations, they were outside the hierarchy of Tudor society, and were seen as an ominous threat to stability.

Draconian laws were ineffective as people began to feel stronger bonds than feudal and religious obligations. They seemed to see more virtue in hanging together than being hanged separately. Edward Hext, a Somerset Justice of the Peace, reported how difficult it was to uphold the law, when even the victims of crime felt more in common with the criminal than the social hierarchy.

> Most commonly the simple Countryman and woman, lokynge no farther then ynto the loss of ther owne goods, are of opynyon that they wold not procure a man's death for all the goods yn the world, others uppon promyse to have ther goods agayne wyll gyve faynt evidence yf they be not stryctly loked ynto by the Justyce. (Kamen, 1976, p. 440)

The way in which the poor were looked on by the Tudor Establishment was with a mixture of unctuous piety and anxious vindictiveness. One of the reasons suggested in 1594 for colonising Ireland was that 'the people poor and seditious, which were a burden to the commonwealth are drawn forth, whereby the matter of sedition is removed out of the city' (Hill, 1975, p. 20). And in Newcastle, in 1633, it was reported that 'people of mean condition . . . are apt to turn every pretence and colour of grievance into uproar and seditious mutiny'. (ibid.). In earlier times, the poor had had an allotted part in society. As in India today, a beggar was giving the donor a chance to redeem his or her soul by giving alms, sometimes on a lavish scale. Thomas Cromwell, 'the Hammer of the Monks', was a link between the two ages. Even though he oversaw the dissolution of the monasteries for Henry VIII, he still retained much of the old Catholicism. He left £46 for masses to be said after his death, and as a later annalist, John Stow, recalled;

> I myself in that declining time of charity have oft seen at the Lord Cromwell's gate in London more than two hundred persons served twice every day with bread, meat and drink sufficient; for he observed that ancient and charitable custom,

as all prelates, noblemen, or men of honour and worship, his predecessors, had done before him. (Kamen, 1976, p. 448)

Nevertheless, the scale of the problem was growing, just as the attitudes to beggars were changing. As Hill says:

the Protestant social conscience and the Protestant respect for labour, produced a new attitude towards begging by regarding it as a social problem, and no longer as either a holy state or a divine necessity. The Act for Dissolution of the Monasteries provided for the maintenance by the purchasers of traditional hospitality. But the lands changed hands many times, and might be sub-divided. As the economic and moral climate changed, the charitable obligations laid on the purchasers were disregarded, and the real burden of the dissolution was placed on the poorest classes. (Hill, 1968, p. 52)

As a result, alms-giving came under legal and social constraints at the very time when need was rising as a result of fundamental economic changes. Begging was restricted from the 1520s onwards, so that it was illegal to give alms to an unlicensed beggar, and able-bodied unemployed were subject to a series of social experiments. Unemployment was seen, not as a result of a lack of work but a lack of moral fibre, so that at various times 'sturdy vagabonds' could be literally enslaved, whipped until bleeding, or sent to houses of correction to stiffen their moral fibre. In 1596, Edward Hext, the magistrate, reported that vagabonds were prepared to confess to felony, and so risk execution, rather than be sent to the houses of correction (Kamen, 1976 p. 451).

Relief, Public and Private – The 1601 Act

The 1597 and 1601 Poor Laws were, in comparison, an enlightened response to the failure of previous experiments. Members of Parliament in 1597 were seriously concerned for the social stability of the country and the implied threat of violent upheaval. Their fears were no doubt exacerbated by the knowledge that discharged soldiers and sailors were among the poor and vagrants. The Poor Relief Act inaugurated the Poor Law principle of public provision for the destitute, and of household rates to pay for it, since previous exhortations to fill the Church poor boxes had gone unheeded.

Elizabeth's government was also concerned to mobilise private resources for the emergency. The Charitable Uses Act of 1597 was intended to ensure that charitable endowments were put to full use. A consequence of the tandem provisions was the creation of a whole class of ratepayers who had a direct financial interest in ensuring that they paid no more rates than they had to – if necessary by enforcing the payment of charitable trusts which as trustees they might otherwise have raided.

The Act gave such interested parties an administrative apparatus to check on bequests 'which have bene and are still like to be most unlawfully and uncharitably converted to the Lucre and Gayne of some fewe greedy and covetous persons, contrary to the true intente and meaning of the givers and disposers thereof' (preamble to the 1597 Act of Charitable Uses). The Act established Charity Commissioners to investigate breaches of trust on a county basis and gave them the power to make binding decrees. Parliament repealed the Act and reissued it in amended form in 1601, following criticism that there was no provision to challenge jurors. This was felt to be contrary to Magna Carta, a document clearly taken more seriously then than now.

Ever since, the preamble to the 1601 Act of Charitable Uses has been used as the basic statement of charitable purposes. Although the Act has been repealed, the preamble is still enshrined in the 1960 Charities Act which declined the opportunity to attempt a modern definition.

The 1601 Act claimed to be concerned with the 'goodly, godly and charitable' uses, but the actual purposes enumerated were aimed at controlling and alleviating vagrancy, poverty and unemployment. It was a literary-minded legal historian in the nineteenth century who noticed the similarity of the objects listed in the preamble to the list given in *Piers Plowman* several centuries before. It is surprising that it took so long for the resemblance to be noticed, since the preamble must be one of the most scrutinised, parsed and dissected paragraphs on the statute books.

The relevant part of the preamble reads:

'Whereas Landes Tenementes Rentes Annuities Profittes Heriditamentes, Goodes Chattels Money and Stockes of Money, have bene heretofore given limitted appointed and assigned, as well by the Queenes most excellent Majestie and her most noble Progenitors, as by sondrie other well disposed persons, some

for Relief of aged, impotent, and poore people, some for
Maintenance of sicke and maymed Souldiers and Marriners,
Schooles of Learninge, Free Schooles and Schollers in
Universities, some for Repaire of Bridges Ports Havens
Causwaies Churches Seabanks and Highewaies, some for
Educacion and prefermente of Orphans, some for or towardes
Reliefe Stocke or Maintenance of Howses of Correccion, some
for Mariages of poor Maides, some for Supportacion Ayde and
Helpe of younge tradesmen, Handicraftesmen and persons
decayed, and others for releife or redemption of Prisoners or
Captives, and for aide or ease of any poore inhabitants
concerninge paymente of Fifteens, setting out of Souldiers, and
other Taxes; Whiche Landes Tenementes Rents, Annuities,
Profitts, Hereditamentes Goodes Chattelles Money and Stockes
of Money nevertheles have not byn imployed accordinge to the
charitable intente of the givers and founders thereof, by reason
of Fraudes, breaches of Truste and Negligence in those that
shoulde pay, delyver and imploy the same.' (Preamble to the
Charitable Uses Act (1601))

Are Churches Charitable?

The list of objects was godly, goodly, and very timely, consisting as
it did of a programme of welfare relief and public works, which
would be financed without direct calls upon the Exchequer or even
upon the local authorities. Most noticeable is the omission of
religion, although subsequent decisions have made its advancement
a head of charity in its own right. The only mention of religion is in
the form of church buildings which could easily be taken in the
context of public works. As Barbara Smoker of the National Secular
Society pointed out the 'promotion of transport' is a better founded
head of charity than the promotion of religion, if the preamble is
taken as the guide it is claimed to be. Havens, causeways, ports and
roads overwhelm the solitary mention of churches.

In fact, Francis Moore, the Elizabethan jurist and member of the
Commons, pointed out that the maintenance of the parish church
as a public building was charged upon the inhabitants of the parish
(Jones, 1969, p. 33). Charitable gifts for that purpose reduced the
tax burden which is why they were charitable rather than because
of any religious connotations. The upkeep of a cathedral was the
responsibility of the bishop, dean and chapter – and the implication

was that they had their own means of support from the Church's own endowments, which is why these were kept outside the statute. Even the funding of a chaplain for divine service was construed as possibly tending towards illegal superstitious uses.

Moore was involved in drawing up the statute and implied that the omission from it of such forms of religious activity was not accidental. It was a conscious attempt by a Protestant parliament to pre-empt religious backsliding by future monarchs and churchmen. 'The statute was cautiously penned in much particulars with the express purpose of avoiding all cowle of approval of superstitious uses which can be gleaned by a liberal construction of Instruction in Divinity, Reading, lectures, preaching etc' (ibid.). The position of religion then was as contentious as that of politics is now. The schism between Puritan and Erastian supporters had reinforced the contemporary identity between politics and religion. Political arguments were fought in religious terms, and heresy and subversion were inseparably linked.

In 1606, a less fervently Protestant Chancellor finally ruled that the upkeep of a chaplain was charitable. Although it was outside the statute, he claimed ancient precedent to enforce what the Charity Commissioners could not or would not.

By contrast, in 1639, the Lord Keeper set aside a bequest for a preaching minister and put the money towards a school. It appears that the local gentry were unhappy with the particular preacher being supported, and had conveyed their apprehensions to the local judiciary who in turn persuaded the Lord Keeper. They had warned that if the ministry had been supported it would 'have beene a disturbaunce in that place both to the church and the Commonwealth' (*Pember v. Kington* (1639) analysed in Jones, 1969, p. 34). (Some legal reports of the case recorded the decision as being the exact opposite, which should warn against undue reliance on ancient precedents (see Tudor, 1984, p. 61).

Perhaps one of the more telling testaments to the degree of public affection for the Established Church came from Bishop Cooper, in 1589, who reported 'The loathsome contempt, hatred and disdain that *the most part of men* in these days bear . . . towards the Ministers of the Church of God' (Hill, 1975, p. 28).

The national schism and the unwillingness of parishioners to support a minister who might not be of their persuasion were thus reflected in even greater secularisation of the concept of charity. To make their decisions, the commissioners had to empanel a jury of 'twelve good men and true' of the county to decide any contested claims. As happens at times of political unrest, juries were prone to interpret the law in the way which best matched their political perspectives. They were developing the peculiar antipathy to household rates, beyond what can be explained by the economic burden, which has infected the English middle classes ever since. It even seems to have helped impel the Pilgrim Fathers to flee to New England. One of them, John Robinson, is reported as inveighing against the payment of rates, 'which should more fitly be called a malevolence, for the ill will it is paid with' (Inglis, 1972, p. 45).

Thomas Dekker, in 1622, testified to the reluctance of the rate-paying classes of South East England; 'Though the number of the Poore do dailie increase, all things worketh for the worst in their behalfe. For there hath been no collection for them, no not these seven yeares in many parishes of this land especiallie in countrie towns' (Kamen, 1976, p. 451).

In general, the ratepayers who formed the juries for the Charity Commissions all had an interest in finding charitable objects if these could reduce the rates. One jury in Bratlington, Surrey was reported as accepting an inscription on a tombstone as evidence of charitable intent. As Jones (1969, p. 53) says: 'The Council in Westminster and the individual parishioner upon whom the burden of supporting the vagrant fell were united in their desire to fulfil the aspirations of the poor relief legislators, and it was this spirit of co-operation and interested dedication which vitalised the [charity] commission procedure and ensured its original triumph.'

The Rich Get in on the Act

Moral obligation, reinforced by political and fiscal expediency at national and local level, made the relief of poverty the paramount objective of a charity. As early as 1612 it was held that, 'where no use is mentioned or directed in a deed, it shall be decreed to the use of the poor.' It was a position which was changed considerably during the following centuries. The loophole through which later judges allowed charities which effectively excluded the poor was that of incidental benefit to the rich.

For example, one of the charitable objectives described by Francis Moore included the provision of bows and arrows for young people of 7 to 17, regardless of whether they were rich or poor. He commented that if they felt it necessary, the commissioners could restrict such an endowment and 'can order the employment solely to the poor if they think fit, without any violation, and thereby rectify the intent of the gift and the statute' (Moore's 'Reading'). It was accepted that if the relief of the poor were incidentally to help the rich, then that was the unavoidable but still charitable price which had to be paid. However, it was clear that to benefit the rich alone was not in itself charitable.

A contemporary revival of that doctrine, so close to the fountainhead of charity law, would, of course, have serious implications for public schools and private hospitals, which will be dealt with later in the relevant chapters. Over the centuries, the ingenuity of judges and legislators muddied the stream with a flow of decisions which effectively let the poor settle in the sediment at the bottom. Existing corporations, like cities, towns, colleges and cathedrals were not bound by the statute, because as corporate bodies they were presumed capable of, and willing to, implement charitable bequests made to them.

Ownership and control of other non-corporate Charitable Uses was in a sense 'vague'. It belonged to the trustees on condition that they fulfilled their charitable obligations. The monarch took upon himself the duty as *pater patriae* to enforce the purposes against fraud and usurpation through the commissioners. In general, however, the corporate exemptions meant that these were effectively self-policing. That implied a degree of optimism about their probity which the Victorian Commissions later demonstrated was scarcely justified. Even now, the colleges of Winchester and Eton and the universities are exempted from the commissioners' jurisdiction, although they have all the privileges of charities.

The Tudor and Stuart periods established the basic framework of charities and welfare provision in a context of feudal social and religious obligations. Charity's relationship to religion and the church was, as we saw, as much a matter of pragmatic politics as of moral imperatives.

The law was very much shaped by decisions on bequests – not necessarily because that was the main source of finance for charities but because that was where most of the litigation arose. In such cases, there were often relatives willing to contest a will which gave away money and land which would otherwise have come to them. The changing sensibilities of the age were expressed by Francis Bacon who said of those who saved their charity till death, 'he that doth so is rather liberal of another man's than of his own'. (*Essays*, 'Of Riches'). That outlook later developed almost the full force of law as the residual piety of his age was submerged by Georgian practicality.

In the Restoration period, there was a distinct diminution of social obligation – in so far as it affected the poor. As the century wore on the commissioners became less active, and the diminished vigour in defence of the poor began to anticipate later standards. In 1671, Beauchamp, a trustee arraigned for diverting charitable endowments, told the plaintiffs, the 'Poor of St Dunstan', that as soon as all their witnesses were dead he would appeal against the commissioners' decision. In those times of local grandees' power, it was a brave pauper who took action in the face of such veiled threats. For charity, as we see in the next chapter, it was the beginning of a Brave New World which had many such people in it.

2

The Age of *Noblesse Oblige?*

By the eighteenth century, piety, real or feigned, was rapidly disappearing as a factor in social relations. This was not an age of sympathy for the poor and the legislative results showed it in a dramatic fashion: between 1688 and 1820 the number of hanging offences grew from fifty to 200 (Hay, 1977, p. 18). Added as casual riders to otherwise innocuous Acts of Parliament, the laws were a practical implementation of John Locke's thesis that 'Government has no other end but the preservation of property'. Thus, even in acts to incorporate commercial companies, 'the death penalty was routinely added to protect their investments' (ibid., p. 21).

As Hay pointed out:

> The Glorious Revolution of 1688 established the freedom, not of men, but of men of property ... Henceforth among triumphant Whigs, and indeed all men on the right side of the great gulf between rich and poor, there was little pretence that civil society was concerned primarily with peace or justice or charity. Even interests of state and the Divine Will had disappeared. Property had swallowed them all (ibid., p. 18).

There was obviously not much room in such a society for those who had no property to protect. Indeed, the corollary was that those without posed a threat to those with. At worst charitable bequests were seen as a threat to property; or, at best, Lord Northington put it disapprovingly in 1764 as 'perpetuating the memory and gratifying the vanity of testators'.

Moreover, charity served to justify the very repression and savagery which would appear to be its antithesis. In classical European law, it had been recognised that it was no crime for a starving person to steal food. Sir William Blackstone recognised the principle in his *Commentaries* while denying its implementation in England. It applied on the Continent 'where the parsimonious industry of the natives orders everyone to work or starve', but in England it was obsolete because 'charity is reduced to a system, and interwoven in our very constitution'. (vol. IV, p. 31).

The privilege which charity had had 'in equity and conscience', as Lord Chancellor Bromley had said in 1583, that legacies to the poor should be paid first out of a will, became obsolete in the eighteenth century. Debts were settled first and private and charitable bequests were treated on a par if there were insufficient resources to meet them (Jones, 1969, p. 156). Lord Harcourt expressed the social ambience of the age in 1721, when he confessed that he 'liked charity well but he would not steal leather to make poor men's shoes'.

In 1988, Douglas Hurd evoked this age of *noblesse oblige*, suitable for emulation and restoration. 'In previous centuries, when full political rights were enjoyed by few, the tradition of social obligation acted as a restraining influence upon the powerful minority' (*New Statesman* 9 April 1988).

It was presumably with just such a sense of social obligation that Lord Chancellor Hardwicke said, in 1736, that he 'would not oppress any man for the sake of charity', and bitterly regretted the precedents of his predecessors in favour of it. (A century later, Sir Francis Palgrave identified his views as 'bigoted' and claimed that they had 'caused much mischief to charitable uses'.)

Indeed, there is a constant frustration evident in the words of judges of the period, who found themselves genuinely unable to understand what had motivated their pre-Restoration predecessors, so great was the change in sensibilities. Lord Hardwicke's comments on the trustees of the period are an epitaph to the effectively dead Charity Commissions' efficiency: 'The instances of the trustees abusing the trust of charity are so frequent that they are sufficient warning to reasonable men not to leave their estates under such uncertainty as to put them absolutely under a person's power, and then trust to his generosity for the disposing of them in charity.'

Mortmain: Protection for Property Against Charitable Excess

The Mortmain Act of 1736 codified this distrust of charity and sought to preserve the perceived natural rights of the heir against the capriciously benevolent whims of the testator. Although now repealed, its effects live on. The Act invalidated any charitable bequest of land which was made in the twelve months before death, or without two witnesses – and provided for it to revert to the heirs at law. The meaning of mortmain is 'dead hand', an adequate reflection of what the age thought about land being encumbered with charitable trusts by the worthy but thoughtless deceased. The Act was alleged to have been motivated by what was seen as the plain stupidity of Sir Thomas Guy in endowing the hospital which now bears his name. The distrust of charity was exacerbated by a profound anticlericalism. The official position of the Church was buttressed by law but its popular standing was eroded by dissent and disbelief, while the archetypal churchman was seen as a venal tithe gobbler.

Medieval mortmain legislation had some credible claim to public interest, since in feudal times land given to pious causes was not available to support military service. By contrast, the 1736 Act was in the public interest only if the public were assumed to be those who had the money and power in the society. In the passing of the Act charities were rounded upon in intemperate tones. It was stated that these devises were 'to the prejudice of the common good of this kingdom', envisaging a future where

> too great part of the lands in this kingdom may soon come to be in mortmain, to the prejudice of the nation in general and to the ruin or unjust disappointment of many a man's poor relations, for I cannot but think that a man's heirs-at-law have some sort of natural right to succeed after his death, at least to his land estate ... The giving of such charity I shall always look on rather as an act of injustice towards the heir at law than as an act of charity in the donor

said one, as he helped pass into law the passing thoughts of Bacon a century before.

Another noble perorated:

> To assist the widow and the fatherless, to nourish the tender infant and succour the helpless old, in short to relieve the poor distressed who cannot provide for themselves is a duty incumbent upon every society, as well as upon every private man; but my Lords, this duty is to be discharged with great caution, and with great circumspection; for if we mistake the objects of our charity, if by giving what we call charity we

encourage laziness, idleness and extravagance, in the persons to whom we give it, or in others, the action is so far from being pious, charitable or commendable that it becomes impious, ridiculous, and injurious to our native country ... The funds for relief of deserving poor are sufficient. (Jones, 1969, p. 110)

Yet the members were disinterested enough to grant exemptions for the more deserving poor – the colleges of Eton, Winchester, Westminster, Oxford and Cambridge, which were said to be the only public foundations 'either useful or necessary in this Kingdom'. This collective bow to the interests of their old schools maintained the continuity which has left those institutions effectively unregulated over the centuries.

Charity by Other Names

The Mortmain Act was significant in more ways than the provision of a historical dipstick for the wells of Christian charity. It also proved crucial for the expansion of the definition, if not necessarily the scope, of charity. Even as they denied charity resources, successive judges liberalised its legal meaning. It was not to keep the ancient law up to date with social developments, nor to extend the privileges of charity to wider benevolent causes. It was because judges, wishing to protect potential heirs from disinheritance by eccentrically generous testators, had to prove that it was a *charitable* bequest of land so that they could overturn it under the Mortmain Act. In 1801, for example, a gift for a botanical garden was declared to be a good charitable object – and so the bequest fell to the heirs.

The Mortmain Act only applied to land, not to cash, and so the judges were just as assiduous in overturning cash bequests as non-charitable, for exactly the same reason as they found cases involving land to be charitable. The result in both cases was the reversion of the bequest to the natural heirs.

Gareth Jones claims that there is no recorded case involving the Mortmain Act which declared a bequest not to be charitable: that would have automatically allowed the bequest to stand as outside the purpose of the Act. This led to charities claiming *not* to be so, to avoid being trammelled up by Mortmain. For example, the British Museum unsuccessfully argued in 1826 that it was not a charity in order to be excluded from the provisions of the Mortmain Act. The Master of the Rolls was not going to let technicalities deprive heirs of their due, and declared that 'every gift for a public purpose whether local or general' was covered by the Act.

Although the different judgments were motivated by the same uncharitable end, the precedents they left tended to be in confusing opposition. Clearly, the interests of the beneficiaries were not a significant factor in the process. The ground for the chaos of modern charity law was well prepared. As Edmund Burke, theoretician for the Establishment of the time, said of human laws, 'Where mystery begins, justice ends.'

We tend to think of the medieval period as the one when abstruse arguments were the norm, but medieval scholastics would have been quite at home with the artificial niceties introduced into charity law by the judges in the Age of Reason. For instance, in 1767, Lord Camden defined a charitable gift as a 'gift to a general public use which extends to the poor as well as the rich, of which there are many instances in the statute – as for building bridges'. However, as charity was extended, the benefit of the poor tended to diminish throughout the eighteenth and early nineteenth centuries up to the first Reform Act. In the end, a bridge which charged tolls beyond the practical reach of the poor would have been a good charitable object by analogy with the fee paying schools.

The turning point for the old view of charity came in the case of *Morice v. the Bishop of Durham*, in 1805. A woman had left money in her will for 'such objects of benevolence and liberality as the Bishop of Durham should most approve'. At one time, a bequest to the Church *ad pias causas* would have been unimpeachable. Even if it had not been to the Church but for lay charitable purposes, judges in earlier times would not have allowed a gift to charity to be voided by imprecise wording. Because the bequest did not come under the terms of the Mortmain Act, Sir Samuel Romilly, acting for the heir, sought to *restrict* the meaning of charity rather than extend it in order to benefit his client. He invented the four heads of charity which he purported to have extracted from the preamble to the 1601 statute. 'First, relief of the indigent; in various ways: money: provisions: education: medical assistance; etc. Secondly, the advancement of learning: Thirdly, the advancement of religion; and fourthly, which is most difficult, the advancement of objects of general public utility' (*Morice v. Bishop of Durham* (1805)). In 1891, the 'four heads' were plagiarised and resurrected definitively by Lord Macnaghten in the Pemsel case, and are now quoted with all the authority which only an oft-repeated invention can have.

The gift was declared to be not charitable because the judge, supported by Lord Chancellor Eldon, drew a distinction between a trust which is charitable, and for the public benefit, and one which merely benefits the public! Charity, he ruled, was distinct from benevolence and liberality. This marked a low point in charity law from which it has never recovered. The original statute had been derived from medieval principles which preserved a sense of care for the community while, it is true, being expediently useful for the contemporary problems of poverty. As exemplified in this case, the overriding concept of care for the wider community had disappeared completely to be replaced by sterile distinctions worthy of Byzantine theology.

Lord Eldon – Determined Hostility

Perhaps the tendentious standards applied by the judiciary are explained – they are certainly exemplified – by Lord Eldon, who was the Lord Chancellor for most of the first quarter of the nineteenth century. According to the *Dictionary of National Biography*, Eldon's 'normal attitude towards innovations of all kinds continued to be one of determined hostility'. He opposed Catholic Emancipation, the freeing of slaves and all forms of political reform, and was widely held to be ultimately responsible for the Peterloo Massacre and the six 'Gagging Acts'. Shelley felt strongly about his legal record.

> Next came Fraud, and he had on
> Like Eldon, an ermined gown;
> His big tears, for he wept well,
> Turned to mill-stones as they fell.

> And the little children who
> Round his feet played to and fro,
> Thinking every tear a gem,
> Had their brains knocked out by them'
> *The Mask of Anarchy*

Eldon, however, was happy to join in the general spirit of innovation which characterised his contemporaries on the bench in the treatment of charity. Admittedly, he refused Leeds Grammar School permission, as a charity, to vary its trust, and forbade its use of any part of its endowment for teaching French or German – since the school was founded to teach the 'learned' languages.

But Eldon helped mould the concept of charity nearer to the form his social peers wished. His era laid the foundations for the charitable status of private schools in their modern form; for bequests to 'poor relations'; and even the decision which was to form the basis of the later doctrine against 'political activity' by charities. In the *De Themmines v. De Bonneval* case of 1828, anti-Catholic sentiment established a precedent which was cited a century and half later to rule that Amnesty International was not charitable.

Eldon stood firm in the face of parliaments which had liberal lapses even in that reactionary period. In 1817, he retrospectively overturned a bequest which had been made in 1701 because it was to a Unitarian Meeting House and therefore against the Trinity (*AG v. Pearson*, 1817). He felt that the Act of Toleration, which had recently been extended to Unitarians, did not obstruct the Common Law's position against them.

In 1815, Eldon showed that he was no more charitable in his law than in his politics. With heavy sarcasm he was forced to admit: 'The general intention of this testatrix, who seems to have been saturated and satiated with the idea of charity, and yet not to have had mind enough herself to determine upon the particular objects, was to devote her property to charity' (*Moggridge v. Thackwell*). He was reluctant to declare that the woman's bequest should go to charity when it was so imprecise but, as he had said in another case, he felt bound by precedents laid down when 'this court was in the habit of deciding monstrous propositions in favour of charity'.

Perhaps influenced by his repugnance with the general idea of charity, Eldon was not even speedy with his judgments, which helped establish the dismal reputation of the Court of Chancery as the Bermuda Triangle of the legal system, into which cases disappeared seemingly without trace. The last Charity Commission under the 1601 Act was empanelled in 1787, as a result of which a petition went to the Lord Chancellor in 1804 to confirm the commissioners' decree. In 1818, Eldon was still deciding on the exceptions taken by the defaulting trustees. The case was doubtless in Sir Samuel Romilly's mind when he later said, 'It was impossible, through the court of Chancery, to obtain redress for the abuses of charitable institutions.'

Complainants had to be both long-lived and rich, as the 'relator's' name had to be attached to the case. Eldon explained that since costs could not be awarded against the Crown, it would be unfair to the plaintiffs not to have someone who could pay as party to the proceedings against them. As a result, the trustees charged with misappropriation could charge their costs to the charity, while any public spirited citizen who took it upon himself to lay information before the court could be ruined by the costs of the exercise.

Henry Brougham, the nineteenth-century reformer, gave details of the case of a charity from Yeovil (Hansard, xxxviii, 1221ff), from whose income of £2,000 only £30 to £40 was going to charitable purposes. The three churchwardens of the parish had spent eight years in the Court of Chancery trying to get the money restored. They had supported costs of thousands without getting full restitution from the townspeople, who would, of course be paying heavily in poor rates to sustain the cost of the cheating.

Brougham described with irony the course of another case. After many months of adjournment

> It was appointed positively for the 29th of February, there being but 28 days in that month. It was of course again deferred, and then again. On a subsequent day it was mentioned. This word 'mentioned' is a light and airy word in that House, but in the court of Chancery it was attended with fees for the counsel, fees to the agents, fees to the shorthand writer – in short a 'mention' was not the most unexpensive and agreeable proceeding that could befall a suitor. (ibid.)

And so it went on for years in a legal system run by the people whom Byron attacked, 'When a proposal is made to emancipate or relieve, you hesitate, you deliberate for years, you temporize and tamper with the minds of men; but a death-bill must be passed off hand, without a thought of the consequences' (speech to the Lords against the Frame-breaking Bill, 1812).

Several attempts to revive the commissioners and expedite proceedings were vitiated by opposition from all those with a vested interest, which by then included anyone who drew an income from the law. Misbehaving trustees were either too strong locally, or the judiciary seem to have regarded their depredations with a benign tolerance.

For example, R. E. Peach wrote about Bath's oldest charity; 'At that period, the Bath citizens were a long-suffering race, and a pious hypocrite (as usually every Chapman was) could and did rob them with impunity' (quoted in *The Independent* of 31 December 1988). He added, 'It was not that successive clerical incumbents were not giving to the poor brethren and sisters *all* to which they were entitled, but for years they ignored their obligations altogether and pocketed the whole of the plunder, or shared it with the "worthy mayor" for the time being.' Elizabeth I had given Bath Corporation the patronage to appoint the Master of the hospital of St John, and the clergy. In 1616, they made the Mayor ex officio Master and that led to wholesale depredations on the endowment. In keeping with the Enterprise culture of the time, they appreciated that the paupers would not be too religious, so they converted the chapel into an alehouse. The fraud had continued for three centuries; the Cross Bath charity was raided by the local worthies from 1552 until a successful Bill in Chancery in 1864.

The four heads which Romilly extrapolated from the statute had repercussions in their implied diminution of the other doctrine, that charities must benefit the poor. The incidental benefit of the rich was strengthened. If, as Romilly said, the advancement of learning was in itself charitable, then it followed that it was so even if the poor were excluded. In 1827, it was accepted that the Advancement of Learning was in itself charitable without necessarily being of even residual benefit to the poor. In the words of Sir John Leach, 'The institution of a school for the sons of gentlemen is not, in popular language, a charity; but in the view of the Statute of Elizabeth, all schools for learning are so to be considered' (*AG v. Lonsdale* (1827)).

Reform in the Air

So, as we enter the Victorian era, the separation of the legal concept of charity from its historical and common usages is well established. The preamble, from being a list of examples by way of illustration, has become a restricted list, against which new objects of charity had to be tested for analogy. As a contemporary textbook wrote, 'the limits assigned to the statute of Elizabeth are sufficiently extensive to take in almost every act, purpose or object which can be considered as having any legitimate connection with charity' (Boyle, 1837).

However, the temper of the age was changing. Reform was in the
air and charities were not excluded, especially since, in the absence
of any state provision, they provided most of the nation's
educational system. In 1816, Henry Brougham's Commission into
the Education of the Lower Orders reported extensively on the
behaviour of the upper orders, 'In several cases as at Huntingdon
and St Bees, the land has been leased to the trustees at ridiculously
low rents, while the income was used for political purposes.
Pocklington School... still boasted a headmaster, but the building
was used for storing lumber, and one pupil was discovered
working in a saw-pit' (Garratt p. 105).

A determined reformer, Brougham was instrumental in establishing a commission to examine the state of charitable endowments.
The Brougham Commission's efforts were soon frustrated by the
'social obligations' of the 'powerful minority'. The commission
began work in 1818 and exceeded its rather generous deadline of
1830 by five years. In the course of their investigations they
produced what has been called a 'Domesday Book' of charitable
endowments, although in fact they omitted many. The 30,000 they
examined had nearly 450,000 acres of land, £6.5 million in cash,
and drew £1.2 million in income.

The universities and major public schools were protected from
the overview. Lord Eldon, of course, was prominent in the blocking
even though the commission had some early successes. 'The
Provost of Eton and the Fellows of Winchester were made to
produce their accounts. The arcana of College Bursaries at Oxford
and Cambridge were dragged out into the open. The master of St
John's College was so upset by his cross examination about the
disposal of fellowships that he burst into tears' (ibid.). Well he
might – St John's was responsible for overseeing the Pocklington
School.

Berkhamsted Free Grammar School was afforded some un-
welcome publicity. In the well-endowed school

> Your Committee find a Master and an Usher, the latter the son
> of the Master, and appointed by him when a minor, the
> incorporated Trustees of the charity property receiving to their
> own use considerable stipends, the school house dilapidated,
> no boys on the foundation, and the surplus revenue so
> exhausted by law and other expenses as to leave an uncertain
> trifle for the relief of the poor. (Brougham Commission
> report)

The Select Committee of 1835 reported on the basis of the voluminous commission reports, and clearly established a need for action. An action in Chancery, to change trustees, recover misappropriated money, or even to replace dead trustees 'consumes, under the present mode, upon an average, from five to ten years of time, and can only be effected at a ruinous sacrifice of the funds of the Charity' (quoted in Nathan, 1952).

The need for action, however, is not necessarily transmuted into the desire for it, and the determined opposition of vested interests ensured the defeat of no less than thirteen bills before the 1853 Charitable Trusts Act was enacted. In 1860, the re-established Charity Commissioners were finally given powers 'to make such effectual orders as may now be made by any judge of the court of Chancery'. Nonetheless, it was their lamentable task to oversee a body of law which had been distorted like a medieval gargoyle. They were also subject to new ideological and moral pressures to meet the changed spirit of the age, which disapproved of the actual objects of many endowed charities.

3

Crying in the Wilderness

The greatest bequest to charity from the period dealt with in the previous chapter is confusion. The clear conception of charity, of concern for fellow men, had disappeared in the Age of Reason, leaving the jurists to dissect a body of law from which the soul had fled. Judges examined each case with no conception of the ideological framework which had held the pre-Restoration conception together, and made *ad hoc* decisions based on their view of the world. That view was the protection of the property rights and political power of the class from which they were drawn.

Looked at in that light, their precedents represent a consistent attempt to bend a Tudor framework of altruism and charity to eighteenth-century conceptions whose only bow to theology was texts such as: 'To what purpose is this waste?' (Matthew, xxvi, 8) and 'unto everyone that hath shall be given, and he shall have abundance' (Matthew, xxv, 29).

Regardless of the motivation for the decisions, they are still binding, and so are now frequently subject to a form of historical revisionism. The past must be rationalised and protected from criticism in order to defend the present legal system derived from it. However, exasperation with the field does find strong expression.

The whole law relating to charitable trusts has been well described as a 'wilderness', and it provides one of the worst examples in our law of endless technical distinctions which have no relation to reality or common sense, and which again and again succeed only in frustrating the intentions, to the prejudice of the public interest, of benevolently minded testators. Faith and Hope are highly necessary virtues in all courts of law, but in the chancery division, charity is the least and not 'the greatest of these'. (Allen, 1964, p. 394).

28

This chapter examines how the period dealt with earlier resulted in that 'wilderness'.

Four Just Heads?

After Eldon's judgment in *Morice v. the Bishop of Durham*, that the 1601 preamble was a definitive guide, the four heads of charity Romilly had adduced seem to have remained in the minds of judges as a useful classification. In 1891, Lord Macnaghten plagiarised them (without acknowledgement) and his codification is now accepted and quoted as definitive. 'Charity in the legal sense comprises four principal divisions; trusts for the advancement of education; trusts for the relief of poverty; trusts for the advancement of religion; and trusts for other purposes beneficial to the community not falling under any of the preceding heads' (*Special Commissioners of Income Tax v. Pemsel*).

Macnaghten's firmness of tone disguises the flimsiness of his extrapolation. The only head which could be reasonably derived from the preamble is the relief of poverty. As we saw, religion was excluded from it entirely, and purposefully so. Macnaghten was in fact formulating current practice rather than any great legal or ethical principles.

'Purposes beneficial to the community' had by then given the blessings of charity status to many bodies, for instance, to what is now the RSPCA, which would have totally bemused the Tudor Commons which had passed the preamble. Adding a new eddy to the meanderings of jurisprudence was a change of motivation for law suits. Previously, most cases arose from aggrieved heirs trying to get their hands on bequests to charity. The Victorian era saw a new impetus for bringing cases to court. The Inland Revenue was now trying to *disprove* charitable status in order to restrict tax concessions.

Despite its frequent invocation, Macnaghten's codification did not really clarify matters, rather it gave judges a spurious rationalisation for decisions whch they would have probably taken anyway. Only a few years afterwards, another judge confessed, 'After all, the best that can be done is to consider each case as it arises, upon its own special circumstances' (*Re Foveaux* (1895)). His honesty was not appreciated and his precedent was later overturned.

Lord Sterndale, in 1924, found himself lost and the four heads no compass points to journey by. He was, he said:

Unable to find any principle which will guide one easily and safely through the tangle of cases to what is and what is not a charitable gift. If it is possible, I hope sincerely that at some time or other a principle will be laid down ... When one takes gifts which have been held to be charitable, and compares them with gifts which have held not to be charitable, it is very difficult to see what the principle is on which the distinction rests. I confess I find considerable difficulty in understanding the exact reason why a gift for the benefit of animals, and for the prevention of cruelty to animals generally should be a good charitable gift, while a gift for philanthropic purposes which I take it, is for the benefit of mankind generally, should be bad as a charitable gift.

The gift for the benefit of animals apparently is held to be valid because it is educative of mankind, it being good for mankind that they should be taught not to be cruel but kind to animals, and one would quite agree with that. But if the benefit of mankind on that particular side makes a good charitable gift, it is a little difficult to see why any philanthropic purpose to benefit mankind on all sides is a bad one. (*Re Tetley*)

The intervening decades have done little or nothing to resolve those difficulties. In 1941, Judge McKinnon, with more than a hint of judicial exasperation commented: 'Thanks to the industry of counsel I have made my first acquaintance with a number of authorities in which the manifest intentions of various testators seem to me to have been defeated by their artless use of language' (*Re Ward*).

Lord Simonds said, in 1955:

There is no limit to the number and diversity of the ways in which man will seek to benefit his fellow men. To determine whether the privileges, now considerable, which are accorded to charity in its legal sense are to be granted or refused in a particular case is often a matter of great nicety, and I think that this house can perform no more useful function in this branch of the law than to discourage a further excess of refinement where already so many fine distinctions have been made. (*IRC v. Baddeley*).

The one tenuous thread holding them all together is the

assertion that charity *always* involves the relief of poverty (see Halsbury, 1974).

The Name of the Game: Analogy

Nevertheless, successive commissions and governments have declared that the present mode of definition is satisfactory! The various principles which have been used could almost make a pleasant parlour game. Contestants could exercise their intellectual dexterity in trying to perceive how poverty is relieved by phrenology, dowsing, looking after sick hedgehogs, the Church Commissioners, or publishing Joanna Southcott's works, all of which are held to be good charitable objects deserving the indulgence of the taxman and the protection of the law.

They could search the 1601 preamble to discern how the charitable status accorded to the Unification Church, or the Children of God, the temples, mosques and synagogues of Hindus, Moslems and Jews could be extrapolated from the preamble's single mention of churches as buildings, or indeed what part they play in the relief of poverty. When they tire of looking for what is not there, contestants can play the Analogy Game, as played often in court rooms across the realm.

The examples are stimulating – the provision of crematoria is 'analogous' to the provision of burial grounds, which is analogous to the upkeep of churchyards, which is in turn analogous to the repair of churches, said Lord Russell (*Scottish Burial Reform and Cremation Society Ltd v. Glasgow Corporation* (1968)). 'I can understand it,' the same judge lamented in a later case, 'when you say that the preservation of sea walls is for the safety of lives and property, and therefore by analogy, the voluntary provision of lifeboats and fire brigades are charitable. I can even follow you as far as crematoria. But these other generalities teach me nothing' (*Incorporated Society for Law Reporting of England and Wales v. the Attorney-General* (1972).

That case itself was a delicious example of paradox: was it a charitable purpose and for the public benefit to record the decisions of learned judges, whose circumlocutory precedents were held up and scrutinised to indicate what was, or was not, a charitable purpose? Somewhat against the historical evidence, it was unanimously held to be so by the Court of Appeal.

The process of analogisation could be carried to further heights.

The provision of harbours could mean that airports were charitable. That could mean rocket launching sites were charitable, and so perhaps space stations. Or one could adopt Barbara Smoker's half-humorous elicitation of a general principle of the 'Advancement of Travel' from the headings in the 1601 preamble and deduce from it that travel agents were potentially charitable, along with holiday camps and charabanc tours. Another possibility, less far-fetched in the Thatcherite era, is to bid for the building and running of the prisons, by analogy with the 'Howses of Correccion' mentioned in the preamble. Will dating agencies cite the 'Mariages of poore Maides', or will it be possible to pay the poll tax of the poor, 'for aide or ease of any poore Inhabitantes concerning paymente of Fifteenes . . . or other taxes'?

With such a job creation scheme for the legal profession, it is perhaps no wonder that the Nathan Commission reported in 1951 that lawyers were against a new definition and preferred adopting Macnaghten's four heads. 'Broadly speaking, the witnesses who were lawyers were against, and those not lawyers began by being in favour of, a new definition' (Nathan, 1952, p. 32).

Perhaps the most scandalous twentieth-century example of how good intentions could fall foul of definitions to the benefit of the legal profession, was the Diplock case. Just before the Second World War, Caleb Diplock left the residue of his estate of over £250,000 to 'such charitable institution or institutions or charitable or other benevolent object or objects in England as his trustees should select'. To a lay person – or more precisely to a disinterested lay person who did not feel cheated of a large inheritance – that seems eminently reasonable, straightforward and commendable.

It was contested, however, and in 1940 the judge upheld the gift as charitable, which was a great relief to the executors. The trustees had by then honoured Caleb Diplock's intentions by endowing an old people's home in Polegate and had distributed the rest of the largesse to no less than 139 charitable institutions in furtherance of the deceased's wishes. But the heir appealed against the decision and in 1941 it was reversed. In 1944, the Lords took time off from waging the war for freedom to consider, and dismiss, an appeal by the Diocese of Chichester, one of the beneficiaries, and by 1948 the heirs were pursuing actions to recover the money from the charities. As late as 1951 the Ministry of Health, as the successor to the charitable hospitals, fought and lost a battle to retain the money which they had been given by Diplock's executors.

One of the executors, faced with personal liability for the sums earlier given to good causes, committed suicide. The death sentence for him, and for common sense, was the one that contained 'or' instead of 'and'. If Caleb had used the right conjunction, he could have rested charitably *and* benevolently in his grave and not dragged his executor after him.

Lord Goddard said in judgment:

> For myself, owing perhaps to the fact that I was not brought up in this branch of the law, I cannot feel any enthusiasm for this rule. Indeed when I find a rule which says that if a property is left to trustees to give to charitable *and* benevolent purposes that is good, but if it is for charitable *or* benevolent purposes it is not, I regard it with some distaste. (*Chichester Diocesan Fund v. Simpson* 1944))

Law-making by the Courts

The importance of the question of definition is greater than whether or not someone's wishes are posthumously respected. Charity based upon money raised from the living is now more important than those based on bequests from the dead. Nonetheless, definitions of charity hammered out in squabbles over wills have power over modern charities and would-be charities which depend upon living donors to carry out their work.

It is frequently said that the accumulation of case law has allowed flexibility to the boundaries, as courts interpret modern social conditions. But that puts considerable social and political power into the hands of a body, the judiciary, whose previous judgments have not always justified a total faith in its wisdom. A judge reading the runes, like any good soothsayer, could discern the message which he wanted to hear from the shades of the departed jurists.

Lord Russell, in the 1972 case cited above (*ICLR v. AG* (1972)), described the process with more candour than we are accustomed to from his profession.

> When considering Lord Macnaghten's fourth category in Pemsel's case of 'other purposes beneficial to the community' [or, as phrased by Sir Samuel Romilly... 'objects of general public utility'] the courts in consistently saying that not all such are necessarily charitable in law, are in substance accepting

that if a purpose is shown to be beneficial or of such utility, it is prima facie charitable in law, but have left open a line of retreat based on the Equity of the Statute in case they are faced with a purpose (e.g. a political purpose) which could not have been within the contemplation of the statute, even if the then legislators had been endowed with the gift of foresight into the circumstances of later centuries.

In other words, a judge could exclude matters which would fit all the definitions of general utility but which he for whatever reason deemed unsuitable. This is most clearly demonstrated in the case of political purposes, which is dealt with at some length below, where imaginative decisions by judges have tended to express the prejudices of their peers in a legally binding form, without the intervention of electors or their representatives. The general pattern of decisions leads to the inescapable conclusion that in the eyes of the judiciary, the status quo is always to the public benefit. Keeton pointed out in 1949:

> The judge, in deciding charity cases, is really making a decision, often of great importance upon the trend of public policy. He indicates the channels into which private philanthropy can be directed with the greatest effect. In form he may appear to follow earlier decisions, but except where the terms of a later gift are identical with that of a gift in a reported case, his margin of freedom is wide, and it is impossible to exclude the personal factor in the choice between competing analogies. That is why, except in cases where a decision on an identical gift already exists, it is often almost impossible for a draftsman to predict whether the gift will take effect or not.

The growth of the voluntary sector, dependent upon the respectability of charitable status to secure grants from public and private bodies, has expanded the significance of the definition beyond that of 'private philanthropy', and into an important public issue. However, as Keeton noted, – the judges' subjective decisions are clearly paramount in this process. Since most judges went to public schools, and attended older universities, it is not maligning them too much to suggest that their backgrounds have coloured their decisions in this most subjective of fields. Is it entirely unrelated that the law favours private schools and hospitals and prefers religion to politics, human rights and campaigning? Could the traditional Anglican, public school, Oxbridge college, and now BUPA, membership of the judiciary not have coloured their views of the public benefit of such things? After all, their predecessors' common membership of the landowning classes clearly formed their views in the period which moulded the present case law so firmly.

The judgments themselves give a flavour of the social background which formed them. In 1958, in the Court of Appeal, Judge Romer considered *Re Cole*. The benefactor had bequeathed two houses, the income of which was to go for 'the general benefit and general welfare of the children for the time being in Southdown House', which was a home for children in need of care and protection.

The court dismissed the gift's charitable status on the following grounds:

> It is permissible to suppose that at any given time, all, or a considerable proportion of the children in the home may consist of juvenile delinquents, children who are beyond their parents' control and children who have been exposed to moral danger. It would appear to me that the provision of a television set, or a gramophone and records and the like, might well be regarded as being for the general benefit of such children... I cannot regard the provision of television sets etc. for the benefit of such persons as juvenile delinquents and refractory children in Southdown House as coming within any conception of charity which is to be found in the Preamble.
>
> If it were, then I suppose a gift to provide the inmates of a Borstal Institution with amenities would be charitable, which would appear to me to be an impossible contention.

It is worth noting that since 1915 (*Re Mariette*) it had been held that the provision of a fives court, or squash racquet court to a public school was a good and charitable gift, and in 1925 it was decided (*Re Gray*) by Romer's father that a gift to promote sport in a regiment was equally acceptable. *Re Mariette* was cited as a precedent!

To Define, or not to?

With so many distinguished judges expressing their discomfort in their best legal prose, one would have thought that there was a heavy pressure to reform the law. However, the Nathan Commission in 1952, and the 1960 Charities Act based upon it, both baulked at the task of clearing up the confusion. The Act set up machinery to regulate charities – without defining what they were. On the one hand, it removed the last vestiges of the 1601 Act from the statutes by repealing the 1888 Mortmain Act which had incorporated the preamble. On the other hand, it accepted the validity of all the legal precedents based upon it. More importantly, the legislature's failure to redefine charity abdicated responsibility for the future development of law. It left it in the unelected hands of the very courts which had so often obscured the issues.

As the 1960 Act put it, '"Charity" means any institution, corporate or not, which is established for charitable purposes, and is subject to the control of the High Court in the exercise of the court's jurisdiction with respect to charities' (Section 45). In other words, charities are whatever the High Court rules to be so. The precedents were such a melange of *ad hoc* decisions and *post hoc* rationalisations that no one could draw up a definition which did not either exclude existing vested interests or include what current establishment thinking considered undesirable. In 1970, Judge Foster exclaimed; 'I find it incredible that the law on this subject is still derived from the Preamble to the Statute of Elizabeth I, long since repealed and long since out of date, and in modern times applied by analogy upon analogy upon analogy. It is time this branch of law was considered, rationalised and modernised' (*Incorporated Society for Law Reporting in England and Wales v. AG*).

Later, in the seventies, the Goodman Committee was set up by the National Council For Social Service (now the National Council For Voluntary Organisations). During its deliberations it was invested by ministers with almost parliamentary significance, and some of its recommendations have since been endorsed by government – although not those on definition.

The majority report included a shopping list of headings from A to Z (literally) which in effect attempted to itemise all currently accepted charitable objects and activities (Goodman, 1976 p. 123). It was in fact a heterogeneous update of the 1601 preamble · rather than an elucidation of basic principles. Yet it was never implemented, perhaps because it was in fact irrelevant – merely reiterating existing practice without prejudice to existing case law.

During the seventies, many voluntary organisations agreed, publicly, that there was indeed a need for a statutory redefinition, which they hoped would free them from arcane limitations on their powers and allow new forms of work. However in the eighties, there are no such calls from the voluntary sector, and the people one would have expected to make them explained why – privately. Their reasoning was simple and convincing. Throughout the eighties, Margaret Thatcher's Cabinet would have had a hand in the exercise. It was widely felt that Week's charity for providing kindling for heretics would return into its own, while many more worthy objects of charity would lose their status if subjected to the caprices of the Conservative Party. Far from looking to reform, most of them breathed a deep sigh of relief, when the 1989 White Paper came out with no specific plans for tightening up on 'political activities' or of reformulating a definition.

It was not that those involved in voluntary work were *happy* with the situation – more that they feared the likely future which would result from changes under the present regime. There was an added undercurrent, that to shout too much about the present restrictions on charitable activity would imply a desire to step across them. That would, in turn, imply that a charity which complained was already operating in the hazy borderline between what is legally charitable and what is not. Therefore, to advocate change too vociferously was to invite attacks from MPs, complaints to the Charity Commissioners, and hostile scrutiny of public funding.

That publicly Panglossian view was perhaps epitomised by Michael Brophy of the Charities Aid Foundation who wrote about (*The Independent*, 4 February 1989) what he called the 'present healthy consensus on charitable status'. He continued:

> We do not want a redefinition of this; we do not want a charitable status redefined in parliament, or elsewhere. It has evolved over the centuries in an entirely satisfactory way . . .
> This is not the time to make charitable status and objects a political football. It is the time for preserving, indeed treasuring the scope and to some extent the idiosyncrasy of British Laws.

Robin Guthrie, who took up office as the Chief Charity Commissioner in 1987, sees advantages in the present system of updating the law, and is confident that the process of precedent will modernise the concept in line with modern conditions, although he does worry that the lack of new cases is hindering this process. At least part of his confidence is derived from his own legal victory, in his previous capacity as head of the Rowntree Memorial Trust, over his predecessor as Charity Commissioner.

In that case (*Joseph Rowntree Memorial Trust Hospital Association v. AG* (1983)) it was accepted that there were implied commas in the 'aged impotent and poor' of the 1601 preamble, so the provision of housing for the aged, which is what the trust did, was in itself charitable without the added qualifications of impotence (in the Tudor sense) and poverty. The case also established that the relief could take the form of a contract, a 'bargain' rather than 'bounty'. This was a common-sense decision which Guthrie rightly feels reflects credit on Peter Gibson, the judge involved.

Guthrie is 'against a statutory definition – on the whole. The law has changed over time, and that has been one of its virtues. The trouble with it, very often, is that consistency is not its greatest virtue, but case law does have some capacity to reflect changing circumstances and social mores' (personal interview with author).

He is also concerned that the 'four heads' could become a constraint, rather than an enablement, and would prefer to see the concept of 'public benefit' expanded. He clearly welcomed the developments under his predecessor, Denis Peach, when there was a steady expansion of the legal field of charity, overriding, or rather circumlocuting, some earlier precedents. In 1983, the commission laid down that in some circumstances the 'provision of employment could be directed to a charitable purpose' and that 'promoting good race relations, endeavouring to eliminate discrimination on the grounds of race, and encouraging equality of opportunity' were charitable purposes (CC, Report 1983, pp. 8–10).

Although the commission's decisions are disguised as interpretation of *existing* law, it is clear that they were in fact overturning existing decisions. However, the time it took to overturn patently absurd decisions, and the tortuous methods required, do not really inspire confidence in the process.

The decision that the improvement of race relations was not charitable was made in 1949, as a result of a bequest (*Re Strakosch* (1949)) for the appeasement of racial feelings in South Africa. The bequest was perhaps questionable in its choice of priorities, since its subject was racial feelings between English-speaking and Afrikaaner whites in South Africa, just as apartheid was being systematised. The result deterred bodies like Community Relations Councils from registering as charities, or at least from declaring their real aims when they did. The South Africans must have been very pleased with the result in both places.

After Denis Peach became Chief Charity Commissioner, the commission was impelled to look at the ruling afresh. After all, in 1981, Toxteth, Brixton and Moss Side had provided convincing evidence that *bad* race relations were certainly not to the public benefit. In 1983, in its capacity as a branch of the High Court, the commission decided that improving race relations was 'analogous to purposes which the court have held to be charitable', citing decisions that it was analogous with 'the preservation of public order and the prevention of breaches of the peace' (*IRC v. City of Glasgow Police Athletic Association*), and the 'mental and moral improvement of man on the basis that discrimination on grounds of colour is immoral (*Re Hood*)' as well as the 'promotion of equality of women with men (*Halpin v. Sear*)' (CC, Report, 1983).

However, the need for such a convoluted intellectual process to legitimise what had already been established as public policy by Equal Opportunities legislation, and which was clearly for the public benefit, may be held rather as an example of the bankruptcy of the process than as a vindication of it. The fact that men of broad sympathies like Peach and Guthrie have enough weight in the Establishment to bend the law in a sensible and progressive direction carries with it the corollary that a modern day Lord Eldon placed in their position could bend it right back again. A stable system should not depend on the good will and good health of an individual incumbent.

Radical Reform Blocked

While it is easy, indeed irresistible, to mock and criticise the existing state of the law, it is difficult to suggest alternatives. First, any mere tampering, as suggested by the Goodman Commission, is like wallpapering and painting a house which is about to fall down. It does not prolong its life but engenders a false sense of security.

The more radical and effective suggestions begin with demolition. These upset conservatives and conservationists, and disturb those who think that demolition may provide a building site for altogether the wrong firm of architects.

Ben Whitaker's Minority Report to the Goodman Committee (NCSS, 1976, p. 143) took the radical line. What Whitaker said still rings true – if one excludes the discordant note from Downing Street. He quoted Sir Arthur Hobhouse, a Victorian Charity

Commissioner who spoke against 'dead hands from the grave'. 'Why should a man, whose opinion no one regarded in life, be able to dictate how posterity shall use part of the wealth they make centuries after he is dead?' He did not add, why should the judgments of deceased judges have any more power to rule subsequent charities than dead testators?

Whitaker (1979) wrote:

The ideal criterion for charitable status would be any purpose beneficial to the community – provided always any such benefit was easily accessible to all members of the community who wish to avail themselves of it. But since charitable resources and the public's ability to give tax relief are both limited, I believe the first priority should be to concentrate these primarily on *deprivation and the disadvantaged.*

These should be interpreted to include the results of not only poverty and sickness (physical and mental), but also of lack of human rights and education. While the duty of mutual care in human society is shared by and extends to the whole community, I consider it right that if the public is to be compulsorily taxed, it should be able to determine the priorities to which limited supplies of public funds are devoted. Private benefactors who prefer to help those people who are not disadvantaged should, of course, be free to do so, but they ought not to assume that the remainder of society should compulsorily be made to assist them.

He instanced examples of funds for officers' mess silver, and the many 'distressed gentlefolk' charities as examples of those which should not get the fiscal benefits.

He went even further by advocating that religion as such should not be a charitable object, but should only have the status of charity in so far as 'they carry out otherwise charitable activities; e.g. for their work in relieving poverty, but not for providing vestments'. If, on the other hand, religions were to retain their charitable status, it should also be open for other ethical and political philosophies to gain it. He cited the precedent of government funding for the major political parties as an indication of the need to consider it for political groups, and thus to end the moral panic over such activities.

While successive commissions, parliamentary inquiries and individuals had expressed their doubts about the charitability of public schools and private hospitals, most had compromised with the status quo. Whitaker suggested, with firm historical precedent, that charitable status should only be given to 'those institutions whose work is intended by its objects directly and primarily (but not exclusively) to be of benefit to the poor, and which does not charge fees to any or all those persons intended to benefit from the work of the institution at such a level that the effect in practice is to exclude those with average or below average incomes'

Since most of those making the major political and social decisions in our society come from a background with above average income, and went to schools operating on a fee paying principle, it is not entirely surprising that his suggestions were not adopted with enthusiasm. Even less well regarded was the Charity Law Reform Committee, which was active in the early seventies. It arose as a result of the *cause célèbre* of the Inland Revenue's attempt to take away the charitable status of the South Place Ethical Society. The case, which we deal with in more detail later, highlighted the anomalies rather than the analogies of what was and what was not charitable. It was perhaps exacerbated by the excuse sometimes given for other, more acceptably religious, anomalies on the register, which is that the 1960 Act was accompanied by an implied promise in Parliament that existing anomalies would be allowed to continue.

For example, the campaigning 'political' activities of the Lord's Day Observance Society have been widely cited as something which would prevent their registration with the commissioners if they were to try registering afresh now. In the early seventies, the commissioners had purged the Rationalist Press Association, the Ethical Union, and the British Humanist Association from the register, but the Lord's Day Observance Society was untouched.

The CLRC advocated the replacement of 'charity' in the legal sense by Non-Profit-Distributing Organisations, which would allow political, religious (or anti-religious) purposes the privileges of charities. As they said in reply to the Goodman Committee's dismissal of their arguments: 'We live in a plural society with many different sets of values. It is invidious for any small group of people, and in particular civil servants, to apply any specific set of values to the exclusion of others. No new definition of "Charity" can possibly meet the evident need for fairness, clarity and certainty' (*The New Humanist*, November–December, 1976).

The arguments of Whitaker and the CLRC are difficult to refute on any grounds except pragmatism and precedent – but both of those are powerful determinants of policy, perhaps more so in Britain than elsewhere. One argument against their suggestions was that this would extend fiscal privileges too widely. Yet it would be difficult to extend such privileges further than the ingenious – and almost totally unchecked – tax-avoidance schemes which characterise some of the foundations on the Charity Commissioners' Register. The proposed strengthening of the commission's powers in the 1989 White Paper should deal with most of such abuses, and there is no reason to suppose that they would not be effective against NPDOs in a reformed regime.

However, there is more to the arguments over definition than technical mechanisms for administering and defining charities. The concept of charity, as refined by the courts, has an underlying social philosophy which has remained intact and has influenced the whole of our society's view of social welfare provision. Running consistently through the decisions is the idea of 'bounty'. 'Bounty' in the legal context means more than just liberality. Preserved within it, like a fly in amber, is a concept of social relations in which some people are active agents and others just passive recipients.

That sense reached its evangelical apotheosis during the Victorian age but shows disturbing signs of a revival now. The next chapter looks at that age and its effect on the ideology of charity and public welfare.

4

Eminent Victorians

From its inception, one of the distinguishing features of Thatcherism has been a sentimentally nostalgic view of the Victorian age. Home Secretary Douglas Hurd epitomised it in 1988 when he claimed that 'active citizenship' was the key to restoring the 'amazing social cohesion' which, according to him, characterised Victorian England. He concluded: 'During this century the unravelling of this cohesion has gone dangerously far' (speech to the Peel Society, 5 February 1988).

'Cohesion' is not the usual word used by social historians to describe the political and industrial upheavals which punctuated Queen Victoria's reign. Between Chartists and waves of unionisation, riots and Fenian plots, there was little sign of social cohesion if the 'lower orders' are taken into account. But that is, perhaps, the point. They were not 'active citizens'; for much of that period they were disenfranchised by property qualifications and socially disqualified by poverty. Charity and the Poor Law were *about* them, not *by* them, and certainly not *for* them, unless they passed rigorous tests of acceptability.

Blaming the Poor

Beatrice Webb identified the 'belief – it may almost be called an obsession – that the mass misery of great cities arose mainly, if not entirely, from spasmodic indiscriminate and unconditional doles, whether in the form of Alms or that of Poor Law Relief'. (Webb, 1938, p. 227). The two forms of relief were complementary, in that payment of one usually precluded the other. The government was deeply concerned that no stray impulses of generosity should soften the harsh Poor Law regime, designed as it was to encourage independence.

While 'The organised Charity, scrimped and iced/ In the name of a cautious statistical Christ,' attempted to filter out any 'undeserving' poor from charitable gifts, the unemployed occasionally demonstrated their cohesion to the scheme of things by rioting. In *Major Barbara*, Shaw celebrated the results of this counter-Hurd instinct:

> *Mrs Baines* ... I remember 1886 when you rich gentlemen hardened your hearts against the cry of the poor. They broke the windows of your clubs in Pall Mall.
> *Undershaft* (gleaming with approval of their method) And the Mansion House Fund went up the next day from thirty thousand pound to seventy nine thousand! I remember quite well! (Act II)

Shaw omitted to add that the Hyde Park Riots of 1886 persuaded an apprehensive government to temper the harshness of the 'less eligibility' regime for Poor Law relief, in view of its concern over the social unrest caused by the lower orders refusing to be held morally responsible for the consequences of a trade recession.

A century later, in 1988, Allen Sheppard of Grand Metropolitan had a pragmatic view of which Undershaft would have approved.

> Do-gooding is actually about economic survival. The limiting factor in the South East is labour availability. So we can't afford to have pockets of long-term unemployed. We know that in Tower Hamlets 50% of young people are unemployed; but we also know that companies like ourselves can't find people to be milkmen or work in our betting shops. Through things like Compact and Joblink, unemployed people are being put in touch with the employers. And all these people are our customers too, so anything we can do to get society moving will come back to us in our pubs and betting shops. (*The Guardian* 8 November 1988).

There is strong evidence that the Victorian poor were not content with their lot. Contemporary reports suggest irritation with the moralising cant of the relief workers, and resentment at providing a hobby for the evangelical middle class whose women were precluded by custom from gainful employment.

Overeager missionaries to the inner cities were warned by the Reverend James Aspinall; 'You will have to contend with that fierce spirit of independence, which will brook nothing that it may regard as an influence with its affairs, which will look upon a word of advice as a word unseasonably spoken, and will force you from its habitation in that decided manner which will plainly tell you never to enter there again' (quoted in Simey, 1951, p. 30). Aspinall exhorted the poor to receive such visitors kindly since their attention 'flows from that pure feeling of benevolence which has founded so many charities for your temporal wants'.

They had indeed. Between 1837 and 1880 9,154 new charities were known to the Charity Commissioners and between 1880 and 1900 the number rose to 22,607. In the early part of the century, however, benevolence was abraded from welfare services by government policy and by the law. To the indifference and sectarianism of the eighteenth century was added a reforming and evangelical zeal which at times seemed almost pathologically vindictive against the poor. It was even ruled that no death knell should be tolled for paupers whose bodies were subject to requisition by the anatomists.

The Poor Law, public policy and charity worked in malevolent tandem. For example, in 1858 (*Thrupp v. Collet*), John Romilly, son of the Samuel Romilly who gave us the 'four heads' of charity, held void as contrary to public policy a bequest for procuring the discharge of imprisoned poachers, although the redemption of prisoners is clearly enunciated in the 1601 preamble. To take another example, that of the Liverpool Domestic Mission, their 1838 report reads: 'To the administration of more than one of the local charities, I am always ready to pay a tribute of merited praise; but nothing, I fear, can take from their natural tendency to propagate the very evil they were intended to counteract. While they exist, there will always I think, be one great source of dependency and degradation among the lower class of the poor' (Liverpool Domestic Mission Report, 1838).

Philanthropy in Fashion

In Liverpool, which horrified visitors like Herman Melville with the poverty on its streets (see his *Redburn*), the missionaries thought that 'the existence ... of not fewer than 60,000 individuals who pass from childhood to age without any efficient means of religious culture ought to excite the deepest sympathy on their behalf, and lead to active exertions for the improvement of their moral and social condition' (Simey, 1951, p. 36). They firmly believed that pauperism was a wound self-inflicted by a slovenly soul; attend to the soul, and the poverty would be cured.

However, not all were so concerned. Liverpool was the richest provincial city, the boom town of the Victorian age. The poor casual labourers lived in proximity to rich merchants in a way they did not in other cities more dependent on industry and less on trade. The rich, some of whose ancestral fortunes were made in the slave trade, spent their largesse on art galleries, museums and parks to beautify the city; the poor lived in a squalor remarkable even for Victorian times. So there were visible objects for charity in great numbers, and great wealth to tend to those wants. But the city's rich, who paid more Schedule D tax on profits from business and professions than Birmingham, Bristol, Leeds and Sheffield combined, were not unanimous in their giving. A survey in 1873 showed that out of 20,000 potential contributors to charity in Liverpool, only 6,688 gave, and just over a thousand of them accounted for half of what was collected (Lane, 1987, p. 78).

Moreover, their motives for giving were not necessarily concerned with the spiritual or temporal needs of the poor. Tory Radical Hugh Shimmin ribbed at the Pooteresque behaviour of the middle classes.

> The most fashionable amusement of the present age is philanthropy. Liverpool, which delights in following a fashion of any kind pants and puffs to keep well up with this in especial. But it is a fashion, and we would not have the working man suppose that all the gentlemen and ladies of Liverpool ... really do care quite as much about him or understand his condition and his wants quite as as well as they give out. No small number of these benevolent persons are philanthropic because it is the fashion to be so; because it brings them into passing contact with this Bishop or that Earl, or even with Mr Cropper or Mr Rathbone, or any other of our leading philanthropists. Not a few ladies, who will visit the garret of a workingman's wife, and talk in the most condescending way, and put on the most friendly interest in the progress of the children would quiver to the utmost hoops of their crinolines if asked to sit down to tea with the wife of a grocer. (*Porcupine* 1 June 1861)

It sounds uncannily like the present revived fashion for charity balls among the modern equivalents of the same class. *The Daily Telegraph* (6 May 1989) carried a breathless round-up of charity balls, confiding that those attending the Rose Ball should 'Look out for: Lady Grade and lots of Hons in attendance. The place will be bulging with important sounding names.' Put on your dancing pumps, Pooter!

The popularity of philanthropy during the Victorian age led to 'an outbreak of what was nothing less than ill-informed and ill-inspired meddling with the working classes ... Whoever saw a need was free to meet it according to his fancy' (Simey, 1951). In 1855, the Liverpool Domestic Mission, which was still having difficulties in making its ministrations acceptable, advised that 'courteous visiting will ensure a courteous reception' and deplored the impatience of visitors who wished to force redemption on their flock, forgetting that 'they are in the house of another in the capacity of visitors' (Report, 1855).

A local paper glossed:

The intention of philanthropists is one thing, the manner in which they carry their intentions out – the way in which they meet and mingle with those whom they wish to benefit – is quite another. [The workingmen's] bluntness is often mistaken for impertinence, their earnestness looked upon as vulgarity and their demeanour spoken of as not being at all 'gentle-manly'. (*Porcupine*, 11 December 1860)

Sorting Deserving Wheat from Undeserving Chaff

Far from being an age of social cohesion, this was the age of perceptive Conservatives like Disraeli, who identified two nations divided by an ocean of social and ideological differences. That division indicated the atavism underlying charity – the implied fission between the beneficiaries and the benefactors, between the active affluent, and the passive poor. Margaret Simey summed up the age in her epitaph to William Rathbone, the great philanthropist, and founder of a socially concerned dynasty: 'To him, the "people" to whose welfare he dedicated his life, were never to include himself or his like; the working man however commendable, however admirable, was never to be taken into the bosom of his family, never loved in life nor garlanded with white camellias in death' (Simey, 1951, p. 91).

That sense of alienation from the beneficiaries and recipients often expressed itself in a distrust of their moral probity. Mendicity

and mendacity were seen as inseparable twins. Therefore, organised
charity was as eager to ensure that the undeserving poor did not
get help as it was to relieve the deserving poor – if not more so.
For example, the Liverpool Central Relief and Charity Organisation
Society was founded under the influence of the cotton famine
caused by the Federal blockade of the Confederate States in
America which led to widespread unemployment and distress in
the North West of England.

In 1863, preening itself on the success of its 12,654 visits
resulting in 10,511 cases relieved at an average of 2s 8d each, the
society added that 'it has also been the means of exposing the
nefarious practices of those who made a business of mendicity, and
the stream of charity which is ever ready to flow in the direction of
deserving objects has, there is reason to believe, been materially
protected from being diverted into an opposite channel' (Liverpool
Central Relief and Charity Organisation Society, Annual Report,
1863–4). The society carried a regular reminder from then on that
it was intended to detect and deter the undeserving as much as it
was to succour the worthy poor.

By the turn of the century, the poor were as unamenable as ever
to moral improvement. Bishop Chevasse of Liverpool lamented

> that it was easier to find money for charity than deserving cases
> on which to spend it, the lack of response by the poor to the
> campaign for inducing habits of thrift, their preference for
> starvation in their familiar slum rather than migration under
> the auspices of the Society, all seemed to them to bear witness
> to a deterioration in the moral stamina of the poor. (Simey,
> 1951, p. 137)

However, the Victorian age was not as homogeneous as political
Victorianists of our day present it. There were voices of genuine
charity to set against the priggish self-righteousness of the
evangelists. Across the Pennines in York, less bigoted thinkers like
Joseph Rowntree were overturning patronising principles and
looking at a new conception of charitable and voluntary endeavour.
In Liverpool itself, trade union leaders like Larkin, Connolly and
Sexton were soon to prove very conclusively that the poor had
minds and methods of their own, which were more to do with
secular than spiritual progress and had little to do with social
cohesion.

Brute Beasts that Have no Understanding

However, those whose well-meaning principles, frustrated by the ingratitude of the poor, had other outlets. Ironically, the Victorians' attitude to the poor was accompanied by a greater concern for animal welfare which was first accepted as a charitable object in 1864.

As Chesterman says, animal welfare represents 'perhaps the most extreme instance of charity's drift towards matters peripheral to social welfare' (1979, p. 168). It is not now seriously questioned that animal welfare is a charitable object, even by people who object to the seeming English preference for dogs and cats over children and the old. None the less, the most imaginative exegesis of the 1601 preamble and the four heads of charity would still have difficulty in extrapolating the charitability of animal welfare.

In 1857 (*London University v. Yarrow*), the courts had ruled that a trust to provide a veterinary institute to study and cure the diseases of animals, quadrupeds and birds, which were *useful to man*, was charitable. It made sense for a utilitarian age heavily dependent on horsepower.

In 1864 (*Tathom v. Drummond*), the principle was stretched to modern lengths of compassion. A trust for the relief and protection of animals about to be slaughtered was deemed charitable. The decision took the bequest into the mischief of the 1736 Mortmain Act – and so by being declared charitable it was disallowed. However, although the estate went to the natural heir on this occasion, the 1736 Mortmain Act was thus the long-term benefactor of the animal kingdom, as it was of so many innovative charitable causes.

That is not to say that animals had it all their own way even in that sentimental age. In 1888 (*Re Joy*), it was held not to be charitable to use private prayer to suppress cruelty to animals. In 1915, Judge Swinfen Eady (*Re Wedgwood*) sanctioned a trust for the benefit and protection of animals with particular attention to better methods of slaughtering. All this would have perplexed the MPs who drew up the 1601 Act. Their main interest would have been how most cheaply to convert animals to victuals for the poor, rather than how to provide for indigent donkeys and homeless cats. But Eady rationalised that

A Gift for the benefit and protection of animals tends to

promote and encourage kindness towards them, to discourage cruelty and to ameliorate the condition of the brute creation, and thus to stimulate humane and generous sentiments in man towards the lower animals, and by that means to promote feelings of humanity and morality generally, repress brutality, and thus elevate the human race.

Empirical evidence would not necessarily suggest that animal lovers are therefore kind to humans.

Indeed one only has to look at Judge Romer, who used the same reasoning to declare that a trust to a particular named person looking after the welfare of cats and kittens was charitable (*Re Moss* (1949)). He was the judge who overturned the bequest to a children's home some years later.

By the 1940s the Inland Revenue was pushing hard against the indulgences of earlier decisions, in an attempt to restrict the fiscal privileges of charities. After all, it had a very expensive war to pay for. Wisely, it did not risk public outrage by going for the RSPCA, or the Cats' Protection League, but went for a softer target, the National Anti-Vivisection League. The League had originally been ruled to be in the public benefit in 1895 (*Re Foveaux*). In 1947, the Lords agreed with the taxmen and withdrew charitable status. They felt that there was more benefit to the public from vivisection than from its abolition. It was a singular example of precisely the type of value judgment which the courts have said they cannot make, when rationalising their unwillingness to accept trusts with political objects. It was not just the League's status which was overturned, but also the indulgent precedent set by Judge Chitty (*Re Foveaux*) that testators' benign intentions counted for more than the courts' views of public benefits.

The RSPCA, being royal, is now safe, although its objects include the promotion of legislation. In 1988, it ran a shock horror campaign with heaps of dead dogs pictured in advertisements, which went way beyond a reasoned memorandum, in an attempt to persuade the government to reintroduce dog licensing. This was manifestly a political campaign of the type for which War on Want had been reprimanded. I put a hypothetical complaint to the Charity Commissioners – was this not a political campaign, and as such were the RSPCA trustees not breaking the law? Yes and no, was the answer. The society did call for a change in the law – but under the RSPCA Act of 1932 they had powers to campaign in that manner.

The courts clearly take a more benign view of the politics of the animal kingdom than they do of human welfare. If the revolt in *Animal Farm* were ever to become a possibility, we could expect the bounds of what is allowable to animal charities to be drastically reduced as the brute creation became politicised – and a potential threat.

Different Uses for Man and Beast

However, technically, the latitude is only allowed to animals which can be considered pleasant. As Swinfen Eady said in 1915:

> I can entertain no doubt that if the Court should now be asked to say whether the trustee under this bequest for the protection and benefit of animals was fulfilling his duty in expending the fund upon the preservation of beasts of prey or mad dogs, the Court would not find any difficulty as to the answer which is dictated by reason and common sense. There are, I suppose, very few, if any charities of a wide character, such as, to take an imaginary case, a charity for the relief of poor mechanics, in regard to which it would not be easy for ingenuity to suggest difficulty of discrimination. (*Re Wedgwood* (1915))

Discrimination is an appropriate word. The Charity Commissioners in 1978 could not accept submissions by Amnesty International that 'the abolition of torture or inhuman or degrading treatment or punishment was charitable by analogy with the prevention of cruelty to animals'. The case did not allow moral uplift for people who wished to stop cruelty to humans. The Privy Council restricted such benevolent extension even further by deciding that just because a 'trust for the promotion of kindness towards the animal part of creation is charitable', it should not be taken to imply 'that a trust for the promotion of kindness of man to man is charitable too'. As they added in the classic Eldonian manner, 'no such wide proposition has ever been accepted; on the contrary "philanthropic" and "benevolent" purposes have never been held to be within the conception of charity' (*D'Aguiar v. Guyana Commissioner of Inland Revenue* (1970)).

In this they followed good Victorian precedents, as their

ancestors had originally felt considerable doubt about whether the
National Society for the Prevention of Cruelty to Children was
charitable. The NSPCC survived its formative Victorian years under
the protective wing of the RSPCA, which provided it with office
space. Arising from those anomalous roots, animal charities in 1988
had incomes in excess of 80 million pounds, covering bodies
ranging from the RSPCA to the Donkey Sanctuary, the Cat's
Protection League and the International League for the Protection of
Horses. It was pleasant to note that in 1987 the NSPCC overtook the
RSPCA in income, although it has to be doubted whether this
respresents a long-term trend in the popular consciousness. The
RSPCA still reigns supreme in the thoughts of those approaching
their maker. It netted £12,623,000 in legacies, compared with
£4,186,000 for the NSPCC, and £11,173,000 for Dr Barnado's. In
terms of voluntary income, children as a sector just beat animals by
about 60 million to 52 million pounds (all figures from the
Charities Aid Foundation, 1988).

A century on, animal welfare is probably well within the lay
definition of charity. Few would demur at the principle, although
many may baulk at the sense of priorities implied in, for example,
the scale of legacies. Indeed, there is now an ecological
consciousness, which has expanded the concept of animal welfare
from utilitarian concerns with useful 'quadrupeds and birds', to a
concern with the whole environment and all species no matter how
small and obscure. Naturally, however, Greenpeace, and Friends of
the Earth which epitomised that ecological view, even before
governments discovered the greenhouse effect, are *not* charities.

The thought processes by which lay society reaches conclusions
are several centuries removed from the legal method. Despite
Orwell's fable, animals have never themselves threatened the
position of the Establishment. In the case of humans, the pecking
order has to be maintained if the Establishment is not to be
disestablished, which is no doubt why many good human causes
have met vigorous resistance to charitable status.

It is not just animal welfare which has survived from the Victorian
age into the late twentieth century. The patronising evangelical
attitudes inherent in the legal conception of charity remain strong
forces in the ideology of the voluntary sector.

The ideology of two nations is nowhere better expressed or
perpetuated than in the largest sector of charities, dealt with in the
next chapter. The vindictiveness expressed towards the poor by the

Victorian Establishment, the restrictions placed on making their lives comfortable, stand in sharp contrast to the generosity and leniency shown towards the public schools, then and now.

5

The Advancement of Learning

The 1601 preamble lists as charitable objects, 'Educacion and prefermente *of orphans*' (author's italics), and 'Maintenance of ... Schooles of Learninge, Free Schooles, and Schollers in Universities'. From those items, as we saw, Romilly had extrapolated the 'Advancement of Learning' as one of his four heads of charity, later to be taken up by Macnaghten as 'The Advancement of Education'. Macnaghten's education was a different thing from Romilly's learning: its social context had changed completely. In the intervening century, it had been established by cases that learning in itself was not charitable unless it was shared, that is, made public. A secret research establishment or a political think-tank, for example, were not and are not charitable unless its work is published and open for the education of the public.

That was not the only change during that time. Education, religion, and the relief of poverty and charity had pulled away from each other. The abolition of religious tests had opened up the universities. When London University opened in 1828, Thomas Arnold of Rugby had denounced it as a 'Godless institution' for tolerating Professors who were not practising Christians. The year before, the Lonsdale case had allowed exclusive schools for the sons of gentlemen, which legitimised the separation of education from relief of poverty.

The Advancement of Education now covers many fields, and, in truth, if it has any direct connection with the relief of poverty, it is intellectual rather than financial poverty. Theatres, operas, ballet companies, learned societies, dowsing, Boy Scouts, and goats are just some of the things which have been accepted under the head of education. Few would doubt that the extension is justified – such arguments as there are, are about accessibility. There is still a lingering, albeit almost fossilised, presumption that charitable bodies should be open, even to the poor.

As always there was a large element of subjectivity in the court decisions. The Boy Scouts, pledging fealty to Queen and Country were clearly educational – one doubts whether the Young Communist League or the Young Socialists would be accepted as such. Judge Vaisey decided in 1945 (*Re Duprée's Deed Trusts*) that the promotion of an annual chess tournament in Portsmouth was educational and so charitable, In 1959, the Court of Appeal ruled Chester Zoo charitable. The judge decided that 'A ride on an elephant may be educational; at any rate it brings the reality of the elephant and its uses to the child's mind in lieu of leaving him to mere booklearning' (*Re North of England Zoological Society*).

State of the Art

Judges have used their implied position as practising sociologists to screen out educational causes of which they disapprove. For example, in 1923 (*Re Hummeltenberg*), a gift for the training of spiritualist mediums was found not charitable, on the ground that it was not proved to be for the public benefit. In contrast, in Scotland, in 1870, the 'advancement and diffusion of the science of phrenology' was found to be a good charitable object (*M'Lean v. Henderson's Trustees*).

Judges in this line of work must be prepared to act as art and drama critics as well as experts in social policy. So art galleries may be charitable, but not for the exhibition of just any old work: they must contain masterpieces. In 1965 (*Re Pinion*), a collector's life work was cavalierly dismissed by expert witnesses, one of whom expressed 'his surprise that so voracious a collector should not by hazard have picked up even one meritorious object'. Luckily for the Tate, Carl Andrés controversial bricks were never brought into the court (although they may have been analogised from causeways, bridges, etc!).

On the same principle, a performance of a slight Elizabethan comedy like Dekker's *Shoemakers' Holiday* would probably be charitable on grounds of antiquity – but a recent Festival of Comedy in the North of England suffered the disability of contemporary accessibility. The commissioners gave them a succinct summary of the state of judicial arts appreciation. 'You will be well aware that the presentation of plays and other works of objectively high artistic calibre is charitable.' They quoted the case of the Royal Choral Society: 'In the case of artistic taste, one of the best ways of training it is by presenting works of high class and gradually training people to like them in preference to works of an inferior class' (*RCS v. IRC* 1943)).

The commissioners then qualified, 'But it is not the performance of every dramatic or other work which may be loosely termed artistic which would fall within what the law would regard as educational. The organising of entertainments such as cabarets, circus performances and comedian shows would not qualify.'

The festival organisers' arguments were compelling, but the commissioners were still worried:

> I entirely accept that comedy is a subject to be treated with the same respect that is accorded to other aspects of drama and is as capable of forming the subject matter of a charitable educational trust.
>
> But not every comic work or performance will be educational in a sense known to the law ... We do not accept that individuals involved in or observing performances (regardless of the aesthetic merit of its subject matter) are engaged upon the pursuit of a 'fundamentally educational purpose'. Nor do we accept that each and every experienced and trained performance will educate observers in any meaningful way. Some performances will, if the subject matter is of objectively high aesthetic calibre. Others will not.

The commission felt that the 'Water Sport Extravaganza' did not fit the bill and also had doubts about the 'cartoon exhibition'. The problem was that they were *contemporary* cartoons. If they had been Rowlandson's or Hogarth's, then antiquity would presumably have been, in itself, educative.

In fairness, there seems to have been a pragmatic creep of the boundaries of what is educational and therefore charitable in the arts world – mainly, one suspects, because such matters have not gone to the courts. One can think of many a judge who would not consider a Picasso, a Dali or a Jackson Pollock as of 'objectively high artistic calibre', if anyone were foolish enough to enlist his services as art critic.

The charitable status of the arts has been controversial – on much the same grounds of accessibility as public schools or private hospitals. But the arguments have been less about the indirect subsidy by fiscal privileges, than about the large amount of direct public funding through Arts Council and Local Authority Grants. The biggest consumers of arts cash from public and private sponsors have been prestigious national companies, like the Royal Opera in Covent Garden which took £5.9 million from the Arts Council in 1988. Since these also have some of the highest seat prices, it raises the ethical question of whether this is not in fact a form of subsidy for the rich. Sensitive to such charges, theatres have tended to make much cheaper seats available at the bottom end of the market. This is, in a way, testimony to the moral leverage which the public can have upon bodies with charitable status.

However, what public influence is there on the subsidies received? In the case of the so-called 'independent' schools, there are clear signs that the same moral arguments make a mark, but this is no more than a dent in their armour of social privilege. The courts have consistently held public schools to be educational, although these depend for their appeal on keeping their doors closed to their social inferiors.

How Public Schools Became Private

Public schools are a classic case of how past precedent can defy present common sense. There is no doubt that historically they were charitable – and little doubt that, in function at least, they are no longer so. In 1975, for example, the Commons Public Expenditure Committee stated firmly that there had been 'a failure to grasp the nettle of definition of charity. We are convinced that the nettle must be grasped, and we advocate the adoption of "purpose beneficial to the community" as the overriding criterion'. It continued:

> We have noted that many... independent schools were founded not simply for the advancement of education, but specifically for the education of the poor... We believe that our recommendation to make a test of public benefit the overriding consideration with that of education accords both with the spirit in which our Sixteenth Century public schools were founded and with a widespread public feeling today that charitable activities should not be manifestly devoted to privilege or exclusiveness.

Despite similar attempts over a century, the privileged position of public schools has remained unbreached. Even though they claim it 'only' saves them 30 million pounds a year in tax (ISIS, 1987), the assiduity with which they defend their charitable status is a measure of its importance. Charitable status confers more than financial privileges. Charity is a powerfully benign concept to enhance the other prestigious connotations of the public schools. Noble and self-sacrificing, academic and sporting-like, the play-the-game image of the schools entranced generations who had not, and could not, have attended them.

One would never suspect from those warm images that, to achieve their present dignified status, the older public schools conducted a guerrilla war of caddish spitefulness against non-U scholars; that they abused their endowments, broke the law, and then secured legalisation of all that they had done. To crown their actions, they also plundered charities founded to keep the poor in coal and food. The nineteenth century was not an edifying period for either welfare or education: the aim in both cases was clearly to maintain the social pyramid.

The English education system began as the responsibility of the Church. The ancient establishments all had close links with the Established Church which, of course, functioned as one of the pillars of the state. There was no question of 'independence', the schools were part of, in fact were, the national educational system. Increasing secularisation combined with ecclesiastical corruption to leave the schools in an appalling state.

Criticism of the public schools as educational institutions is not a recent egalitarian trend. In *Joseph Andrews*, Henry Fielding regarded them as the 'nurseries of all vice and immorality' while Cowper's *Tirocinium* was a lengthy indictment of the snobbery, cruelty and patronage he found at Westminster: 'Though from ourself the mischief more proceeds/ For public schools 'tis public folly feeds'.

By the eighteenth century, the deficiencies of the schools were well recognised. In 1795 (*King v. The Archbishop of York*), Lord Kenyon referred to the schools under the Archbishop of York as 'empty walls without scholars, and everything neglected but the receipt of salaries and emoluments. In some instances that have lately come within my own knowledge there was not a single scholar in the schools, though there were very large endowments to them.'

In the industrial areas, new technological developments were transforming the age and laying the economic foundations of the British Empire. But one would be hard put to identify any of those inventors or entrepreneurs with public schools which were often restricted to classical languages.

Exclusive – in Every Sense

By then, fee paying and boarding had become big business for schoolmasters, in compensation for the shrinking value of their ancient endowments and emoluments. In 1807, Eldon had allowed that admitting fee paying pupils to Harrow and Rugby would not affect the charitable privileges they received, based upon their provision for 'poore schollers'. (Although he ruled that Leeds Grammar School could not vary its trust to teach anything other than classical languages!) This caused direct tensions since the poor scholars identified in the founding trusts could not, by definition, pay fees. The older schools were charities because they were free, or at least very cheap, and in the statutes setting them up the phrase 'Pauperes et indigentes' is used to describe their scholars.

In fact, when Henry VI founded Eton, in 1442, the rule laid down was, 'No one having a yearly income of more than five marks (£3–30) shall be eligible', and scholars at Winchester had to swear to their lack of means on reaching the age of 15. Eton had a rule that the sons of serfs should not be admitted, which is usually taken as confirmation that most other grammar schools did admit those of servile origin. To reinforce a generally egalitarian principle, the 1406 Statute of Artificers ruled that 'every man or woman of what state or condition that he be, shall be free to set their son or daughter to take learning at any school that pleaseth them within the realm'.

Eton's statute provided for a Provost, seventy poor scholars, ten Priest fellows, ten chaplains, ten clerks, sixteen choristers, a schoolmaster, an Usher and 'thirteen poor infirm men'. Noblemen's sons and special friends of the college, up to twenty of them, were allowed to sleep and board at the college, provided that no expense was incurred for them beyond their instruction. (This was the loophole which allowed the present day exclusivity; it has to be doubted whether the £7,000 per annum fees for modern pupils buy King Henry's soul much of the remission from purgatory he intended with his pious gift.)

Similarly, when Winchester was established, in 1382, its founder, William of Wykeham, laid down that it was to consist of seventy 'poor and needy' scholars who were to live as a community. But, conscious of the need for support and patronage, he stipulated, 'We allow, however, sons of noble and influential persons, special friends of the said college, to the number of ten, to be instructed and informed in grammar within the said college, without charge to the college, so that by occasion thereof prejudice, loss or scandal in no wise arise to the Warden, priests, scholars, clerks or any of the servants of the same.'

That education was free did not prevent the scholars and their parents from showing their gratitude for the quality of instruction. The founder of Bury Grammar School said in 1625: 'My intent and meaning is not to debar the Master and Usher from that common privilege in all free schools of receiving Presents, Benevolences, Gratuities etc.' Bromsgrove's master's salary was fixed at £7 per annum in the mid-fifteenth century. It was clearly not enough but presumably it could be supplemented – the headmaster in 1818, the Hon. Reverend Joseph Fell, was accused of spending nine consecutive days in a local tavern (Gathorne-Hardy, 1977, p. 56). A more sobre eighteenth-century headmaster, of Blundell's, collected £60,000 by such 'common privileges' in his twenty-three years of office.

What began as a gratuity soon came to be a necessity. By the mid-century, the Public Schools Commission was told that keeping a boarding house had become 'the regular and principal source of income of an assistant master'. This may appear reprehensible but it has to be put in the context of wage freezes lasting centuries. The results *were* reprehensible. The local day school pupils were squeezed out by the socially and financially more acceptable boarders. With the growing class consciousness of the age, the titled and affluent were not going to pay good guineas to have their sons brought up along aside the offspring of mere tradesmen and farmers, let alone the genuine poor.

The evidence of the schools to the various parliamentary commissions indicated some degree of awareness that what they were doing was neither strictly ethical nor legal. Yet they were prodigal, rather than economical, with the truth. Westminster School told the parliamentary commissioners that the statutes providing free places had never been implemented and had not been confirmed by Queen Elizabeth, because, with prescient anticipation of Victorian values, she had disapproved of the rule. That King James afterwards referred to the free scholars of Westminster, or that the terms of the Statute of Uses itself indicated differing mores, did not disturb the smooth flow of convenient lies. Outstanding in its concern for child poverty was Winchester. When the Brougham Commission, in 1818, asked it why there were so many rich boys at a school meant for the poor, the school replied that the boys were in fact very poor indeed. In fact they were totally without money – it was their parents who were rich. Charterhouse, struggling to balance the needs of snobbery with those of the founding statute told the Clarendon Commission of 1861 that the forty-four foundation boys were usually 'persons exceedingly well connected, but really poor'. The Clarendon Commission later summarised:

> The bulk of each school is an accretion upon the original foundation, and consists of boarders received by masters or other persons at their own risk and for their own profit . . . The legal position of the Headmaster of Eton is that of teacher or 'informator' of seventy poor and indigent boys, received and boarded within Eton College; the headmaster of Harrow is legally the master of a daily grammar school, established in a county village for the benefit primarily of its immediate neighbourhood.

Making it difficult for the poor to gain access to the schools was unethical but legal. After 1827, Judge Leach had made it possible to exclude them entirely. 'The institution of a school for the sons of gentlemen is not, in popular language, a charity; but in the view of the statute of Elizabeth, *all schools are so to be considered'* (author's italics) (*AG v. Lord Lonsdale* (1827)). Thus between them, the headmasters, judges and parliamentarians of the nineteenth century achieved what Faustus had to sell his soul for:

> I'll have them fill the public schools with silk
> Wherewith the students shall be bravely clad.

The exclusion of the poor was noted by William Gladstone who, as Chancellor of the Exchequer, tried in 1863 to restrict charities' fiscal privileges as 'an undiscriminating public subsidy for a large group of organisations which were not subject to any adequate form of public scrutiny'. His example was the élite schools 'which had little or nothing to do with educating the poor'. Some later jurists still clung to belief that there must be some residual benefit to the poor in charity. 'I am quite aware that a trust may be charitable, and yet not confined to the poor, but I doubt very much whether a trust would be declared to be charitable which excluded the poor,' said Lord Justice Lindley in 1896 (*Re Macduff*). His faith, even then, was rather touching, but time has dealt even less kindly with it.

Making the Unethical Legal

It is a measure of the strength of the élite that they took hold of parliamentary commissions designed to reform their schools, and transmuted the results into a final exorcism of the poor from their cloisters. The Taunton Commission was set up in 1864 to look at schools other than the nine 'Great Schools' considered earlier by the Clarendon Commission. Perceptively, it noted that

> Boys who can add much to a master's earnings must be boys from a superior class, and they will not be attracted to the school to associate with boys in the same position as those in the national schools. Sometimes even a few boys seem to form an obstacle to the schools becoming attractive to others. If on the other hand the reputation of the master is high, boarders or paying day scholars come but the foundationers are, to say the least, often slighted, and even where well taught, are yet separated from the others by some distinction which is in fact invidious.

Where the free scholars or foundationers were not simply excluded directly, they were made to feel their position with the vindictiveness usually reserved for the poor. At one school, foundationers were not allowed to use the playground or associate with the boarders after hours. At another, they were separated by a glazed partition from the fee payers, even though they sat in the same class room.

The incorporation of boarding – often as a commercial enterprise – within the school establishment was sometimes the motivation, but also a method, of excluding the undesirables. R. H. Tawney (1966, p. 55) described the process in the mid-nineteenth century: 'enterprising grammar schools made haste to fall in with the fashion, sometimes placating their consciences for the diversion of their services from day boys to boarders by supporting cheap day schools for the sons of local residents'.

Rugby and Harrow were outstanding examples of the practice. When John Lyon, a successful hatter, founded Harrow as a local grammar school in 1571, he allowed its master, after providing free places for the locals, to 'receive over and above the youth of the inhabitants within this parish so many foreigners as the whole may be well taught and applied and the place can conveniently contain, and of these foreigners he may take such stipend and wages as he can get'. In the mid-nineteenth century, Harrow established the 'Lower school of John Lyon' which was a continuation of the 'English Form' set up as a day school twenty-three years earlier for the sons of farmers and tradesmen (like founder John Lyon himself). There, boys were given what the Taunton Commission described as 'a commercial education, including French', in a 'humble tenement' socially and physically separated from the boarders and the 'real' school.

Vaughan, the headmaster, had already tried tricks like taking registration just after the midday meal, which the day boys took at home. In case they made it, he forbade them to ride. The school gave additional tuition in the evenings for boarders – and then set examinations on the work done for everybody, including the day boys. By 1864, Harrow's head master was able to assure the Clarendon Commission that there were no longer any tradesmen's sons in the school which had been founded by the generosity and charity of one (by this time Vaughan was no longer headmaster – he had been forced out for sexual irregularities with one of his pupils).

Gathorne-Hardy suggests that Thomas Arnold, the founding saint of the public school as it is known today, abolished Rugby's lower school for one reason only. 'By doing so he effectively prevented lower class local people from entering the school since they couldn't reach a high enough standard to pass into the upper forms – unless they paid for outside schooling. A law case decision said he was wrong. Arnold ignored it' (1977, p. 74). Later, in 1878, the Lower School of Lawrence Sheriff was founded to provide instruction such as 'may be suitable for boys intended for commercial and other similar occupations, and may also qualify them for admission into the higher school'.

To make doubly sure of restricted entry, public schools insisted on competence in Latin before entry which effectively forestalled any remote chance the lower orders may have had, and led to a whole new growth industry of preparatory schools to groom the financially privileged to jump through the social hoops necessary for admission. The results of this policy were evidently not in the national interest. In an increasingly technological age, in which dreadnoughts and artillery won wars rather than cricket and pluck, the schools which educated the Empire's rulers were laughably inadequate. In 1884, Eton employed twenty-eight masters for classics, six for maths, and none at all for science or modern languages. Harrow had twenty-one teaching classics, five maths, two modern languages – and one 'Natural Science'. (It was presumably as a result of this Harrovian toe-hold in the modern world that Stanley Baldwin felt able to announce, in the 1920s, that he had determined that his government should have six Harrovians in the Cabinet (Griggs, 1985 p. 57).)

To the outside observer, bemused and repelled by such clannish élitism, there is some amusement to be drawn from the correspondence between Shrewsbury and Westminster. Shrewsbury had been included in the nine 'Great Schools' at the pushy insistence of its headmaster. He had informed the commissioners that the school's title of 'Free Grammar School' referred to its independence, not the cost of the education. Despite his efforts, when the Shrewsbury Cricket Eleven tried to organise a fixture against Westminster, they were snubbed by the latter because 'Westminster plays no schools except public schools and the general feeling in the school quite co-incides with that of the Committee of the Public School Club, who issue this list of public schools – Charterhouse, Eton, Harrow, Rugby, Westminster and Winchester' (Fleming, 1944, p. 123).

Shrewsbury has since had its revenge. The 1984 *Sunday Times* Survey of Public Schools showed it as having one of the lowest proportions of pupil intake from maintained state schools, a mere 2 per cent.

Managing Reform

Public opinion – or at least the opinion of that part of the public with enough property to vote – was more outraged by other revelations of the various commissions than by their violation of founding statutes. These were the widespread misappropriation of endowments by those who were supposed to be training the nation's élite (and looking at the process of imperial expansion, one can only suspect that they taught their lessons well).

In 1860, the Warden and Fellows of Winchester took half the

college revenues – eight times what was spent on the staff. The Clarendon Commission revealed that Eton had, in twenty years, collected £127,000 of fines on leases which had been divided between the Provost and Fellows. Their defence rested on precedent: the statutes had been ignored for centuries. The Fellows escaped uncharged and unpunished for a crime which was, in modern values, greater than that of the Great Train Robbers. But then, the Taunton Commission (1867) discovered thirty-eight schools in Yorkshire and Durham which were still endowed, but had omitted to enroll any pupils. The commission did its sums, and calculated that the endowments involved were sufficient to form the core of a modern, national, comprehensive education system, with a syllabus equipped to take the country into the twentieth century.

Already, the Great Exhibition had revealed that Britain's technological edge was being blunted in comparison with countries like the USA and Germany. The Endowed Schools Bill, which sought a parallel of the type of reform which Bismarck's Germany was carrying out so successfully, was not well received. It would have had science taught in the schools, admission to which would be by a national competitive examination, while the old endowments would be used to provide free places for the able poor.

In a striking demonstration of the solidarity and power of the public schools, the actual Endowed Schools Act of 1869 reversed the whole trend of the bill which had germinated it. It set up an Endowed Schools Commission with the power to introduce reforms as it saw necessary. Amazingly, the commissioners seemed to find necessary just what the heads of the endowed schools wanted. 'Furious behind the scenes lobbying (not yet fully researched) completely castrated the bill of its radical elements' (Gathorne-Hardy, 1977, p. 99). However, the prime lobbiers were later to set themselves up formally as the Headmasters' Conference. On their behalf old statutes and trust deeds were set aside, blowing away all the old semi-feudal relics – like free places, or provision for the education of the local community – as well as the more necessary removal of restrictions on curricula.

The Endowed Schools Robbery

The Endowed Schools Bill had envisaged rationalising and harnessing the nation's charitable endowments for a grand strategic purpose. The Taunton Commission had seen a future where an educated nation would raise science and industry to great heights, alleviating the problem of poverty. The mechanism for its reforms was carried into law with the 1869 Act, but not its intention. Section 30 of the Act allowed the commissioners to appropriate for educational use

> any endowment which is not an educational endowment as defined by this Act, but the income of which is applicable wholly or partially to any one or more of the following purposes, namely
> Doles in money or kind
> Marriage Portions
> Redemption of prisoners or captives
> Relief of Poor Prisoners for debt
> Loans
> Apprentice fees
> Advancement in life or
> Any purposes which have failed altogether or have become insignificant in comparison with the magnitude of the endowment, if originally given to charitable uses in or before the year of our Lord one thousand eight hundred.

In subsequent legal literature, there is almost a conspiracy of silence over the Endowed Schools Commissioners' activities in diverting old endowments. When their work is mentioned, the type of endowments usually highlighted are the 'Redemption of prisoners and captives', and the 'relief of poor prisoners for debt'. However, contemporary parliamentary reports make it quite clear that the largest amounts were raised from the class of 'doles in money or kind'.

In fact, the Act set in train a defalcation on the scale of the depredations of the Provost and Fellows of Eton, whose £127,000 misappropriation had exercised the surprise but not the punitive action of the authorities. The schemes set up by the Act violated the express wishes of the deceased benefactors, in a way which breached the cy près doctrine. Worse, they took bread from the mouths and coal from the hearths of the poor to fund schools which were mostly for the use of the privileged classes.

One must assume that the commissioners were aware of the controversial nature of what they were doing. At least one MP suggested that their reports to Parliament should include details of the previous endowments and school statutes for comparison with their suggestions. But although otherwise meticulous in their detail, most of their reports did not do so. The Endowed Schools Commission Reports did, however, have to include some details for identification. So in 1870, for example, the Poor's Land Charity and Wolstenholmes's Charity in Whittington were appropriated for education. In Monks Kirkby, Thomas Wales's Charity was taken 'in augmentation of the salary of the Head Master, and payment of a second Master'. In 1873, in Ilkley the 'Dole Charity founded by Joseph Watkinson' and the 'Cow Gate Dole' went to the Grammar School. In Stafford, the poor shivered after the winter of 1873, when Izaak Walton's bequest of '£5 annually for a maidservant or poor man's daughter, and £35 per annum for coals for the poor' and William Farmer's and Rebecca Crompton's charity of '£13 10 shillings for coal for the poor of Stafford and to six poor widows' were taken for the King Edward VI School.

When the commissioners reported to the House of Commons Endowed Schools Committee, in December 1872, they identified income of £8,300 a year which had been, or was in the process of being, diverted from non-educational charities. It was not a negligible sum. For comparison, the eighty nine school schemes which had already been processed had a total income from their endowments of £20,276, so 40 per cent of that was being met from funds diverted from the poor.

One committee member, Power, asked the commissioner, 'Then we may take it that the recipients of these charities to the value of £8,300 a year allowed them to be transformed to educational purposes, without objecting to it?' The reply - 'Broadly speaking, I believe that is so' – could well have been true. There could have been no speedier way to be branded as ungrateful and undeserving poor than for an old widow, or a poor man's daughter, to raise a hue and cry against this form of enclosure, which was often initiated by the great and good of the neighbourhood. It was the trustees, not the beneficiaries, who gave their permission and they could be expected to share the opinion of the Chairman of the Committee, Lord Lyttleton, who pointed out: 'The labouring man will benefit very largely from them, though perhaps not *directly* to the extent that they do now.'

In many areas, especially where endowed elementary schools were being discussed, there were other motives at work. After it was agreed that trustees were remarkably generous with endowments – in 'many other places a considerable amount of non-educational endowments, chiefly dole money has been given up', a committee member, Mr Alderman Lawrence, asked whether the 'amount going to the elementary schools has the effect of lessening the rates paid by the inhabitants towards those schools?' There was only one answer commissioner Stanton could give: 'Yes.' The eagerness of the trustees to hand over their trusts was explained. It relieved them of a burden on their rates at somebody else's expense.

Although the poor themselves were, naturally, not asked their views, they did have representatives – sometimes in the most unlikely quarters. For example, the Lord Mayor and Aldermen of London objected unsuccessfully to the scheme which established the Westminster Schools. They said, 'The scheme would have the effect of diverting a large part of the endowments of the hospital from the education of the poor.' Their objections in that particular case may be taken as an effective summary of the results of the Act. Fighting the case up to the Privy Council, they emphasised, 'The scheme has not due regard to the educational interests of the poor, a class of person whose privileges and educational advantages were thereby abolished or modified.'

Mr Henry Roby, the secretary to the commission, was taxed with this before the Commons Endowed Schools Committee, in 1871. He evaded the issue saying:

> I think that the meaning of the word 'poor' is a very variable one, and as far as I understand it ought always to be treated in reference to the particular endowment ... For instance 'poor' is a term employed in the foundation of Eton and in the foundation of Charterhouse and in the foundation of other schools of the same class. Then again you meet with the word 'poor' obviously in connexion with elementary institutions , or with other words pointing to what would be commonly called the labouring classes.

The *Dictionary of National Biography* describes Roby as a person of 'keen insight, indomitable zeal, and the most genial humour', of which the last must pass as a sample. Perhaps revealing the scale of the victory of the old schools, he is also described as a great educational reformer, one of whose major achievements was a new Latin grammar.

Roby told the parliamentary committee that the commissioners had 'adopted as their maxim that there should be no gratuitous education except as the reward of merit'. 'Then I may take it in a general way that even for orphan asylums you would recommend a test of merit being imposed upon the children before admission to these asylums?' asked Mr Alderman Lawrence. The implacable Mr Roby assented.

The commission thus established the present basis for bursaries and scholarships – that they should generally be awarded as a result of competitive examination rather than because of need. As a result, the status of 'Foundationers' and similar scholarship pupils rose from Untouchable to Brahmin in no time at all. The examinations were open – but the only people who could pass would have had an expensive preparation. There were, and are, very few completely free places, so even a subsidised place was beyond the reach of the majority of the families in the country.

The whole shabby period represents the sequestration, for the use of the privileged, of public assets intended for the poor. The transformation of the old schools into the modern form of public schools is a telling example of a form of Victorian values in which the arrogantly powerful knew what was best for everybody else, and so had no need to consult them.

That attitude, so typical of the general ethos of charity and bounty, became self-perpetuating in the public schools which successfully segregated the offspring of the rich and powerful from the majority of the society which they largely continue to administrate. R. H. Tawney described the effects in the Civil Service – but the same applies to industry, finance, the armed forces, and many of the large charities.

The higher ranges of the British Civil Service have many virtues. What too frequently they lack is not intelligence, or expert knowledge, or public spirit, or devotion to duty. It is personal experience of the conditions of life and habits of thought of those for whose requirements in the matter of health, housing, education, and economic well-being, they are engaged in providing. That deficiency is serious. Yet how, as long as the schools attended by a somewhat high proportion of the individuals concerned are schools which no common child can enter, can they be blamed for suffering from it? (Tawney, 1966, p. 65).

The public schools are certainly responsible for perpetuating the caste barriers in British society. They in turn can foster the lack of empathy which leads to the more objectionably intrusive forms of charity in the field of social welfare. They are in law also charitable. The next chapter considers the question of whether that status of the public schools can be justified.

6

Learning to Advance

Private Schools, Independence – and Publicity

Feepaying and boarding are the most distinctive features of present day public schools. However, although the prestige of many of the schools, and certainly their claim to charitable status, rests on the continuity of their age-old traditions, these features were innovations introduced in the last century.

The privileges claimed by the schools are not nearly so ancient as their original obligations as charities. In Victorian times, many of the schools paid tax on their profits because they were seen in those robustly practical days as carrying on a trade and selling a product. It took years of assiduous lobbying by, particularly, Brighton College to spread the net of privilege wider. That campaign, subsidised by the Headmasters' Conference, was rewarded by Winston Churchill with the 1927 Finance Act which exempted profits from trade if they arose from the primary purpose of the charity. It was the decision which opened the door for fee-paying charities of the kind we now know.

As recently as 1960, the public schools were granted rate relief of 50 per cent – or even more if local authorities were compliant enough to do so, and with implementation of the Poll Tax they will have 80 per cent relief. Anomalously, county schools still pay full rates.

Eton and Winchester are exempt charities which do not even have to register or provide accounts to justify their exemptions. But like all the public schools they benefit from exemption from income and corporation estate duties, capital gains and transfer taxes, covenant tax refunds, non-payment of VAT, and an ability to gain grants from foundations which are restricted to funding charities.

Opposition to public schools has almost as long a pedigree as the present form of the institution. As noted earlier, Gladstone opposed

the tax concessions of élite schools which did not benefit the poor.
In 1931, R. H. Tawney succinctly summed up the main argument
against them: 'The idea that differences of educational opportunity
among children should depend upon differences in wealth among
parents is barbaric.'

However, the system is remarkably resilient. It retains the fiscal
privileges of charity, with its connotations of relief of poverty,
alongside sedulous cultivation of élitism. In 1988, out of 1,365
'independent' schools in the Independent Schools Information
Service Census, 1,102 were educational charities, while 111 were
limited companies and 147 were proprietary. In general, the
secondary, public schools are invariably charities. Indeed, their
100,000 staff represent half the workforce claimed for the charitable
sector, and their fees represent about a quarter, £3,167 million, of
the sector's turnover (see CAF, 1988).

The Creep to Independence

The survival of 'barbarism' on this scale is eloquent testimony to
the power of the public school lobby. This has a formal side, in ISIS
and the Headmasters' Conference, to which we return later. The
core defence is in the 'establishment' itself. There may not be a
public school plot in Whitehall, but it is a striking coincidence that
a series of administrative decisions over the last two decades have
had the cumulative effect of reducing government leverage on the
public schools.

The former head of Winchester, Sir Desmond Lee, told the 1975
Commons Committee on the Charity Commissioners; 'If we are
asked why we should have charitable status, the answer surely is
that education is a charitable purpose, therefore institutions which
are providing education are fulfilling a charitable purpose; if the
definition of charitable purpose were to change, then clearly that
might change as well.' He added, 'If you want to change the law,
after all, you are the law-giving authority of this country. It is up to
you.'

However, the year before, the repeal of the Endowed Schools Act
of 1868 had gone almost unnoticed. As Francis Gladstone says 'The
Labour party seems never to have realised that the Endowed
Schools Act of 1869 enabled Secretaries of State For Education to
impose their will on virtually all public schools' (1982, p. 62).

The transfer of responsibility for educational trusts, including public schools, from the DES to the Charity Commissioners moved them from 'political interference' (or day to day control by accountable elected ministers) to the Charity Commissioners. The Commissioners in their quasi-judicial role are independent of the executive, guardians of centuries of judicial case law.

Margaret Thatcher was the Secretary of State for Education responsible for rolling back this particular boundary of the State, and her junior, Van Straubenzee later boastfully described the move as protecting the independent schools from political interference.

Later Conservative governments disarmed opponents by abandoning the DES procedures for collecting information on the private sector, so that it would be difficult, if not impossible, to assess the advantages the independent sector has in financial terms. While the Conservatives claimed foresight for their actions, in 1977 the Labour government withdrew the DES inspection which had previously recognised the schools as 'efficient'. This was presented as an ending of state subsidy to the private sector – but it was also a further relinquishing of the state's *powers* over it. Was it an initiative suggested by the Civil Service or by the minister, one wonders?

Baker's exemption of the public schools from the National Curriculum 1988 fits the pattern as a 'negative precedent', a conscious decision not to use powers available, in the hope that they would wither on the vine. The process once begun develops a momentum of its own. For example, the Charity Commission decided that 'local education authorities should not be given power to nominate trustees of independent schools unless there were good reasons for maintaining a link with the State system' (CC Report, 1986, p. 13). It was a reasonable, pragmatic decision, which, incidentally, cut another link with the period when the endowed schools were a part of the national education system.

Disarming the Enemy

Two decades of post-war Labour governments have left the public schools safe on their pedestal. One reason was a Fabian–Panglossian glow of confidence in the future, as revealed in the party's NEC decision of 1958.

> At present no scheme for 'taking over' or 'democratising' the public schools shows sufficient merit to justify the large

diversion of public money that would be involved. In time to come when maintained schools are improved, when the prestige of the public schools is consequently diminished, and when substantial changes in the distribution of wealth and in public opinion have occurred, the question, in a changed form, will once more arise. We believe our conclusion is right for the present time.

In fact, Labour's optimism was misplaced. In 1986, Her Majesty's Inspectorate of Schools reported on the state sector: 'Few can take much, if any, pride in a national service within which three tenths of all the lessons seen were unsatisfactory; one fifth was adversely affected by poor accommodation; a quarter was suffering from shortage of equipment... the damaging effects of all this on pupil performance and on the teachers' morale... are showing themselves clearly.' A confidential Department of Education and Science report then showed that two-thirds of state secondary schools' tables and chairs needed immediate attention and 90 per cent of lockers and cupboards were substandard.

Yet by the 1970s, there had been no effective erosion of the privileges of public schools. In 1976, when Roy Jenkins was Labour Home Secretary, the Home Office issued a discussion document on 'Legislation on Human Rights, with particular reference to the European Convention'. The foreword, by Jenkins, said, 'It should also be noted that the obligation to respect the right of parents to ensure education and teaching in conformity with their own religious and philosophical convictions might be held to preclude any measures which would prohibit parents from arranging for their children to be educated privately.'

None the less, in 1981 the Labour Party pledged to take steps to abolish the fee paying schools in a joint party – TUC document. Other steps proposed in transition to abolition included removal of charitable status and imposition of Value Added Tax on fees. In 1986, Labour leader Neil Kinnock said, 'Eventually we hope to make it illegal to charge for education' (*The Spectator*, 29 November, 1986), while Roy Hattersley hoped to 'reduce and eventually abolish fee-paying education'. However, by the 1987 election, it was accepted that the selective imposition of VAT on schools would probably violate European Conventions, as would outright abolition. 'We do not intend to put VAT on school fees or make it illegal to charge fees. We accept that the European Convention does not allow us to close private schools, but we think they should be made to stand on their own two feet, and, for example, pay their whack towards training teachers' (Internal Labour Party election briefing 1987). By 1989, the Labour Party Policy Review had cut back its offensive to the abolition of charitable status.

The main agent for change was the effective public and legal campaign run by ISIS, the Independent Schools Information Service, which has been remarkably efficient in promoting the 'independent' sector. It claims a membership of 25,000, and the support of all the major private school associations for its vociferous campaign. ISIS has redefined the issues in precisely the way Tawney foresaw, in 1943, when he wrote dismissively of the 'venerable device of describing privileges as liberties' (Tawney, 1966). The schools which once vied for the title of 'public' now style themselves 'independent'. The concept is a key part of the schools' defence strategy. It is much easier to sell 'independent' schools to the public than it is to sell 'private' ones. As a title 'public' is dangerous: it now has disturbing connotations of privilege, while carrying within itself disconcerting memories of just why the schools were so called. Indeed, even the Labour Party's practice of referring to the public schools as 'private' connives in this process of ideological privatisation.

Effective though its PR work has been, ISIS's greatest success has been its legal counter-offensive, which has not so much convinced as frustrated those who advocated draconian solutions to privilege. In 1983, Anthony Lester QC and David Pannick produced the legal opinion which demonstrated the difficulties facing some of the simpler proposals advanced by Labour, and which was almost certainly responsible for drawing the teeth of Labour's earlier abolitionism. (It may, or may not, be significant that Anthony Lester was Roy Jenkins' special adviser when Jenkins wrote the foreword anticipating the European Convention's applicability to the schools.)

In the foreword to the ISIS pamphlet (1987 edition), Lord Scarman echoes Jenkins by concluding

> that a future United Kingdom Government would not lawfully be able to prohibit fee-paying, independent education, or to remove the benefits of charitable status or to impose VAT in respect of such education. We note that the content of an earlier version of this Opinion, published before the 1983 General Election, has not been disputed by or on behalf of the Labour Party. In a country which rightly prides itself on respect

for the rule of law, we hope and expect that those who propose taking such action for political reasons will think again in the light of the legal obligation of the United Kingdom under the European Convention on Human Rights and under European Community Law. (Lester and Pannick, 1987)

There is something very distasteful about the invocation of Human Rights to cover the unashamed élitism and caste privilege of the public schools, but Lester and Pannick are unperturbed. They cite Article 2 of the European Convention on Human Rights: 'In the exercise of any functions which it assumes in relation to education and to teaching, the State shall respect the right of parents to ensure such education and teaching in conformity with their own religious and philosophical convictions.' As the two point out, religious and philosophical convictions includes such beliefs 'as are worthy of respect in a democratic society... and are not incompatible with human dignity.'

Against those who incline to Tawney's views on 'barbarism', they assert: 'In fact, Independent schools *serve a wide spectrum of social classes* (author's italics). The parents who choose to pay for their children's education are a heterogeneous group.' Tawney had mocked this same argument forty years before, simply by quoting one of its proponents who referred to the liberal spirit in which the schools admitted the children of 'dentists, bank managers and the more successful shopkeepers' (Tawney, 1966, p. 55).

They go on, with unconscious irony, to quote the West German Basic Law:

The right to establish private schools is guaranteed. Private Schools, as a substitute for state or municipal schools, shall require the approval of the State and shall be subject to the laws of the Laender. This approval must be given if private schools are not inferior to the State or municipal schools in their educational aims, their facilities and the professional training of their teaching staff and *if segregation of pupils according to the means of their parents is not promoted*. (my italics).

It all depends on construction – but that hardly sounds like the precedent to quote in defence of a system whose whole purpose is to segregate the children of the affluent away from their less rich compatriots and contemporaries.

When Labour MP and QC Peter Archer advised the party on the legality of possible measures against public schools, he wisely stressed that they would not necessarily be electorally acceptable.

Possible ways of 'preventing' the financing of public schools from private sources would be:

(a) applying criminal sanctions to those who pay fees;
(b) applying criminal sanctions to those who do not send their children for education in the state system;
(c) penalising children educated in public schools by reducing their chances of obtaining a place on merit at university;
(d) applying criminal sanctions to those who charge the fees.
(Letter to the Labour Party, 19 January 1987)

As Archer pointed out, none of those measures would go down well with the European Court of Human Rights. 'I assume it would be virtually impossible to argue that parents with unusual religious or philosophical convictions were not entitled to make their own provision' (ibid.).

Indeed, apart from pragmatic electoral difficulties, it would be difficult to reconcile such measures with the Labour Party's move towards the more libertarian ideology of 'the enabling State'. The corollary of a legally enforced state monopoly of education implies a monopoly of ideology. In evidence for that, ISIS quoted the speech of M. Titgen, a French delegate to the post-war consultative assembly which drafted the European Convention: 'We are familiar with the suppression of free or private educational institutions, the obligation imposed upon all parents to place their children in the educational institutions of the State. We have seen children brought up from the age of 5 to worship force, violence, racialism and hatred. That is what we wish to avoid.' It is a compelling argument when one has experience of authoritarian central government which believes it holds the franchise on acceptable ideology and morality.

The arguments certainly had the intended effect on Labour Party policy. Without fanfare, abolition was shelved in the face of the legal arguments. It was done so quietly that even the hard left missed the opportunity to attack the leadership over the 'sell-out'. Although Lester and Pannick felt differently, Archer considered that neither the UN nor the European Convention would prevent withdrawal of the fiscal benefits of charitable status (ibid.). Thus arose the Labour Party's 1989 Policy Review pledge to withdraw the public schools' charitable status. As we shall see later, this may be a shortsighted move which actually benefits the public school system.

Public Support for the Public Schools

Adding to Labour difficulties, support for the public schools has come even from people who have no chance of sending their children to them. In May 1987, MORI surveyed parents with children in the 11- to 18-year-old bracket in state schools, and found that 48 per cent of them would send their children to a private school if they could afford it, while 42 per cent would not. There may be many reasons why the 48 per cent said they would: dissatisfaction with the state schools after years of cutbacks, recognition of superior education elsewhere, or simple recognition that if privilege exists, it would be silly not to take advantage of it. But the stubborn fact remains, 93 per cent of children do not attend 'independent' schools, which is of course the big attraction for the parents of the other 7 per cent.

Perhaps more importantly for the survival of the sector, a *Sunday Times* survey in 1982 (*Times Educational Supplement*, 2 April 1982) showed that 90 per cent of Queen's Counsels' children were attending or had attended 'independent' schools. QCs, of course, tend to become judges who decide cases about charitable status. The administration of the greater and lesser departments of state is likely to be in similar hands. The Fulton Civil Service Commission, in 1969, revealed that the results of the interviews conducted for top civil servants' posts showed a consistent pattern. Applicants from state schools who later got firsts at university had often been rejected in favour of public school entrants who only achieved lower seconds or thirds. The interviewers seemed to have a sensitive nose for the indefinable qualities of leadership which one can only acquire in a public school. The same *Sunday Times* report revealed that over 80 per cent of Anglican bishops, often governors of public schools, would have spent their schooldays in one. And in 1979, ten years of Wilsonian meritocracy later, 85 per cent of bishops, 60 per cent of permanent secretaries, and 81 per cent of principal judges had been educated at public school (*New Society*, 4 October 1979).

The armed forces recruit public school men for their officers, and their officers' children for their public schools. Although officers only account for one-seventh of the roll, the MOD pays three times as much in boarding allowances for officers' children as compared with other ranks. It is, of course, understandable that overseas service may need boarding arrangements for children. However, three times as much of the money is spent on behalf of personnel serving at home as abroad. Indeed, the MOD pays a day school allowance to parents of children who stay with relatives or friends while attending a day school. In 1980, it was paid on behalf of a mere 213 children in comparison with 19,787 on boarding allowance. (One deleterious effect of the allowances has been the number of officers who cannot afford to retire until all their children have been through school, which has given the British Armed Forces a top-heavy and ageing command structure.)

Judging the Public Benefit

The charitable status of the public schools is of great political importance to them. However, it is also a potential weapon against them, since it sets a standard of public benefit against which they can be judged. Commercial enterprises can practise élitism in the price structure, but charities are in the public domain and susceptible to public scrutiny. In the seventies, Labour MP Christopher Price took the Charity Commissioners to task for the double standards they applied to public schools compared with other charities. He pointed out that the commissioners take the general view that the use of 'Charity Funds for a purpose now adequately provided out of public rates and taxes is no longer an effective use of resources available' (*The Times*, 29 September 1976). Price's example was the recent commissioners' scheme to divert Edward Harvist's bequest. In 1610, Harvist had left money 'for repairing and amending the highway between Tyburn [Marble Arch] and Edgewarth [Edgware]', and until 1975 this money was passed to the various London Boroughs straddling the road to help repair it. The commissioners then felt that public money was 'supplanting' the bequest, and decided it should be used to help the poor in those boroughs instead.

If public expenditure on roads had supplanted the purpose of the charitable trust, why, Price asked mischievously, did public provision of education not remove the justification of charitable trusts for education? Why could they also not be put to the benefit of the poor? The commissioner was faced with two seemingly contradictory positions, but he was helped by the nuances of the English vocabulary. The public schools were 'supplementing' the educational system, they 'did not relieve public funds in the same direct way'. He admitted that the commission, to make its decision, had made 'both a quantitive and a qualitative assessment' of the state of education. In short – a *subjective* assessment based on several recent centuries of precedent, and maybe even prejudice. The commissioners had made an assessment that Edgware Road was adequately maintained, but that the state education system was not.

However, there are other more serious weaknesses in the schools' case than just overstretched analogy. *Halsbury's Laws of England* (1974, p. 322) reiterate that a trust for education must also be 'for the benefit of a sufficient section of the community' while the general Common Law position is that charity must always 'involve the relief of poverty'.

There can be little doubt that the public schools fail on all counts – of public provision, of public benefit, and public accessibility. Yet it has usually been accepted on good authority – often of the schools themselves – that they do indeed meet those needs. The 1975 parliamentary committee 'did not have time to interview the DES', but accepted the view of the Independent Schools Joint Council that the abolition of charitable status for educational organisations would 'fall most heavily on schools helping those in need in the public sense'. A refreshing flash of honesty amid the humbug came from Dr Rae of Westminster who told *Listener* readers in 1979 that it had always seemed to him 'rather a stupid dishonesty' to pretend that 'this and similar schools do not represent privilege'.

However, the ISJC's statement betrayed more concern for their public image than for truth, or for the poor. The reality of the scholarships open to the Poor and Indigent Scholars of the foundations was revealed by Griggs (1985, p. 38), who found that out of 300 schools a mere ten offered full scholarships. Some of the others offered as little as £50 to set against fees of £3,500 pounds. It is an offer the unemployed could easily refuse; their benefits stood at £34–70 for an adult plus £8–95 per child in April 1989.

Lord Belstead of the ISJC expressed worry that if charitable status were withdrawn from the independent schools, then other institutions, pursuing goals he valued, would forfeit it as well. Whatever the real cause of his worry Belstead did have a point, in that many special schools for the handicapped and orphans enjoy a similar status. Few of those, however, would have difficulty proving public benefit. Such arguments tell strongly against abolition while leaving open the possibility of root and branch reforms in the élitist schools.

Options for Change

Because schools have claimed charitable status, precedents can be changed, and even ancient trusts can be brought up to date. The Schools Inquiry Commission quoted with approbation an earlier report of the 1861 Popular Education Commission.

It seems ... desirable in the interests of charities in general, and of educational charities in particular, that it should be clearly laid down as a principle, that the power to create permanent institutions is granted, and can be granted, only on the condition implied, if not declared, that they be subject to such modification as every succeeding generation of men shall find requisite. This principle has been acted on ever since the Reformation, but it has never been distinctly expressed. Founders have been misled, and the consciences of timid trustees and administrators disturbed, by the supposition that, at least for charitable purposes, proprietorship is eternal, that the land on which its rights have once been exercised can never be relieved from any of the rules and restrictions which have been imposed on it; that thenceforth it is subject, and ever will be subject to the will, not of the living, but of the dead.

Several generations have now felt that change is 'requisite' for these endowments. In 1952, the Nathan Committee considered that a trust to provide a fee paying school should not be charitable, but rejected the idea. The Tenth Expenditure Committee considered it, liked it, but baulked at the task of framing definitive forms of words for such a complex task. The Newsom Committee recommended exemption from fiscal benefits for fee paying schools while leaving their charitable status intact. Even the Goodman Committee of 1976, with its generally anodyne approach, noted:

There was considerable feeling in the committee, however, that a point might be reached when facilities offered by an educational establishment were so expensive or in some other way so exclusive that only a tiny fraction of the community could enjoy those facilities. In such cases there is a strong argument for saying that charitable status should not be granted.

There was, and is, an even more widespread feeling, expressed by Whitaker in his Minority Report to the Goodman Committee, that far from describing a putative future eventuality, that situation had existed for a long time! Fees of over £7,000 per annum are simply beyond the means of many who are comfortably off, let alone the 'poor'.

However, radical reform would not be easy. Poll results over the last twenty-five years consistently show that over half those questioned either 'approve, or see no reason to change public or private schools' (Rentoul, 1989). It indicates a public mistrust of uniformity enforced by the State, which often seems more feared than a uniformity enforced by poverty. One of Margaret Thatcher's distinctive contributions to British populism has been to play upon the electorate's suspicions of the State – even as she strengthens it – and one of the Labour Party's drawbacks has been its identification with statist solutions. So, any action taken against the public schools which involves heavy-handed coercion is unlikely to be politically acceptable to voters.

Even rhetoric about the purchase of privilege does not always ring a chord. Parents who have the facilities and educational background to help their children do better in the state system do not stop doing so because it gives them an unfair advantage over those in poor or illiterate households. Rentoul quotes an interviewee who had children at a state school as saying, 'You expect a better standard of education if you're paying for it. I know I'm paying for his education out of my taxes, but if you pay directly to the school, you think you'd have more say.' Or as Rentoul summarises it, 'Paying for something gives you rights to complain about quality – rights that you wouldn't otherwise have (or have the confidence to assert)' (ibid., p. 40).

This is an interesting reversal of roles. The 'charitable' public school gives fee paying parents the power to bargain, while tax paying parents with children in state schools are to some extent dependent on the bounty of the bureaucracy for what they receive. As a more recent supporter of educational freedom said, 'One of the freedoms enjoyed by the independent sector is freedom from political diktat by those who seek to use education for social engineering.' Of course, Kenneth Baker, the Conservative Education Secretary, when he said that in March 1987, was referring to 'freedom from local education authority diktat', not to freedom from his national curriculum for state schools which dictated an approved positive version of history, grammar and religious education in the 'Christian tradition'. (It is one of society's ironies that the putative iconoclasts of the independent sector exercise what one might call intellectual hegemony over the state sector. Kenneth Baker was educated at St Paul's.)

Indeed his actions towards the state sector have in themselves been one of the more eloquent arguments against state-run education. It is not unthinkable that if current trends were continued, the biggest defections from the state system could be left-wing teachers and parents breaking away from the officially enforced conservatism of the syllabus. If they did, they would invoke the crucial section of the European Convention which provides the right for parents to have provision for education and training 'in conformity with specific religious and philosophical convictions'.

Charitable Status – A Trojan Horse?

There can be no democratic weapons, or democratic objections, against individuals banding together to provide their own schooling for their children, or even against commercial organisations offering training and education. What protects public schools is that they are in many characteristics similar to universities, polytechnics, and even orphanages, which are also self-governing charitable trusts largely financed by fees charged for each student. However, the universities are generally accessible because the State undertakes to pay those fees on behalf of any resident who fulfils admission requirements.

The weak chink in the moral armour of the public schools is their lack of accessibility. In the main, despite government attempts to buffer the reality with Assisted Place Schemes, their intake is determined by the fee paying ability of parents. This is at odds with the basic concepts underlying their charitable status. Lester and Pannick have tried to turn the implications of charitable status from being something of a Trojan horse into a cavalry charge on their behalf.

But the bugles sound only feebly. Lester and Pannick point out that in English law a charitable trust is valid in perpetuity, and if the money were not spent for a charitable purpose, then the cy près doctrine would apply. 'Any legislation to remove charitable status so as to deprive independent schools of their fiscal advantages would need to be carefully drafted to ensure that the trustees could continue to use the school and its assets for charitable purposes,' they say. ISIS itself gives a figure of £1.5 billion as the cost to the State of taking over the assets.

However, that is a wilful avoidance of some of the options which would be legal and politically feasible. With the privileges of charity, comes the burden of responsibility:

> Charitable status is not optional. If an institution is charitable, the consequences of Crown enforcement, perpetuity and fiscal privilege ensue whether the promoters desire them or not. It is sometimes forgotten by those who seek charitable status with only tax relief in mind that its corollary is supervision by the Commissioners to ensure due execution of the trusts (C. P. Hill, 1966, p. 106).

Thus spoke the first of the modern Charity Commisioners, who could have added – due execution of the law, as well.

As charities, the schools are not private institutions but are in the public domain – to be regulated and ordered as the public wishes. If action were taken to 'nationalise' the schools, to replace the trustees, or to insist upon public benefit – to the poor, there would, of course, be an uproar from the older foundations – but as we have seen, they were built and financed with money from the King or the Church – with what was, for its day, public money.

So outright take-over of the charitable schools would not entail compensation since they are not private property, but are in fact in the public domain. Those Direct Grant Schools incorporated into the state system in the seventies were not the subject of compensation. Similarly, the National Health Service's takeover of the voluntary charitable hospitals in 1948 involved no compensation for the simple reason that they were still being used for the same public benefit as before.

A new definition of charity, emphasising the test of public benefit, and which formulated reasonable tests of accessibility for the poor, would do much to transform the institutions. For example, a requirement that endowments should only be used for people in need, and that fees paid by others should reflect the use of endowed charitable capital, would surely help change the schools significantly. Alternatively, a modern Endowed Schools Act could return the endowments to public use as specialist schools, or sixth form colleges, which would preserve their educational uses while being to the public benefit. It could even enforce a comprehensive non-selective entry on the schools.

Such constructive reformation of them would right a historical wrong, and perhaps help build a voluntary, charitable sector, which would look towards a more equal future, rather than to a Victorian and Georgian past. It could reconcile a genuine and desirable independence with genuine public benefit. In the overall context of charities, it would remove perhaps one of the largest power blocs with a vested interest in inhibiting the development of the law of charity to meet conditions of the twentieth and twenty-first centuries.

One immediate effect would be an examination of the analogously anomalous status of the charitable hospitals, and that is what the next chapter considers.

7

Abandoning Alms – the NHS

The modern National Health Service is an indication of what a National Education Service would have been like if the charitable public schools had been integrated into it. Of course, in health care, 'going private' has none of the confusing connotations which 'public' has for education. Public hospitals, like public baths, are open to all, and therefore inherently non-U. Hospitals have never had the caste-asserting role of the public schools; a BUPA policy does not mould the thoughts and fortunes in the way an old school tie does.

This is partly because hospitals are much closer to their charitable roots than the schools. If hospitals had been money-making businesses in 1948 as they are now in the USA, the vested interests ranged against the National Health Service might have proved insuperable (instead of just extremely difficult). As the Labour Health spokesman Robin Cook (1988, p. 1) pointed out:

> Looking back over the debates of forty years ago it is interesting that no one then attempted to argue that the market had a role in allocating health care. True the Conservatives divided the Commons on both the Second Reading and the Third Reading of the National Health Service Bill, but on both occasions the focus of their opposition was a defence, not of the market as the provider of health care, but of charity as the source of hospitals for the poor. As their spokesman expressed it at the Third Reading, the charitable hospitals are 'an outlet for private benevolence – and that is not a thing to be misprised'. The debate was, after all, taking place against a background of health care which was in the main left to the market and no one could be found to defend the consequences.
>
> Nor were those consequences solely that for the poor the reality of private health care was charity health care.

Contemporary health care plans represent a neat inversion of the concept of charity. On the one hand, private patients get five star comfort in charitable hospitals, funded by the private benevolence once invoked for the public welfare. On the other hand, even now there is more than a whiff of the more degrading aspects of charity in the publicly owned sector, although the ethos of much of the service is charitable in its best, philanthropic, sense.

This chapter examines the development of charitable hospitals and the metamorphosis of most of them into NHS hospitals. It considers both the positive and negative aspects of that heritage, and how the ethos of the eighties has strengthened the 'charitable' nature of the NHS.

A Place Not to Live, But to Die

In earlier times, rich people would not be seen dead in a hospital – that was a dubious privilege left to the poor. The OED's definition of that sense of 'hospital' (which it optimistically describes as obsolete) is 'a charitable institution for the housing and maintenance of the needy; an asylum for the destitute, infirm, or aged'.

The charitable hospitals were for the chronically ill and poor, and were endowed as such. As the 1601 preamble says, endowments were given 'some for relief of aged, impotent and poor people, some for maintenance of sick and maimed soldiers and mariners'. In terms of general health care, public midwives were also accepted as charitable in the days before male gynaecologists established their stranglehold on the delivery business. The difference between hospitals then and now was made morbidly plain by Sir Thomas Browne in *Religio Medici*: 'For the world, I count it not an Inne, but an Hospitall, a place not to live, but to die.' For most of the centuries of the existence of the hospitals, medicine, even more than today, justified Voltaire's comment that its purpose was to entertain the patient as nature effected the cure – or not.

Nevertheless, asepsis and anaesthesis began to make hospitals places where the comfortably off could get treatment denied them at home. Surgeons transmuted professionally from barbers to consultants, who dispensed their services to both the rich, who paid, and the poor who could not pay but were good practice. Even for employees, the rigid hierarchy of a hospital reflects the days when upper class ladies doing voluntary service 'organised' lower-

and middle-class women who may have needed to make a living out of nursing. In the nineteenth century, Jane Stewart, a colleague of Florence Nightingale, expressed it well: 'The improver must live among those she endeavours to improve and to train, one of them, tho' superior to them.' That the meeting of the classes could be a great strain is suggested by her tone of patrician forebearance, 'It is not good that a nurse who has just behaved, for instance, with deceit, or gross insubordination, should sit down to dinner with the superintendent' (see Anne Summers, *History Today*, February 1989). It is not surprising that disaffected nurses denounced her to the War Office! While some of that class consciousness has gone, the rigid hierarchy is still evident in many hospitals.

A Service for, or of, the People?

When the health service was set up, there were difficulties with all the vested interests. The consultants wanted the run of the hospitals, and private practices. GPs wanted – and got – control of referrals to consultants, and private patients. They also secured all the benefits of self-employment, combined with the security of a staff job, and as a bonus, the right to moonlight with private practice. It has been disputed whether Aneurin Bevan actually said that he stuffed their mouths with gold, but there is no doubt that that is just what he did. Quite apart from the package for those in service, £66 million was put aside to compensate doctors who wanted to quit.

The customers were assumed to be so grateful for the largesse of the state that they need not have a voice in what they wanted – and anyway, their voices were muted by the strident shouts of the BMA as it lobbied for better terms.

The popular opinion, cited in connection with education, that those who pay directly for a service are in a stronger bargaining position than those who get it 'for nothing', is equally applicable to health care. Of course, it is not 'for nothing'. Taxes and National Insurance contributions mean that most NHS customers have paid, are paying or will pay for their treatment. However, while a client can refuse to pay a private clinician if the service is not up to standard, the fate of those who refuse to pay taxes is not so easy.

During the 1987 election campaign, Margaret Thatcher defended her use of private medical services in terms which succinctly summed up what people would like the NHS to offer: 'to see the doctor I want, on the day that I want, at the time that I want'. It did not excite as much indignation as it should have, possibly because so many NHS clients themselves accept that in reality they would have to pay for that kind of service, rather than expect it on the NHS in return for their taxes. There is nothing more comforting than knowing that the NHS is there in case of emergencies – there is little more uncomfortable than waiting around the NHS for non-emergency treatment.

Both patient and doctor are locked in a system in which it is bounty not bargain which determines the relationship. One detached American view of the NHS identified the system as dominated by doctors rather than lay representatives who could be taken to stand for the clients (Eckstein, 1959). Certainly, the management boards from the beginning were appointed rather than elected, perhaps exacerbating the 'bounty' principle, since the only effective voice the patient had was via Parliament and the Minister of Health who appointed the committees. This was seen at the time as an important retention of the 'voluntary principle'. 'The hospital service has been "nationalised", but its administration in the field has been entrusted to voluntary committees,' claimed the National Council For Social Service in 1952 (Norman, 1952).

It is worth looking more closely at what the NCSS committee meant by that:

It is frequently argued that this method of appointment is undemocratic. This argument implies that a committee can only be democratic if it consists of elected representatives, which seems to us to be a narrow interpretation of the term. It is our belief that the true democratic element, which defies precise definition, is maintained through the voluntary status, irrespective of the method of appointment, and that the members of voluntary boards and committees entrusted with statutory responsibilities are, *except in the methods of their appointment* (author's italics) representative of the people whose interests they serve (ibid.).

This is clear exposition of the 'Lady Bountiful' principle as applied to public service. There is an ominous parallel in the way fundamental changes were made to the NHS in the eighties, with the purging of the very last representatives who could in any way be termed elected.

Since more than a third of the existing 78,000 hospital beds in

1948 were still administered under Poor Law terms, it is perhaps
not entirely surprising that the expectations of potential patients
were easily satisfied, and that few objections were raised to this
paternalistic approach. One lobby which *was* listened to was the
trade unions. They used their influence to ensure that the Manor
House and Inverforth hospitals were left outside the system when
the other hospitals which the service wanted were nationalised (the
277 which were not wanted were 'disclaimed'; some were
unwanted because of disuse, others belonged to religious orders –
or as in the case of the Royal Masonic, the freemasons). As the
private hospital of the Labour movement, Manor House has since
proven to be private medicine's best weapon in muffling Labour
opposition.

While the establishment of the NHS is correctly seen as a social
revolution, it also set an important precedent for charities. The NHS
expropriated the property of all the voluntary hospitals, in effect
confiscating the endowments left by benefactors living and dead.
Hospitals moved from being for the public benefit, in the public
domain, into the public sector. Although as has been noted, the
public control was effected at a fairly remote level, it is, none the
less, a significant precedent for any future government wishing to
reform the position of the public schools.

Health for Rich and Poor Alike
– So Long as They Can Pay

Before the establishment of the NHS, the major voluntary hospitals
faced serious problems. As with the schools, the implication of the
1601 statute and all the flow of precedent afterwards was that a
charitable hospital was for the poor, not for the rich. The genuinely
charitable aspect of hospitals survived longer because the rich were
not clamouring to enter them on the same scale as they had done
with the charitable schools.

The lack of an affluent clientele left the law unclear, and it was
not solidified until 1969 when a bequest was made to 'the sisters of
Charity... so long as they shall conduct St Vincent's Private
Hospital'. In fact the clarification obscured the issue: the principle
of accessibility to the poor was restated, while in practice their
exclusion was accepted. Lord Wilberforce said (*Re Resch* (1969), 'A
gift for the purpose of a hospital is prima facie a good charitable
gift... because the provision of medical care for the sick is, in

modern times, accepted as a public benefit suitable to attract the privileges given to charitable instructions.' However, he qualified that unequivocal statement at some length:

> To provide, in response to public need, medical treatment otherwise inaccessible but in its nature expensive, without any profit motive, might well be charitable; on the other hand, to limit admission to a nursing home to the rich would not be so. The test is essentially one of public benefit, and indirect as well as direct benefit enters into the account.
>
> In the present case, the element of public benefit is strongly present. It is not disputed that a need exists to provide accommodation and medical treatment in conditions of greater privacy and relaxation than would be possible in a general hospital and as a supplement to the facilities of a general hospital. This is what the private hospital does and it does so at, approximately, cost price. The service is *needed by all* (author's italics), not only the well to do. So far as its nature permits, it is open to all: the charges are not low, but the evidence shows that it cannot be said the poor are excluded; such exclusion as there is, is of some of the poor – namely those who have (a) not contributed sufficiently to a medical benefit scheme or, (b) need to stay longer in the hospital than their benefits will cover, or (c) cannot get a reduction or exemption from the charges. The general benefit to the community of such facilities results from the relief to the beds and medical staff of the general hospital, the availability of a particular type of nursing and treatment which supplements that provided by the general hospital and the benefit to the standard of medical care in the general hospital which arises from the juxtaposition of the two institutions.

In short, the poor are excluded only if they have no money. The case illustrates the drawbacks of law-making through the adversarial process of the courts. The judge's decision is made, ostensibly, on the basis of the cases put forward by those involved in the litigation. The beneficiaries and other interested parties – like the public – do not have an input. In this case, for example, there was no one to raise the possibility that a general hospital might be paying a consultant who would be spending more time with his private patients than with the NHS, thus helping to create the waiting lists which Wilberforce claimed the private hospitals were shortening.

The Resch case may have confused earlier, more definitive judgments which had ruled (*Re Girls' Public Day School Trust Ltd* (1951) and *Re Smith*(1962) that schools and hospitals could not be charitable if they distributed profits. In the Resch case, the hospital did make some profit but it went to the nuns. (Does this imply that a limited company whose shareholders were all members of a religious order could be charitable?)

Lord Wilberforce considered that a 'need' for facilities implied that it was to the public benefit. But, as this monetarist age knows too well, demands and needs are not the same – there is no more *need* for 'greater privacy and relaxation' than there is for Rolls-Royce cars or Pullman trains. One can accept the legitimacy of people wanting, and even being prepared to pay, for such facilities, but it is surely unacceptable to expect the commmunity to subsidise them through the fiscal privileges which attach to charity.

Charging for Charity

As it now stands, organisations like BUPA are not in themselves charitable – but the chain of Nuffield Hospitals, set up by BUPA and largely dependent on its insurance benefits, is so. The decisions which affect BUPA and similar organisations were originally aimed against working men's mutual benefit societies which have not been charitable for over a century. As recently as 1962, the print union, NATSOPA, had its convalescent home and sanatorium for members with consumption ruled uncharitable (*Re Mead's Trust Deed*).

In 1945, Judge Wrottesley had overturned a plan by Lord Nuffield to encourage mutual insurance societies against sickness for working people; he declared them not charitable (*Nuffield v. IRC*). That decision seems to have stuck. On the other hand, in Sheridan and Keeton's phrase (1983, p. 143), he was 'probably wrong' in deciding that hospitals were not charitable if confined to paying patients. One cannot help feeling that Judge Wrottesley actually got it quite right on precedent, but may have erred in not legitimising the existing social practice.

In fact, in 1887 (*St Andrew's Hospital v. Shearsmith*), it had been decided that hospitals, even charities, had to pay income tax on income derived from trading. Hospitals, like schools, benefited from Churchill's 1927 Finance Act which removed the obligation for charities when the income arose from the charitable purpose itself. It was a timely move for the voluntary hospitals whose own resources were failing and who were happy to take in paying patients. Indeed, as their financial problems built up, the hospitals secured the Voluntary Hospitals (Paying Patients) Act 1936, which in some small measure did for the voluntary hospitals what the Endowed and Public Schools Acts had done for the schools – it allowed them to set aside the terms of their original trust deeds and charters so as to provide pay beds, if the Charity Commissioners approved the scheme.

As with the public schools, argument about modern voluntary hospitals is likely to concentrate on the abolition of fee paying. However, this immediately causes problems in the real world of social and political improvement as opposed to the rhetoric of the conference platform. It is not just a medical matter. Many civic repertory theatres, let alone operating theatres, are registered charities, and there is no suggestion that they let everyone in free. However, while many of them offer concessionary tickets to the unemployed, young people and old age pensioners, the private hospitals make even fewer concessions to poverty than the public schools.

There is another aspect to fee paying. For example, the position of women would be radically different were it not for the pioneering and practical work of fee charging groups like the Marie Stopes' Clinics and the British Pregnancy Advisory Service or the Family Planning Association. The platform rhetorician may well claim that such services could and should be available from the State. But they were not, and what moves the State did make in that direction were probably spurred by the voluntary effort.

This brings us to the question of the private hospitals and how charitable they are. The *Re Resch* (1969) decision tends towards the view that to be charitable a hospital must not exclude the poor, and leads on to quite refined matters of personal judgement of what is a 'reasonable' cost. Test cases on charity law have become infrequent during a period when the actual charging of fees for services has been spreading. It is an issue which exercises the minds of Charity Commissioners, lawyers and judges involved in the field. They held a seminar on 24 October 1988 to discuss the development of the law, and concluded:

> If charitable law was vulnerable to the charge that it contained an inbuilt social bias it was in respect of private charitable schools and hospitals which charged for their services with the

result that their benefits were in practice confined to those
who could afford the fees. To what degree could this be said to
be for the public benefit in a charitable sense? How did it sit
with the view that charitable assistance must be by way of
bounty and not bargain?

Suggestions to separate fiscal benefits from charitable status and
to withdraw tax relief from charities which charged were
considered, but generally found too difficult to administer. Those
present concluded: 'Charges should nevertheless be appropriate to
the type of charity and the service provided. Each case should be
examined on its merits to determine whether charging and the
degree of charging was reasonable and consistent with the
fulfilment of the charity's trusts.'

Robin Guthrie, the Chief Charity Commissioner replied, when I
asked him about this issue:

> I absolutely understand the general public's point of view that
> organisations which restrict themselves to the wealthy by
> charging high fees can hardly be regarded as being charitable
> in the public eye. The problem is that you can't possibly stop
> charities charging fees. It's perfectly possible for charities to
> charge them, and in some cases it is absolutely essential that
> they do, while still fulfilling what the ordinary member of the
> public would consider to be perfectly proper activities.
>
> Having failed to distinguish in this way, how can one
> possibly distinguish between those who charge for this that or
> the other service, and those who prevent potential beneficiar-
> ies from gaining access to their benefits by charging. If you
> were to say, 'you may charge, but you must not refuse entry to
> anyone who can't pay', then it makes the whole system
> unworkable – how could a theatre box office operate?

Self Help – or Helping Yourself?

The nearest to a clear point in law then, is that the poor must not
be excluded – so where does that leave the charitable hospital
chains like Nuffield Hospitals? Anyone, except perhaps a learned
judge, would accept that BUPA charges were more than could be
met from unemployment or other supplementary benefits. It is a
point which could be demonstrated quickly by any recipient of

benefit who had the sense of humour to apply for a social fund grant for the purpose.

So in what sense is the Nuffield Hospitals Trust a charity? If it were restricted to BUPA members, it would almost sail dangerously close to the decision which barred the trade union convalescent home from charitable status in *Re Mead*. Is BUPA not a self-help organisation? Of course, the Nuffield Hospitals are not restricted to BUPA members, they are open to whoever can pay, regardless of the source of their money. But any camel without money, a job and a BUPA scheme would find it impossible to get through the eye of this financial needle to enter a Nuffield Hospital.

The private hospital sector is not as large an operation as the public schools, although one suspects that they have similar clientele, in both size and social background. Nine per cent of the population of the UK were covered by private medical insurance according to the 1989 government White Paper 'Working For Patients'. As we have seen, around 7 per cent of school age children are in the private schools.

The White Paper reported that 28 per cent of all hip replacements were carried out in private beds, which implies either that there is a statistical affinity between private patients and hip problems, or that the waiting lists on the NHS are so large that patients are driven to pay for the operation.

The independent charitable acute hospitals include the London Clinic, the Royal Masonic, and Manor House, with a total of 1,884 beds. The Nuffield group's thirty-two BUPA hospitals offer 1,264 beds, while BPAS and Marie Stopes add 193 to the total. Religious hospitals provide 1,334 beds, mostly from the Roman Catholic nursing orders.

How accessible are they? Nuffield's Lancaster hospital offers fixed cost surgery. In 1989, a tonsilectomy would have cost £872, an adult circumcision would cost £624, while a hip replacement would cost £3,812.

Someone in work could raise a bank loan, or pay cash for such operations, if the alternative were long periods of discomfort and loss of earnings, waiting for the NHS. A family with a breadwinner aged between 30 and 49 could take out one of the cheaper health insurance plans for £34–£39 a month. But no one who qualifies even for a generous extension of the term poverty could possibly afford premia or fees.

The Nuffield Hospitals offer no discounts to the needy. Mr Sargeant, their marketing manager, claimed, 'Waiting lists are not the big issue. People want to have the private facilities available. A lot of them come on word of mouth recommendation. They want to see the consultant that their friend or neighbour saw.' The many companies and individuals who donated to establish the hospitals get no benefit, no discount or preferential treatment in return, just a bid for posterity with their name on a plaque or a door. In all, the income from donations and covenants is £1,800,000 a year.

But what are the motives of, for example, members of the medical profession who make donations to set up hospitals? Is there not a large element of self-interest in providing facilities in which they can considerably enhance their income? Bob Russell, fund-raising manager of the Nuffield hospitals discerned 'enlightened self-interest' as the motive for many charitable donations. He pointed to donor firms like Marks & Spencer, whose staff are on health schemes and which would clearly like a network of hospitals which serviced their staff.

The other benefit Russell adduced is employment. Lancaster employs 100 staff in a depressed region, while Nuffield overall employs almost 4,000 staff if the part-timers are included. Yet, as the Charity Commissioners have pointed out, the provision of employment is not, in itself, a charitable object.

The publicity material for the Chester Nuffield Hospital, the Grosvenor, shows how a particular section of the public sees the public benefit of private hospital provision.

> Our story began in the 1970s, when a group of residents realised, with some concern, that there was a serious lack of beds for private treatment in the area.
>
> As soon as Nuffield Hospitals heard about this problem, we agreed to design, build and run a small private hospital providing land could be found ... Thanks to the enthusiasm and enterprise of this committee, we soon exceeded our appeal target.
>
> And our good luck continued! His grace the Duke of Westminster offered us an idyllic setting for our hospital.

So far, this sounds almost like a latter day version of the efforts of the Rochdale Pioneers to set up the first consumer cooperative. But this was a charity. The facility was not intended to benefit the poor; it was targeted specifically at a group which could afford and wanted a certain type of medical attention. Nuffield Hospitals' fund-raising manager, Bob Russell was articulate in defence of this provision, and quoted a poor 70-year-old lady in one of their hospitals who spoke to him after her hip replacement operation, obviously considering the relief from pain to be a near miracle. Her sons, she revealed, had clubbed together to pay for the operation. Yet a strict definition of poor would exclude someone whose relatives could raise £4,000.

The steering committee for the Grosvenor Hospital included four consultants and two general practitioners who had joined with a retired Liverpool stockbroker to establish the facility, because there were only seventy-four beds for private patients in the area, in the early seventies.

The money was raised quite quickly, even though the appeal 'required and obtained greater financial support than any other voluntary fund raising operation mounted in the same area'. The fund-raising report singles out the Chester and Wrexham hospital consultants who jointly presented £41,367.

In the early eighties, the facility was extended with an appeal for a further million. The money for the extra development was raised from trusts, which donated £48,050, industry, which donated £274,935, the medical profession which donated £138,302, other professions, £57,924, and individuals who gave £30,212.

The companies tended to be those which offered BUPA or similar schemes for the staff; the consultants could, one presumes, have a chance of providing services for the new hospital; and the individuals and other professionals might well have been members of a health plan also. In that cynical view of the case, the only purely disinterested donations would have come from the trusts. However, even they are often administered by the kind of people who also are in BUPA. Indeed, most charitable trusts could not have made donations unless the Nuffield Hospitals were recognised as a charity.

If the initiators of the Grosvenor Hospital had been a group of trade union members, they would have been considered by the type of legal precedents we saw earlier to be a closed group, unable to qualify for the privileges of charity. However, since they did not share the common bond of a few coppers a week union dues, and were only distinguished from their fellow citizens by wealth, they were not a closed self-help group.

Cutting the Gordian Knot

As in the case of state education and public schools, there are clear conflicts between attempts at the universal provision of health services and the private sector. Similarly, while the conflicts appear to be clear, the means of reconciling them are not. To 'nationalise' medicine and make the NHS, as it were, compulsory would be a gross attack on human rights. Moreover, control of orthodox practitioners over the NHS would mean that many forms of alternative treatment would in some sense become 'illegal'. Homoeopathy has been squeezed out of the system over the decades (homoeopathy's results, it may be argued, are scientifically questionable, but homoeopathy has not, for example, cursed millions with addiction to tranquillisers in the way more orthodox treatment has). 'Fringe' disciplines like acupuncture and hypnotherapy are becoming increasingly acceptable to the public, but are not often available on the NHS.

Barring prohibition or renationalisation, neither of which is likely to be politically or legally acceptable, the issue of private medicine boils down to the question whether, in any sense, the private medical system merits charitable status.

That there is some disquiet about the legal situation can be gauged by, for example, the London Clinic's provision of some concessionary (but not free) beds. However, an unpleasant corollary for charitable hospitals is that having become charities, they cannot escape the responsibilities accruing to being part of the public domain. They cannot now switch back to being commercial enterprises because that would alienate the endowment of the trusts, although it does appear that managements in the sector are considering the possibility of running the hospitals on a commercial rather than charitable basis.

It is perfectly feasible, therefore, that Parliament could at some time feel the need to define precisely what the charitable private hospitals must do to perform their charitable duties, as was suggested earlier in the case of public schools. At the moment, it is almost as if the users and providers of limousines had come together to provide a maintenance and sales service for the luxury end of the market. Any poor person with the money to buy a Rolls-Royce would qualify to join – and after all, some poor people do win the pools don't they?

However, decisions on 'Metal Box' type trusts have tended to specify a minimum of 25 per cent 'outside' beneficiaries to retain charity status. For example, in 1954 (*Koetggen's Will Trusts*), trustees were directed to give preference to employees' families for scholarships – provided that no more than 75 per cent of the overall cost went to them. Judge Upjohn upheld it because it was 'uncertain' that the closed beneficiaries would in any year exceed the quota.

A ruling that a proportion of the patients should come from those whose poverty normally inhibits their access to such facilities is feasible and probably desirable. Politically, it would be hard for the governors of such hospitals to make out a case against it without wrong-footing it. The biggest opposition would probably come from within the Labour left's knee-jerk reactionaries, who occasionally want to see people suffer to prove principles.

In fact, more people object to NHS facilities being diverted to private practice while the service itself is being starved, than object to private practice itself. As John Rentoul (1989, p. 70) says, 'People feel much more warmly about the NHS than about state schools or council housing. But private provision is not usually frowned on, not even when it's thought of as damaging the NHS – and it is only natural to have it as personal prosperity increases.' He quotes an ex-Labour but now Tory voting bank clerk: 'Anyone with money would. It would be the same as having a car or holidays abroad; if you've got the money, you would have it.' However, while 46 per cent of those interviewed (British Social Attitudes Survey quoted by Rentoul) thought that private treatment should be encouraged – 57 per cent thought that NHS doctors should not take on private patients and that private treatment should not be allowed in hospitals. And as the crucial rejoinder to the whole drift of Thatcherite policies Gallup reported that 59 per cent were prepared to pay more in taxes if it were 'earmarked to increase spending on the NHS'.

Ideally, of course, the NHS would be divested of the remnants of its Poor Law ethos. Patients would not have to sleep in converted workhouse dormitories, and privacy and dignity could be obtained without going private. NHS patients could choose their doctors and consultants, and see them at the time they wanted, on the day they wanted. Realising the difficulty with uncritical defence of existing health service practice, Labour health spokesman Robin Cook called for personalisation as opposed to privatisation; for a patients' charter which

> provides a checklist against which they can measure any
> hospital. Did it provide an individual appointment time? Was it

kept to? Was the reception welcome and reassuring? Were there childcare facilities? Did the consultant or junior explain their diagnosis and discuss alternative forms of treatment? How flexible were the visiting hours?

In the second reading debate [on the NHS Bill] Bevan observed that he would rather recover in the sterile efficiency of a large hospital than expire in a warm gush of sympathy in a small one. But is there any reason why we cannot devise methods of personalisation that give us general hospitals with both efficiency and warmth? (Cook, 1988, p. 12)

An Uncertain Future

However, that particular appointment with destiny seems a long way off, and receding further as the 1989 White Paper augured the dismemberment of the NHS: 'In short, every hospital in the NHS should offer what the best offer now. These improvements will bring greater appreciation and recognition from patients and their families for all the care that the Health Service provides.' It called for individual appointments, quiet and pleasant waiting areas, rapid test results, 'and a wider range of optional extras and amenities for patients who want to pay for them – such as single rooms, personal telephones, televisions and a wider choice of meals', in a vision that is somehow realistic and threatening at the same time.

Was the White Paper a precursor to privatisation? Will all patients have to pay 'hotel costs' like meals and linen? Or why should all patients not get such amenities on the NHS? The proposals need examination in the context of wider government policies. The clarion calls to self-reliance and active citizenship scarcely conjured up images of plush waiting rooms and coffee for all. They seem far more likely to presage the development of a two tier service within the NHS. The NHS Hospital Trusts sound very much like a revival of the old voluntary hospitals. 'The Government believes that self-government for hospitals will encourage a stronger sense of local ownership and pride, building on the enormous fund of goodwill that exists in local communities ... Supported by a funding system in which successful hospitals can flourish, it will encourage local initiative and greater competition.'

Who will own and control them? The White Paper suggests that the chairman of a proposed hospital trust should be appointed by the secretary of state who will then 'consult' with him to appoint all the other non-executive directors. Except, that is, for two 'community' directors appointed by the RHA from the 'hospital Leagues of Friends and similar organisations'. 'The executive directors will include the general manager, a medical director, the senior nurse manager and a finance director.'

Taken together it is hardly a stunning example of patient power. With income 'coming from GP practices with their own budgets, private patients or their insurance companies, employers and perhaps other NHS Hospital Trusts', it is easy to see a situation where hospitals in wealthy communities will expand while others shrink or are reduced to providing lesser services.

The proposed trusts bear a remarkable resemblance to the pseudo-charities which have already been set up by health authorities (see Chapter 8). They seem to preserve all the worst features of the Lady Bountiful principles of the Poor Law as inherited by the NHS, with few if any of the safeguards. The trusts will be able to dispose of assets, and will probably be free to concentrate more on private patients if that is where the money is. It is worth considering the implications of the qualification that the trusts must also continue to provide essential services to the local population, including accident and emergency services 'where no alternative provision exists'.

That suspicion is clearer when one looks at those who can initiate the process of converting an NHS hospital to a self-governing trust. They could 'include the District Health Authority, the hospital management team, a group of staff, or people from the local community who are active in the hospital's support'. It is a social grouping uncannily similar to those who initiated the Grosvenor Nuffield Hospital – and for the same complex of reasons.

The government envisages a future where the former NHS and the 'independent' hospitals will have grown so similar that they will be indistinguishable. It must be more than a fair bet that the end envisaged is an end to the 'Nanny State' with self-reliance forced on those who can take it and Poor Law standards for those who cannot. A look at the more enterprising culture of the US shows what the future may look like here: 40 per cent of personal bankruptcies are caused by medical care debts, often to 'charitable' hospitals.

8

Alms for Health Care – the Future Now

After the foundation of the NHS, fund-raising activity on behalf of local hospitals continued irrepressibly. Local enthusiasm and pride, as well as gratitude for treatment, all ensured a flow of money. It was money which originally was to be for trimmings. The principle of national funding for the main business of hospitals was firmly fixed. With time, however, the appeals moved up the scale in their objects, from television sets for patients, to scanners, to specialist surgical units – and eventually in the case of Great Ormond Street, a whole new hospital.

As well as attracting charitable funds into hospitals, administrators had, even before the 1989 White Paper, begun to hive off activities from the health service to charities. This chapter looks at the ways in which health service funding and the charitable sector are coming closer together.

The pre-NHS voluntary hospitals were the products of local enthusiasms and subscriptions, which put terms like 'Hospital Saturday' in the dictionary to describe some of the original flag days. Their endowments varied from area to area as did their resources – and they were all appropriated by the Ministry of Health. The teaching hospitals, as part of the process of wooing the higher castes of the medical profession, retained their own endowments.

The move did cause some resentment at state interference in local affairs, but the obvious benefits of state funding for the flagging finances of the voluntary hospitals outweighed such parochial attitudes. Still, one can sympathise with those who had entered into covenants for a particular hospital. At the inauguration of the service, some of them cancelled, only to be requested forcibly to continue their legally binding obligation – but to send their cheques directly to the ministry.

The various endowments were collected in the Hospitals Endowment Fund and distributed to localities on a per bed basis. But the charitable urge is often benefactor-driven rather than beneficiary-driven. The hospitals found that people often wanted to carry on helping, and this led to new funds being raised. Naturally such people were not raising money for the Ministry of Health, no matter how much they approved of the new system. Nor were they concerned to reduce the National Debt or National Insurance charges. They were keen to continue supporting their local hospital as they had done hitherto.

It was appreciated that members of the public might well resent being asked for voluntary contributions to hospitals in a national service whose expenditure was met from Exchequer funds to which they contributed through taxation and insurance contributions. Direct appeals to the public have therefore ceased, but many hospitals have the active support of such bodies as 'Friends of the Hospital.' (Norman, 1952 p. 112)

That was, of course, in the first flush of enthusiasm for the NHS. The flag days which used to provide better amenities for patients and staff have now changed completely. With technological developments in medicine, nurses and junior doctors can spend their days off jangling collection cans for projects which until recently would have been regarded as the sole province of the NHS and the State.

Suffer Little Children

Such activity can be controversial, like the appeal for the redevelopment of the Hospital for Sick Children in Great Ormond Street, in 1988. To start with, the ideal place for a new children's hospital is surely somewhere accessible, in country surroundings with clean air, and on a relatively cheap site. The last place one would pick would be a constrained site in the middle of a highly polluted and congested area, where atmospheric lead and the oxides of sulphur, nitrogen and carbon rise to heights only matched by land and labour costs. Unless, of course, one were a consultant with a private practice in Harley Street, a quick hop away. This was pointed out by Dr Gerry Bulger, an East London GP who sits on the board of Great Ormond Street as an observer, and who told the *The Guardian* (14 September 1988): 'There was a good case for selling the site and relocating the hospital somewhere on the M25, and they wouldn't have needed the appeal. But all the consultants want to be near Harley Street.' In fact there was a site which fitted the bill perfectly: Tadworth Court. This was actually owned by Great Ormond Street until they divested themselves of it before launching their appeal to finance their city centre rebuilding. (It is not surprising that the hospital is one of the more likely to opt out under the White Paper provisions.)

The appeal itself caused many undercurrents of unease which exemplify the problems of reliance on charitable funding for essential services. The prestige of the Great Ormond Street Hospital persuaded the advertising industry to offer free spaces; poster hoardings were made available across the country to exhort contributions to the 'Wishing Well Appeal'. There was great resentment in provincial towns when their own cash-starved children's hospitals were confronted with posters calling for help for their well-heeled Metropolitan counterpart, as happened to Booth Hall Children's Hospital in Manchester. In Liverpool, angry nurses confronted supermarket chain managers who put on special Wishing Well appeals. Some hospitals were understandably miffed when collectors for the Great Ormond Street appeal appeared even in their own premises. For collectors, it was, of course, a dream appeal to work on: sick children fill the cans like nothing else. But not everybody was swept away in a euphoric tidal wave of fund-raising teardrops. Dr Bill Beswick of the Salford Health Authority commented to the *Guardian* (14 September 1988):

> They have a degree of privilege although they're no different from us in their activities, apart from being less broadly based. We've nearly half as many patients as they have, but we get £7 million a year in running costs while they get £35 million ... We've only sent a dozen children down to them in ten years. They do create an aura that they're the only children's hospital.

In the charity world itself, resentment was caused because of a suspected moving goalpost. Cynics assumed that the failure to report on progress meant that the appeal kept going after it had already passed its target. Indeed, the target itself was raised from £30 million to £42 million to 'cover inflation and unforeseen costs'.

The government, always keen to be charitable with public money rather than to squander it in inflationary public spending, was going to add another £30 million to the appeal. This appeared generous, but it was the Department of Health's parsimony in refusing to fund the rebuilding which made the appeal seem necessary to those who wanted the hospital redeveloped on the site. Lord Prior, Chairman of the Wishing Well Appeal, rather unctuously hoped, in the *The Daily Telegraph* (12 January 1989), that other fund-raising events would go ahead, 'and that the money raised would be given to other children's hospitals'. The success of the appeal was followed by Kings College Hospital's announcement that it was opening an appeal for £20 to £30 million to rebuild its facilities.

The mechanism was explained by the Wishing Well fund raiser, Marion Allford, in an interview with Christine Doyle of the *The Daily Telegraph* (17 January 1989):

> Who you are, who you know, and how persuasively you can approach them were what mattered when choosing people for the prestigious committees drawn from the City, and commerce, the institutions and marketing world. Those close to retirement or 'whose influence is going' were unlikely to be asked.
>
> Allford explained, 'We aimed as in other big appeals to raise one third of the money before the big public launch, so that the appeal is seen to be a big success from the start. Getting the Prince and Princess of Wales as patrons clinched the "top brass" appeal.'

The appeal disturbed even Bernard Levin who commented in the *The Times* (13 January 1989);

> The Great Ormond Street appeal succeeded not only because it was well-planned and well-run but also because the institution was well-known and well-loved. But what about the Lesser Ormond St Hospital in Muckleton-on-the-Marsh? It too urgently needs funds for renovation, new equipment and more room for parents when their children are being treated there ... Only, you see, the Muckleton Hospital doesn't have *famous* friends'.

He concluded that necessary private money for vital or important institutions should not 'depend upon the number of famous faces which appear on the appeal posters, but it does. Worth and need cannot be measured by glamour but they are.' However, it is not only glamour but also patronage and power that achieves ends. The government, despite ministerial pronouncements to the contrary, still puts most of the coins in the collecting boxes. As the NHS worried about lack of finance for basics, the government announced a £6 million pound grant to a charity, the Cyclotron Trust, for an expensive piece of equipment of disputable therapeutic and experimental value. Labour MP Harriet Harman alleged that 'the Government has ignored medical and research advice in its hurry to tip public funds into private health care initiatives', (*The Independent*, 11 January 1989). Other commentators saw it as a straight whim of the Prime Minister. It appeared that she had overridden the advice of both the government's own experts, and of the evaluation team at the Hammersmith hospital, to make the grant. One of the main movers was, coincidentally, the Premier's own eye surgeon, whose clear-sighted advice outweighed that of everybody else. The rallying cry was 'partnership between public and private', although it appeared that the public end of the bargain was to provide money for a private facility. 'The equivalent of the annual equipment bill for two NHS regions,' commented one opponent.

Margaret Thatcher's plans were, however, perhaps fortunately, tempered by a sense of the politically possible. The NHS represented all that she detested about the 'Nanny State' – but it was immensely popular with the people she needed to re-elect her. So her policy on the NHS had an occasional element of the Victorian value expressed so cogently by Arthur Hugh Clough in the *Modern Decalogue*, 'Thou shalt not kill but needst not strive/ Officiously to keep alive.'

The White Paper's 'internal market' proposals were a halfway stage in the process of dismantling the NHS and enforcing self-sufficiency on the overdependent electorate. According to David Hencke in the *Guardian* (1 March 1989), Thatcher had fought down her own instincts and the pre-emptive abolitionist toadying of John Moore. It is alleged that he had come up with a proposal for compulsory private insurance which, if implemented precipitately, would have been an electoral disaster. It was squashed at the time, but that does not detract from its attractions as a future aim.

'Charitisation' – The Acceptable Face of Privatisation?

In the meantime, the 1989 proposals for self-government for hospitals, and indeed for GPs' surgeries, represented a step forward to the aim of privatisation, or, in a sense, backward, to the old voluntary hospital system. The opted-out hospitals are envisaged as competing with existing private hospitals for patients funded initially by the State. It is even possible that at some point the hospitals, as happened to the Trustee Savings Bank and similar quasi-charities, will be sold off. But the model of the self appointed charity, run by its adminstrators and consultants with no public input, is one that will do just as well as a strictly commercial enterprise.

The Regional and District Health Authorities have already been effectively depoliticiocd, in the sense that even appointed members from elected bodies are being squeezed out. It recalled what had happened to elected representatives on the Water Authorities once their privatisation had been decided upon.

Already within the NHS, there were harbingers of the process of 'charitisation', a process in which facilities were removed from the NHS and placed under the control of quasi-charities, set up by the health authorities themselves. In 1988, a spate of local press reports across the country heralded a policy which was being implemented in many health authorities. It appeared that the NHS was surreptitiously pulling out of free long-term, in-patient care for the chronically ill. One of the clearest examples was in the Mersey Region where the DHAs were reported to be closing long-term wards for the elderly and mentally ill, and transferring their elderly patients to residential homes run by charities which the DHAs themselves were establishing.

The DHAs made savings by transferring costs to the Department of Social Security. Patients in hospital wards cannot claim Income Support Benefits, whereas in the residential homes, not run by the NHS directly, they can – if they are eligible under means-testing regulations. However, after six months residence, capital assets of more than £6,000 would debar patients from benefit. This meant that they could face having to sell their homes to finance their care – or returning home before they are medically ready. Ironically, the transition was financed by grants for 'Care in the Community' arrangements, designed to reduce the dependence of long-term patients so that wherever possible they could be cared for in their own homes and communities.

The attractions of 'voluntarisation' were obvious. For cash-strapped DHAs it was a creative and imaginative use of DSS regulations which released funds for use elsewhere. For most of the patients, or users, it can offer a move from wards with more than a whiff of the workhouse to purpose-built accommodation, sometimes with single rooms and almost certainly better facilities. But the implied shift from long term care by the NHS raises questions for those who fall into the gaps between what the DSS is prepared to finance and what the NHS was pulling out of.

Perhaps for fear that publicity could alert the DSS to change the rules, there is no clear information on how many health authorities are involved. Certainly in 1988 several such schemes were running in the Mersey Regional Health Authority which had made available £400,000 to finance 'Care in the Community' packages for each of its constituent districts, as I reported in *The Independent* (30 December 1988). In Southport, the District Health Authority was actively involved in setting up the Avondale Trust, a company limited by guarantee which was applying to the Charity Commissioners for registration as a charity.

In the Halton District Health Authority, covering Widnes and Runcorn, the policy was more advanced than many others. Community Integrated Care Ltd is a company limited by guarantee, and was registered as a charity in March 1988. Its stated aims allowed it to 'relieve illness, suffering and homelessness' and to 'establish maintain and conduct residential and nursing homes and day care and home care services'. Although CIC Ltd and the District Health Authority claimed an arms-length relationship, its founding trustees included three existing and one former employee of the DHA, and almost all its staff were employed by the NHS but contracted to CIC Ltd.

Within months, CIC Ltd had undertaken the responsibility for several wards full of long-term mentally ill and elderly patients, and had branched out into the nearby St Helens and South Sefton Health Authorities. With a staff in the hundreds, it was at the end of 1988 looking after 154 patients and anticipated doubling the number within twelve months.

The South Sefton Health Authority was closing three long-stay hospital wards and building a new forty-eight-bed nursing home on a former hospital site which will be managed 'on a peppercorn rent' by CIC Ltd. John Woods from the Health Authority said, 'Instead of old wards in old buildings, they will have single rooms in a much better environment.' But when asked about the potential patients not eligible for DSS benefits he was clear that 'We don't influence that – it's the government which lays down the regulations. Our job is to maximise the resources available for patient care, which this does.' While admitting the possibility that the government could move the goalposts over benefit rules, Woods said, 'We operate the best we can within the rules available.' Neil Whalley, Chief Executive of CIC Ltd was previously the Finance Manager of Halton Health Authority, but he preferred to stress his long involvement with MIND, the mental health charity, as more important. 'The Care in the Community schemes dried up ... As a company, we can borrow from banks and building societies. We've built places with more of a community scale.' Asked about the problem of those who do not qualify for DSS benefits, he replied, with the insouciance of a bureaucrat, 'That's the law of the land.'

Roger French, the General Manager of Halton District Health Authority, was more explicit about the policy implications, although he still tried to imply that the rise of CIC Ltd was purely coincidental to the authority's strategy. Halton was 'at least as far ahead as any other authority' with the policy. He pointed to the capital available for developments by charities, and asked, 'Are we talking about medical care or social care? Is it the job of the NHS to be "warehousing" at-risk groups?'

Staff at other voluntary groups and charities wondered why the NHS could not provide similar facilities itself, since the State is in any case funding the same staff and planners as before. It posed the question of whether the much vaunted Care in the Community exercise was to be reduced to a book-keeping manoeuvre with patients being transferred from one government department's columns to another.

Edward Murphy, Director of the Liverpool Council for Voluntary Service, explained the worries of some of the other local charities, and incidentally reflected a deeper and more widespread concern about the direction of government thinking: 'If new charities are established as mere handmaidens to a transient government view of what the NHS is for, they risk destroying the public support on which all charities depend.'

The change-over was tacitly encouraged by the Department of Health, which admitted that Mersey Region was one of the most advanced in its use of the tactic, but said it was widespread in most regions.

We have been encouraging Health Authorities to make such
sorts of provision where it is felt that patients are more in need
of residential than hospital care, but we have yet to decide on
general guidelines following the Griffiths report on Care in the
Community. However, we have given legal advice to authorities setting up such schemes – we wouldn't want them to do
anything illegal.

Since the whole drift of government measures in the health
services had been that management could only deliver its best with
cash incentives, it is not perhaps unduly cynical to see similar
motives in the move to charitisation. It seemed highly probable that
one reason for the popularity of the move among administrators
was the new results-based pay scheme for them. Since 1986,
according to the DHSS circular (PM (86)7), managers could be
awarded higher basic salaries for achievements like 'substantial
movements from hospital based to community based provision', or
'substantial closure programmes', and 'substantial relocations'. In
addition, they later secured additional payment for performance
'above normal expectations'. There is no hint that it is the
customers' expectations which are being assessed. One need look
no further for reasons for the amazing osmotic spread of the
concept of voluntarisation.

The charities are technically independent. Just like private
'charitable hospitals', or public schools, they are accountable only
to their trustees, not to their clients or beneficiaries. Wage rates for
staff are, in the end, open to 'market conditions' as is the service
provided for the customers who have possibly even less power of
influence than they did before the tenuous means of popular
control over the NHS.

The definitive model was Tadworth Children's Hospital in Surrey
which was transferred out of the NHS in 1983. (It had a 60 acre site
in Surrey which would doubtless have been ideal for a children's
hospital, but Great Ormond Street decided to sell for reasons of
their own – like rebuilding in London.) Tadworth Court went
independent, without getting any of the £16 million raised from the
sale of some of the land for housing. The Spastics Society headed
the consortium which led the opt out and found that it was much
more difficult to raise the funds. David Brindle in the *The Guardian*
(28 January 1989) reported that only 13 per cent of income was
being raised from appeals and donations, as fee paying became a
more and more significant share of revenue. One of the first actions

taken was the withdrawal of union negotiating rights for the 190 staff and dropping out from national Whitley Council pay and conditions.

This is, of course, the subtext in some of the Prime Minister's ambivalence to the NHS – a conviction that large nationalised bodies give the unions too much power. The atomisation of the service achieves the diffusion of that power. As against that simplistic picture, the big attraction of opting out for managers is precisely their ability to reward themselves in excess of nationally agreed pay scales.

Tim Yeo, then Director of the Spastics Society and now Tory MP for Suffolk South, said, 'Unknowingly we actually provided a model for this whole opt-out procedure long before anybody thought of it'.

Perhaps in that context it is worth looking at what Barry Hassell, the Hospital's Chief Executive said, before endorsing it as a model. 'We actively seek funding from the statutory authorities for these children. It is not the parents' responsibility to pay. But we have never refused admission to any of our ongoing older patients because of a lack of funding. I have to say, though, that we are much stricter with new patients.'

That could be taken as an accurate forecast of the future for the NHS and its patients as the cumulative changes erode the basic principles which motivated its inauguration. The models of opting out, or voluntarisation, both involve replacement of the service by a form of charity. In that they are helped because the law on charities and their traditional social practice recognises no voice for the beneficiaries. None of the proposals for hospitals to 'opt out' has suggested that the customers, the patients and potential patients, the catchment community, should be consulted. None of the proposals envisages giving them a voice afterwards. 'Organised charity, cold as ice', on the one hand, and the Poor Law on the other.

9

Saints, Sects
and Secular Societies

One of the ironies of modern charity law is that the privileges which the Established Church once jealously guarded for itself have now been extended to almost all other religions and cults. Indeed, it was the enthusiastically ecumenical Church of England and the British Council of Churches which sprang to the defence of the Moonies under the guise of protecting 'religious freedom'. This chapter argues that in fact it was the defence of religious *privilege*, not freedom.

The chapter looks at the confusion of roles assigned to religion in law; at how religions are allowed privileges of political activity denied secular charities; and at how the modern churches find themselves in political and social opposition to an unctuously pious government.

From Faggots to Forebearance

Charity law in relation to religion and the law on blasphemy share a common origin in protection for the Established Church. Those who blasphemed were guilty more of subverting the political order than of shocking religious sensibilities. Similarly, the Doctrine of Superstitious Uses, and later the concept of 'public policy', sought to exclude politically unacceptable beliefs and organisations from charitable status. As Lord Justice Denning said of blasphemy in 1949, 'The reason for this law was because it was thought that a denial of Christianity was liable to shake the fabric of society, which was itself founded on the Christian religion. There is no such danger to society now, and the offence of blasphemy is a dead letter' (until, of course, Mary Whitehouse proved him wrong by successfully prosecuting *Gay News*).

112

Before the Reformation, a gift to religious charity was the same as a gift to the Church. Week's Charity served as a stark reminder of the fate of anyone who left money for another religion. The Protestant ascendancy was only marginally more tolerant in what it allowed as charity. Religion and politics were bound together so that unorthodoxy in one field betokened it in the other. As late as 1754 (*Da Costa v. De Pas*), Lord Hardwicke overturned a bequest for Jewish religious purposes, without returning it to the natural heir as was the commmon pattern of the century under the Mortmain Act. In a decision which evoked memories of the *Merchant of Venice*, Hardwicke reasoned that the gift was indeed charitable, but it was void under the superstitious uses doctrine as contrary to established religion, it therefore reverted to the crown to find a suitable outlet for the charitable intentions of the testator. So he directed that the bequest should go to the Foundling Hospital for bringing up children on good Anglican principles.

When the bounds of acceptable religious activity were extended under the various Toleration Acts, political reasons were prominent in the methods of registering and ensuring the charitable status of the places of worship of other faiths. Indeed, Section 11 of the Places of Worship Act of 1812, which is apparently still in force, made it an offence to hold any form of religious meeting behind closed doors, for reasons of public security.

As a result of the extension of religious toleration, places of worship do not have to register with the Charity Commissioners, so their accounts are not available for public scrutiny. The local churches are overseen by their denominational authorities, which effectively removes the right of interference by the Charity Commissioners. In addition, places of worship are exempted from rates. For Anglican churches, the exemption dates from the very beginning of the rating system in the Elizabethan Poor Laws, and derived as much from the fact that they were public buildings as from their religious role. The parish, with the church as its centre, was until recently as much a secular administrative unit as a religious concept.

The Act which extended rate relief to non-established churches, and by extension the benefits of charitable status, was the Poor Law Relief Act of 1833 and the quid pro quo was the registration of the premises which gave the authorities a measure of control and surveillance.

The conjunction of religious and political outlooks could be seen in the *De Themmines* case in 1828. The judge ruled that it was

'against the policy of the country to encourage, by the establishment of a charity, the publication of any work which asserts the
absolute supremacy of the Pope in ecclesiastical matters over the
sovereignty of the state'.

Tolerance in religion developed from then, so for example,
Romilly decided in 1862 (*Thornton v. Howe*) that a gift for the
'printing, publishing and propagation of the sacred writings of the
late Joanna Southcott' was charitable, even though he held her to
be 'a foolish and ignorant woman'. In case this looks like a
remarkably tolerant attitude for a high Victorian judge, it should be
remembered that the 1736 Mortmain Act was in force – and the
bequest fell. However, like the animal welfare decisions of the
same period, later jurists worked on the principle that Romilly
meant what he *said* rather than what he *did*.

Judge Gavin Duffy, in Ireland, later held that Southcott was 'a
patently demented visionary, whose sectaries had practically
disappeared after her death'. He thought the writings were foolish –
but indubitably religious.

As society changed, the impulses of a different age began to work
on the precedents; there was a manifest tension between the social
ends the judges now wanted and the earlier reasoning in the cases.
Indeed, the case law seemed as dependent on revelation as the
religions themselves.

While accepting tolerance for other religions, in 1917, Lord
Parker cited the *De Themmines* case when he drew the line in
Bowman v. Secular Society Ltd: 'The abolition of religious tests, the
disestablishment of the Church, the secularisation of education, the
alteration of the law touching religion or marriage, or the
observation of the Sabbath are purely political matters. Equity has
always refused to recognise such objects as charitable.' His decision
was clearly motivated by his distaste for the irreligious message of
the Secular Society. To justify it he mustered the early precedents
against unorthodoxy in religion. Ever since, his decision has
effectively equated political activity by charities with the now
redundant doctrine of superstitious uses. If the early reasoning of
the case law is followed, political activity is heretical.

God on Our Side? Liberal Theology, Orthodox Politics

An objective reading of Parker's judgment, far from justifying the
extension of charitable status to other religions, should clearly

debar many of them; they could all be presumed to oppose the aspects of 'public policy' he enumerated. 'Religious tests' were, after all, the means of excluding all who were not members of the Established Church.

Similarly, the many Hindu and Islamic charities now on the Charity Commission register would have had the earlier law-makers stirring in the afterlife. However, once the boundaries crept past the Established Church it was very difficult for the judges to see how or where they could draw the line. Earlier restrictions of charitable status to monotheism have been quietly put aside. One sticking point, however, is that theism, whether poly or mono, is firmly established as the benchmark test.

The other test is that it is not the practice of religion, as worship, which is charitable, but the *advancement* of religion. Private services and private prayers are not charitable, which demonstrates a Protestant ethic still visible through the decisions. Some authorities insist on a further test of 'public benefit', which functions as a form of small print for judges to exclude what they consider undesirable. It allows much latitude for religion since, as Lord Plowman held in 1973, the courts could not distinguish between one set of tenets and another, unless they 'were subversive of all morality'. The effect of the indulgence is that the present appearance of the law is like a palimpsest of pragmatic decisions. The original ones have been almost erased and overwritten, but still show through the dusty parchment at inopportune moments. In the words of Sheridan and Keeton (1983, p. 66); 'The law as to religious charities is now tolerant, but in an unholy mess.'

The Church as Activist

The privileged position now accorded to all religions sits strangely with contemporary views on political purposes as applied to secular charities. The Roman Catholic Church participated in campaigns to repeal the Abortion Acts, which would have had Tory backbenchers calling for action by the commissioners if it had been a secular charity. The Lord's Day Observance Society devotes considerable tax exempt funds to making the Sabbath miserable for all. Most interestingly, the Church of England, once seen as the Conservative Party at prayer, has increasingly taken not just a political stance but one at odds with the Thatcher government over the effects of its policies and actions. From being the definitive

benchmark of 'public policy' and religious and political acceptability, it has become increasingly suspect in the eyes of the
government.

In his biography of Margaret Thatcher, Hugo Young advances the
idea that she has, ideologically at least, adhered to the muscular
monetarist Judaism of Chief Rabbi Immanuel Jakobovits, 'in effect
the spiritual leader of Thatcherite Britain'. Many Conservatives seem
to file 'Faith in the City' on the same shelf as State and Revolution.

Of course, political activity ancillary to the main purpose of a
charity is acceptable – and since the main concerns of all religions
cover eternity and infinity, it could easily be said that all human life,
and therefore politics, is ancillary to God's purpose.

The rationalist Barbara Smoker remembers using this equivalent
of the archaic legal form of sanctuary to help set up RAP – Radical
Alternatives to Prison. As she says, it was difficult to conceive of a
more political project, going as it did against the grain of all those
Conservative Party speeches from the platform which get the blue
rinse set so excited. 'I chaired its inaugural meeting and most of the
other founder members were atheists, agnostics, or something
tenuous and unorthodox,' she said (interview with author
December 1988). But it had become a project of Christian Action so
that it could benefit from that body's religious charity status and
attract funding from the major trusts, which are mostly prohibited
from making grants to bodies without charitable status. To preserve
the fiction, she resigned from RAP's executive in case anyone drew
attention to the incompatibility of her being President of the
National Secular Society and an activist in Christian Action!

Her experience points to a development which has probably
gone much farther since then. The churches can no longer rely
upon captive audiences, and in the atomised communities which
were left by post-war social engineering they are often the only
non-governmental bodies able to help the dispossessed organise
themselves. In 1988 and until the police stormed the church and
removed him, Sri Lankan Viraj Mendis's attempt to resist deportation led him to 'claim sanctuary' in the Church of the Ascension in
Manchester. The episode headlined a conflict between Church and
State, but the less publicised local Churches' Work Scheme
underlined a usurpation of the former role of the Welfare State – it
had become the biggest employer in Hulme and Moss Side apart
from Manchester City Council itself.

The Victorian Anglicans had built no less than eleven churches to
evangelise the inner city working-class district of Hulme in

Manchester – a work for which government grants were available. The Sea of Faith receded, leaving its Gothic pebbles stranded around what became Europe's largest inner city redevelopment. In Hulme, the only thing swinging in the sixties was the demolition contractor's ball and chain. The Church of the Ascension arose to replace its eleven predecessors, its concrete walls blending in with the sixties tenement blocks which surround it.

The building's bare modernity is relieved by William Morris stained glass rescued from a church endowed by the Dunlop family, depicting workers making rubber tyres. Morris's reaction to the aesthetic bleakness of the modern environment could have been matched by that of the locals to pictures of people working. In February 1989, over 60 per cent of them did not.

Over 300 of those who did were employed by the Churches' Work Scheme. The project was started in collaboration with St Wilfred's, the nearby RC church, whose priest, Philip Sumners, was the employment specialist of the partnership. What others saw as modernity, and Marxism, Ascension's Rector John Methuen saw as the traditional role of the churches: 'We've never entirely given up our secular role. Just look at the church schools. In fact, the State has only undertaken many of these functions for a few generations – we've been doing it for centuries longer' (interviews with author, March 1989).

Father Philip saw employment as the biggest need unmet by the state. As a junior seminarian he had known the Hulme of BC (Before Clearance). 'Hardly any of those people are left now. I found some press cuttings from one of my predecessors warning the council of the consequences of dispersing communities the disastrous way they did.'

He was trained as a canon lawyer which had helped his dealings with the Department of Employment over the Churches' 'Firmstart' Scheme. 'A lot of people we've trained don't have the £1,000 necessary to get the Enterprise Allowance. The idea was that they'd work in our workshop, with all the backup we could give. They'd carry on getting dole, while we'd hold anything they made in a trust, and then make a grant of the thousand afterwards.' The DoE, with logic-chopping worthy of a Chancery judge, considered that this would make the participants unavailable for jobs, although there were no vacancies in the neighbourhood.

Less contentious schemes included the Furniture Project, which rehabilitated furniture for distribution to people in the neighbourhood, and Community Engineering, which had begun with the repair of old tools for countries like Tanzania, and had developed expertise in welding, and making wrought iron and security bars. One of the most successful in placing trainees was the computer scheme based in the Church of the Ascension itself. Other activities include waste recycling, fitting security devices on doors and windows, painting and decorating.

Most of the trainees had never worked before, so the most basic skill to acquire was getting up in the morning. 'A great deal of pastoral care is needed just to keep someone in the business,' Father Philip commented drily.

In a sense, the projects epitomised the problems of voluntary organisation among the dispossessed. The social stratification on the council estates had led to a shortage of the managerial and organisational experience which was once a by-product of trade unions, co-ops and friendly societies. Social security payments did not leave much for the raising of capital or running costs for self-help organisations, so the schemes were dependent on funding by local and national government. They in turn wanted to see responsible management which forced the churches into the position of overseers as well as instigators. In the latter role there was potential for mistrust by the beneficiaries, while in the former the government saw a danger to their essentially passive plans for the inner city inhabitants.

So what did the Church get out of it? Father Philip said, 'The Church is seen to care, to be doing something, and that gives our worshipping congregations a degree of pride.' As a marginal effect, he also detected a higher rate of christenings in St Wilfred's, 'But we RCs tend to baptise everything that moves. Father John has a stricter policy!' For the Anglicans, Father John Methuen claimed about a dozen regular new churchgoers as the result of the Viraj Mendis affair, and far more black funerals and weddings held in the church. 'Not that marriage is a boom industry in the neighbourhood,' he added smiling.

The increased black involvement in the congregations had left them open to charges of white middle-class missionary activity in an area with a high black population. Pastor Blake, from the African Methodist Evangelical Church, insisted that the Churches' Work Scheme had 'outgrown the ideas which I as a grass-roots person wanted to foster' and described it as 'empire building'. It seemed as if the success of the project was in itself a subject for reproach, especially if a white priest played a part. 'One of the biggest problems,' said Father Sumner, 'has been the "Hulme and Moss

Side disease" – if you try something positive, others will try to knock it down. There's so much disenchantment here!'

Their Victorian predecessors would not count a few extra christenings and marriages as a triumphant success, although they might have been happy that the scheme employed more people than the local brewery. But Father John identified a special role for the Established Church which recalled its politico- religious origins.

> The Church of England is a parochial church. There is not a square foot in England which is not in someone's parish boundaries, which have been an integral part of life since the Vikings. So we feel a responsibility for everyone in our parish of over 20,000, whatever their denomination.
>
> John Wesley said the world was his parish – I think I have enough to do in Hulme itself! But what we do, we do for the benefit of those who live here, which is why we became involved in the Viraj Mendis Sanctuary affair, and in the work scheme.

Applications for places on the Work Scheme came through the Job Centre, so there is no way, even if they had wanted, by which the fathers could have developed a latter day cargo cult, packaging gospel and jobs together. Father Methuen defends what others would call political involvement: 'In the end, it comes down to the nature of Christian faith – our belief in a God who comes here and becomes a human being – and so is interested in human beings and this world.'

He had once been chaplain to Eton College and was sensitive to charges that the churches' activities represent a white middle-class mission to the natives. In fact, when he recently returned to Eton to give a lecture on Church and State at the height of the Mendis deportation uproar, he 'was treated like a returning hero. They're not exactly the Socialist Workers Party, but it's certainly not a Thatcherite paradise either.'

Despite intellectual currents at Eton, did the churches' role in places like Hulme augur a revival of the churches' secular role? For decades, they had contented themselves with pointing out new fields for government intervention and giving the Welfare State their blessing.

Initiatives like those in Hulme should have been exactly what the Cabinet ordered as it exhorted 'Active Citizenship' to fill the gaps in social spending. But schemes like this were more likely to be seen as rendering a reproach to a neglectful Caesar rather than an attempt to usurp his functions. Father Methuen summarised: 'We think the State was right to take up those responsibilities, and wrong to relinquish them – but if it does, then it's our duty to do what we can.' It almost seemed that in its rearlong rush to the Victorian and Georgian ages, the government had overshot its target and reached the medieval period, when charity and 'pious causes' were one and the same.

10

Sects and Sinners

'Cult' is an emotive and derogatory word with connotations of un-British enthusiasm and unthinking devotion. None the less, it is difficult to frame an objective formula which could distinguish between cults and mainstream religions.

Cults are sometimes called 'new religious movements' by their apologists to emphasise their identity with the mainstream. Whatever they are termed, it is clear that they are fringe organisations whose novelty makes them stand out from other religious bodies. We are so imbued with the religious ideas which permeate society, that even those who assume that this is a predominantly secular society take the position accorded to religion for granted. Therefore, examination of cults as something outside our experience gives a useful platform from which to look at how the more established religions ('mainstream cults') are treated in law.

The Gold-bricked Road

For a cult, the blessings of religious and charitable status are manifold. Religious status offers fiscal advantages in all countries following Common Law systems. Similarly, 'Registered Charity' on a letterhead lends a respectability to activities. The public assumes that the organisation and its methods and objects have been approved and thoroughly vetted. Yet, as the Charity Commissioners admit, their only real point of contact and discipline is at the point of registration.

In the more tolerant atmosphere of the USA, the Universal Life Church pursued the legal privileges of charity to happy absurdity. According to the *New Humanist* (July 1980) the church, founded in 1962, 'believes in what is right, and that all people have the right to determine what beliefs are right for them, as long as they do not

interfere with the rights of others'. This right-on church ordained
many a draft dodger to avoid call up, but in 1966 the IRS refused to
grant religious tax exempt status. In 1974, this was overturned by a
federal district judge who said that 'neither this court nor any
branch of this government will consider the merits or fallacies of a
religion. Nor will the court praise or condemn a religion. Were the
court to do so, it would impinge upon the guarantees of the First
Amendment.'

Church founder Kirby J. Hensley was actually opposed to tax
exemptions for churches, but considered, in an eminently reasonable and ecumenical manner, that 'if the government is going to
give a free ride to Billy Graham and the Pope, then why not let
everybody participate in these blessings?' This prescient ecumenism
predated the late eighties when the Swaggarts and Falwells trod
precisely such a gold-bricked road to Heaven.

However, amusement at such foibles should not obscure the fact
that those same privileged standards which allow Anglican,
Methodist or Roman Catholic political activity, enable groups like
the Moonies to maintain a network of actively right-wing political
fronts, like the Collegiate Association for Research into Principle
(CARP) or the American Freedom Coalition. Tax tripped up the
Moonie establishment, of course, since in 1985 Sun Myung Moon,
the cult founder, completed a thirteen month gaol sentence for tax
evasion in the USA.

Internal speeches reveal Moon's interest to be more overtly
political than theological.

The Time is here now for the work of CAUSA and AFC, Father
[himself] has already laid the grassroots foundations in order
to reach National and State politicians. If we had enough
seminary graduates, we could mobilise them a lot ... This time
your frontline missions will be your hometowns ... when you
go back to your homelands you can utilise all the church's
organisations that already have been established. The foundations of these organisations are substantial and you have to
connect with and work with them, helping to reach people
from the Christian Culture, patriotic conservatives, and retired
military personnel and veterans. (*Time Out*, 23 November
1988)

The Moonies provided an object lesson in the legal problems
facing opponents of cults. They sued the *Daily Mail* for libel – and

lost disastrously. The jury in the case not only exonerated the newspaper on 4 April 1981, but also added a rider recommending an investigation into the entitlement of the Unification Church to charitable status. The jurors felt that the Moonies' activities were not only harmful but political and so should not have charitable status. However, the Charity Commissioners set aside the jury's recommendation. As they read the law, the advancement of religion was almost automatically charitable. Thus they had no grounds for effective action against the registered Moonie charities, the Sun Myung Moon Foundation and the Holy Spirit Association for the Unification of World Christianity. Under public pressure the commissioners reconsidered – but in the end returned to their original conclusion. As an earlier commissioners's report had confessed: 'Charity law is not always governed by logic nor are the decisions entirely consistent' (1967).

The commisioners' report on the Moonies was accurate and clear – it was the law which was not.

(11) Inclusion in the register of Charities carries with it no moral or social approval of the purpose of an institution or of the manner in which it is administered; it is simply a recognition that the institution has objects which are charitable in law.
(12) It seemed to the Commissioners that as a matter of law the teaching and practices of Divine Principle which is referred to in the objects of the two institutions do not go beyond the very wide bounds which have been applied by the Court for the purposes of ascertaining whether or not the propagation and practice of any particular religious creed is charitable in law. (1982 Appendix C).

The Attorney-General appealed against their decision but in 1986 somewhat shamefacedly dropped the action. Many backbenchers were livid that an organisation which they saw as an attack on the values of family life, as sinister, secretive and dishonest, should maintain charitable status. However, there is little doubt that the commissioners were right, even if the Moonies were wrong. It was difficult to describe the Unification Church in a way which was different from the mainstream religions.

Each objection to the Moonies' practice could, by charity law's favourite tool, analogy, be matched with a similar one to more established churches. Foreign control: was it any worse to be controlled from Korea than from Rome? A Guru, or autocratic head: what about the Queen as head of the Church, or the Pope? Political involvement: try testing the Archbishop of Canterbury's or the Bishop of Durham's pronouncements, or the Chief Rabbi's forthright views on social affairs, or the Roman Catholic campaigns on abortion. Money-making involvement – see the Vatican's business empire and the Church Commissioners! Cults split up families and take children away from their parents – in the Roman Catholic church they call it a vocation. Irrational beliefs, such as that God spoke in Korean – was that any less plausible than his being monolingual in Hebrew, Latin or Arabic? And would any dispassionate observer accept, without faith, the doctrines of resurrection, or the Athanasian Creed?

It is no wonder that the government abandoned its case against the Unification Church. The main saving grace of the established churches was that their seniority had bred familiarity and contentment with their practices. However, one can assume that the mainstream churches saw an identification, since they flung a protective arm around their bizarrely heretic sister church. The Anglicans and the British Council of Churches saw it as a defence of religious freedom.

In fact, of course, there was no threat to the *freedom* of the Moonies, or to that of the churches. They would have exactly the same rights as secular, ethical or political groups to fight for the hearts and minds of citizens. What might be lost would be the privileged, legal and fiscal position from which they were accustomed to fight their good fight.

Scientology – Religio ad Absurdum

One organisation which has tried desperately to achieve worldwide recognition as a religion, and has in fact had several of its front organisations registered with the Charity Commission, is the so-called 'Church of Scientology'. In the words of Mr Justice Latey, it is 'corrupt', 'sinister' and 'dangerous'. In 1968, the Minister of Health, Kenneth Robinson had said:

> The government is satisfied, having reviewed all the available evidence, that Scientology is socially harmful. It alienates members of families from each other and attributes squalid and disgraceful motives to all who oppose it; its authoritarian

principles and practices are a potential menace to the
personality and well being of those so deluded as to become
its followers; above all its methods can be a danger to the
health of those who submit to them.

The Scientologists' struggles to be accepted as a religion illustrate
how desirable such status is – and how close the organisation got to
it. Unusually for 'religions', we have direct testimony as to the
somewhat unspiritual motives of the founder. When the Scientologists tried to register their 'chapel' in East Grinstead as a place of
worship, they had good legal advice – the counsel in the
proceedings was Quintin Hogg, later to be Lord Chancellor.
However, whatever talents later took him to those giddy heights he
lost in the case (*Re Segerdal* (1969)).

Under the 1855 Act, the Registrar General maintained a register
of buildings for religious worship. Once he had registered a
building it was exempt from poor law rates and also from the
supervision of the Charity Commissioners.

Mr Hogg argued that the Registrar-General had no option but to
register an applicant place of worship; that he had no supervisory
powers but could only rubber stamp the application. To the great
benefit of ratepayers everywhere, Judge Ashworth rejected this
view:

> The effect of registration is not merely to relieve persons from
> penalties for practising their religious belief; on the contrary,
> registration opens the door to other advantages and, in my
> view, Parliament cannot be supposed to have intended that
> such advantages were to be obtained merely on the certificate
> of the persons most interested in obtaining them, without any
> provision being made for checking the correctness of the
> certificate.

On the question of whether Scientology was a religion, Ashworth
was not going to make judicial history. 'As has been said before,
while it may be difficult to draw the line, it may not be difficult to
say on which side of the line a given case falls.' The issue in the
case was not the question of public benefit but whether the
Scientologists worshipped a deity.

If it had been a standard charity case, the judge might have
invoked some of the small print in the precedents to decide on
public benefit, or even superstitious uses. In this case, the judge

decided that they did not have a deity, and that was enough.

The Scientologists' case was complicated because although they do indeed believe in a supernatural being, they also believe in charging proselytes up to £130,000 to get 'Up the Bridge' and attain that knowledge. This particular belief is held with such religious rigour that they certainly would not have told the judge unless he joined up and paid.

Scientology teaches those with sufficient money and gullibility that 75 million years ago Earth was part of Galactic Confederation of seventy planets. The ruler, Xenu, rounded up all 'artists, revolutionaries and criminals' and transported them to Earth, where he dropped nuclear weapons on them. Their spirits survive, reincarnated in humans and causing 'enturbulation', but they can be overcome with the help of 'auditing'. This imaginative cross between Flash Gordon-style science fiction and psychotherapy is amusing, and may be no more or less plausible than the Virgin Birth and resurrection of the body. However, the costs of involvement are no laughing matter.

In 1988, a bankruptcy court in Tunbridge Wells was told that a computer analyst, Adrian Thomas Hayman, gave more than £175,000 to the church in fourteen years, and had in fact borrowed heavily to do so; £71,000 had gone in a little over a year (*East Grinstead Courier*, 12 May 1988). One of L. Ron Hubbard's more forceful policy statements to his disciples was, 'Make money, make more money ... make other people produce so as to make money.'

There is every reason to believe that Hubbard's deity bears an uncanny resemblance to Mammon, and that the superfical veneer of 'churchdom' is intended to obtain the fiscal privileges which accrue to a religion. In 1987, there was an attempt to argue that 'The Church was not a tax dodge. It was a means of giving Hubbard's auditors the freedom of American Hospitals and to stop the psychiatrists hounding them' (BBC Radio 4, August 1987, *Ruthless Adventure*).

In fact, Hubbard wrote to his secretary, Helen O'Brien, on the 10 April 1953, the year before the incorporation of the 'Church':

We don't want a clinic. We want one in operation but not in name ... It is a problem in practical business. I await your direction on the religion angle. In my opinion we couldn't get worse public opinion than we have had or have less customers with what we've got to sell. A religious charter would be necessary in Pennsylvania or NJ to make it stick. But I sure could make it stick. If we were able to return there [to Phoenix], we'd be able to count 10 to 15 preclears per week at $500 for 24 hours processing. That is real money... Charge enough and we'd be swamped (Atack, 1989).

As a conversion on the road to Damascus, it lacks spirituality. 'If a man really wanted to make a million dollars, the best way to do it would be to start a religion,' L. Ron himself said, with a rare lucidity. And as he had written to Helen O'Brien so it came to pass. Six months after his letter to her, he incorporated the Church of American Science, the Church of Scientology, and the Church of Spiritual Engineering – in New Jersey. Within two months the Church of Scientology of California was launched.

Russell Miller (1987, p. 220) sums it up:

Hubbard had been quietly planning the conversion of Scientology into a religion for more than twelve months, ever since... the autumn of 1953. It made sense financially, for there were substantial tax concessions available to churches, and it made sense pragmatically for he was convinced that as a religion Scientology would be less vulnerable to attack by the enemies he was convinced were constantly trying to encircle him.

After Hubbard's revelation that his operations had deep religious significance, his officers began to call themselves ministers and the 'Hubbard Association of Scientologists International' transformed into sister churches of the Church of Scientology of California, which had been incorporated in February 1954. The advantages were obvious – one of his most notorious memos to his followers advised that if any Scientologist were to be arrested in the course of 'church' activities, such as harassing defectors and opponents, they should file for massive damages for molestation of 'a Man of God going about his business'.

Business was, of course, the operative word. Hubbard was soon on a fixed percentage of the very large takings of the 'church'.

Eventually, an Australian High Court decision won the cult recognition as a religion there, which is why their Saint Hill headquarters in East Grinstead, in England, loudly proclaims that the church is 'Incorporated in South Australia'. To paraphrase another figure from the sixties, 'It would be, wouldn't it.'

The 'church' has never advertised the *Segerdal* decision against it, even though the judge so carefully refrained from discussion of any of the pejorative opinions which circulated among his colleagues, unlike Mr Justice Latey who ignored the South Australian precedent and accurately summed up the cult in 1984, 'Mr Hubbard is a charlatan and worse,' he declared, and the 'Church' was

> corrupt because it is based on lies and deceit and had as its real objective money and power for Mr Hubbard, his wife and those close to him at the top. It is sinister because it indulges in infamous practices both to its adherents who do not toe the line unquestioningly and to those outside who criticize or oppose it. It is dangerous because it is out to capture people, especially children and impressionable young people and indoctrinate and brainwash them so that they become the unquestioning captives and tools of the cult, withdrawn from ordinary thought, living and relationship with others.

In 1988, the US Supreme Court finally overruled the church's claim for tax exempt status there, on the grounds that, 'Certainly if language reflects reality, the petitioner had a substantial commercial activity since it described its activities in highly commercial terms, calling parishioners "customers", missions "franchises", and churches "organisations".' The judges added: 'The goal of money-making permeated all of the petitioner's activities – its services, its pricing policies, its dissemination practices and its management decisions.' It finally ruled that the 'church' did not qualify for tax exemption 'because it violated well-defined standards of public policy by conspiring to prevent the IRS from assessing and collecting taxes', and that 'it is operated for a substantial commercial purpose and because its net earnings benefit L. Ron Hubbard, his family and OTC, a private non-charitable corporation controlled by key Scientology officials'.

For their members and potential converts, the 'church' maintained the power of positive thinking by ignoring the major defeats and trumpeting the minor victories. 'Scientology is definitely a religion. Courts and other official government bodies all over the world have recognised this fact,' they claimed. But the only one they adduce is 'a major court case in the District Court in Stuttgart, Germany ruled that the Church of Scientology is a religion'.

The consensus of decisions, however, favoured the Spanish judge, Ximenes, who in 1988 ordered the arrest of many Scientologists including their international head, 'Reverend' Heber

Jentzsch. He characterised it as 'a multinational organisation whose sole aim is to make quick money under the guise of doing good'. He was investigating charges of fraud, forgery, tax swindles, extortion and threats.

Although it is almost forty years since the conversion, the 'church' has not had much success in gaining recognition or respectability, partly because of the evidently distasteful nature of its activities. But mostly, one suspects, it is because Hubbard only belatedly grafted on spurious religious trappings to a clearly secular con-trick which was already up and running. It is, in fact, the difference between a conversion and a purpose built job. If, like the Unification Church, Hubbard had incorporated the trappings of Christianity, he is likely to have been more successful in gaining the recognition, and privilege, for which he fought

Charity Shall Cover the Multitude of Sins

With so many judges and ministers, here and abroad, vociferously aware of the nature of Scientology, it may surprise some people, that the 'church' has several fronts which are registered as charities. The Charity Commissioners can only rule effectively on the stated objects of a charity. They have as yet no power to vet trustees for suitability, although that might change as a result of the White Paper.

In East Grinstead, Scientologists run their own charitable school. Greenfield School has been demonstrated to be under the control of the cult, and despite some complaints to the Charity Commissioners remains so – because it is in effect a fee paying public school for the children of Scientologists in good standing. 'Good standing' is the operative phrase. Marcus Allen, a Scientologist, was Chairman of the Trustees, but wilfully persisted in speaking to people whom the church had 'declared' or excommunicated. As a result, in 1984, not only was he removed as trustee but his son was expelled from the school just before taking his GCEs. The reason was his father's refusal to toe the line in the purge which was then proceeding in Scientology. The school at the time had twenty-seven staff – and a total staff bill of £58,593, which in effect meant that the staff were working at charitable rates – an average of around £40 per week.

The school's counsel's advice was, 'If Greenfields were to do something that closed the group it catered to, and thus not be for the public benefit, then it could result in difficulties regarding charitable status ... No doubt a child could be expelled for his or her behaviour but I see no legal base for expelling a child because of a parent's behaviour.'

So while the school's behaviour was very likely to be uncharitable in a strict reading of the law, 'by analogy' it was not substantially different from that of more established public schools catering for religious groups. After all, there are Jewish, Catholic, Quaker and even Muslim schools which would be unlikely to welcome the offspring of apostates, even if they did not go so far as to have a policy of exclusion like the Exclusive Brethren or of Declaring like the Scientologists (see 'Sweet Charity', *New Statesman*, 27 November 1987).

Another Scientology-controlled charity was 'Narconon' which claims to be able to cure drug addiction. In his otherwise comprehensive condemnation of Scientology, Justice Latey had said, 'I have searched, and searched carefully for anything good, some redeeming feature in Scientology. I can find nothing, unless it be such participation as there has been in the drug abuse campaign.' One feels sure that the learned judge will be happy to know that his fears were unfounded – Narconon, the Scientologists' 'anti-drug abuse' charity is as much a scam as the rest of the operation. But it is a registered scam! Narconon lays great stress on its charitable status in the begging letters it has been sending out to companies, most of whom would consider it to be a certificate of good faith by the Charity Commission (see *Private Eye*, Cult Corner, 29 November 1987).

The therapy Narconon advocates is massive doses of vitamins, in a treatment which bears a strong resemblance to much derided Hubbard claims to be able to treat radiation sickness. It includes a 'Megavitamin detoxification programme' and a 'Purification programme of nutrition, exercise and sauna to cleanse the body of any accumulated drugs or chemicals'. The scientific credentials of the Scientologists for undertaking medical work can be assessed by Hubbard's statement that 'Leukaemia is evidently psychosomatic in origin' (The Old Man's Casebook 1953, *The Journal of Scientology*). In 1958, the FDA seized and destroyed 21,000 multivitamin tablets of 'Dianazene' which Hubbard was labelling as a cure for radiation sickness.

The Scientologist's newspaper *The Auditor* called upon members: 'SoCo are also looking for Narconon lecturers and staff. The aim is to get Narconon fully operational in the UK and revert the current drug problem.' SoCo is Social Coordination, the church's front organisation bureau. Its head at the time, Sheila Gaiman, was the correspondent with the Charity Commission over Narconon. Her husband, David, as 'Deputy Gaiman', ordered the planting of false information in US Security Agency computers, for which the FBI would very much like to see him (see Lamont,1986). SoCo is described in internal bulletins as 'developed in 1975 to carry Scientology into the Society and create a recognition of the indispensability of Scientology Technology within the Society itself'. There may be subsidiary motivations. The Gaimans happen to own G&G Foods, a health food shop – which sells a very nice line in vitamins. David Gaiman described the business as, 'A nutrition company I have an interest in, with an all-Scientology exec structure, has been in a screaming affluence for years. This has been entirely due to LRH admin tech and good people who apply it' (*The Auditor*, no. 209). There is little mention there of charity, or for that matter of religion.

The Advancement of Education

Travellers on the London Underground may have seen an announcement headed 'Philosophy' and subtitled '12 discussions on Practical Philosophy'. At the bottom of the poster they will see the subscript 'Registered Charity established 1937'.

While the Scientologists scour the globe for complaisant judges to declare them a religion, the School of Economic Science is a religious cult which purports to be for the advancement of education. Those who survive the twelve lectures will be invited to more, and will eventually be donating considerable amounts of money and time to the 'charitable' work of the school. The SES began as a group supporting nineteenth century economist Henry George who held that a land tax was the solution to most economic ills. Add in a touch of theosophy, and more lately meditation, and one has a strange syncretic system of Victorian values and Hinduism.

An SES woman's place is in the home – except when ministering to the cult and its leader, Leon MacLaren, who has all the attributes of a guru. MacLaren had met the 'Shankaracharya', an Indian guru, and it is his branch of Hinduism which the former economic and philosophical study group adopted. Like the Scientologists, the cult runs private schools for children, where vegetarian wholefoods and

Sanskrit are the order of the day. They are run by the cult's subsidiary, the Independent Educational Association Ltd, a registered charity.

'The vital common link is that both organisations have looked to Mr MacLaren and his conversations for philosophic guidance,' explained Roger Pincham, the former Chairman of the Liberal Party and an SES member. It would be difficult to squeeze Sanskrit and meditation into a state school syllabus under Kenneth Baker's National Curriculum. The schools were founded 'to give their own and other children the opportunity to receive the simple truths upon which teaching in the schools is founded at an early age' (quoted Hounam and Hogg, 1985, p. 281).

The Hinduism in the schools was none of your namby-pamby Gandhian variety. In this robust reinterpretation of meditation, children from the age of 4 were forced into boxing matches, and corporal punishment was the norm, interspersed with punitive cold showers. The women had to have long hair and long skirts, and the children's food was generally uncooked and vegetarian. The cult is distinguished also by its reluctance to recruit disabled people since it appears that they are paying the price for misdemeanours in previous lives.

That people should wish to delude themselves in this way is their right. But should they be subsidised by the State for it? If the Workers Revolutionary Party tried to set up a school, for either adults or children, they would stand little chance of being accepted as charitable. Indeed, in 1982, the Charity Commissioners refused registration to 'Youth Training' precisely because there was evidence which suggested that the WRP was intending to use it for political purposes (Charity Commissioners, 1982).

Anyone who has had contact with the WRP would know that it did indeed have many of the characteristics of a religious cult, in which Leon Trotsky is the deity, and General Secretary Gerry Healy is his prophet. It operates on revelation as much as any charismatic cult, and the internal disciplines are every bit as strong.

However, because its philosophy does not invoke a deity acceptable to the judges and commissioners, it cannot get charitable status for schools which propound its policies. The SES (and the Scientologists in the case of Greenfield) can, even though they advance a definite political line in connection with Henry George, and have very specific views on how society should behave. In *The Secret Cult*, Peter Hounam and Andrew Hogg (1985) detail the SES's attempt at political influence through the Liberal

Party. The school claimed it as merely political activity from individual members, but the basic premise of Henry George's land tax is highly political – and was very influential in other English-speaking countries. Roger Pincham admitted that the school had

> a great interest in the land question and the extent to which other forms of taxation could be reduced if only revenue available from communally-created land values were collected ... However it should be emphasised that neither then nor at any time since has the economics course been conducted in support of any political party or for any political purpose. Not only did the Charitable Rules forbid it but everyone concerned respected the objective of trying to discover the truth about the subject which would then be available to everyone of whatever Party. (ibid , p. 285)

In fact he is guilty of a major error. Commissioners and judges have consistently defined 'political activity' as including attempts to change the law – and reforming the nation's fiscal system may be presumed to include at least a Finance Act!

Once distanced from the old established Church, looking at the cults raises the question, not whether charitable and religious privilege is desirable for them, but whether any religious body should be privileged in a society which polls show is predominantly secular. If the propounding of one set of philosophical doctrines, under the guise of religion, is to have charitable status, then why should not other bodies with philosophical and ethical systems which are not supernaturally inspired?

Rational – but Wrong: The Secular Societies

While the cults push religious toleration to the limits of credulity, the secular societies reveal the system's inbuilt bent to the supernatural. While the courts have determined Joanna Southcott's writings to be irrational but charitable, the Rationalist Press Association, for example, did not benefit from such a broad judicial view. First registered as an educational charity in 1963, it was struck off by the Charity Commissioners in 1971. It was not alone, the Ethical Union and the British Humanist Association had already suffered from an excess of evangelical fervour on the part of the Charity Commissioners.

They did not have the cash to fight the decision in the High Court and they were well aware that the law was not in their favour. 'As between religions, the law stands neutral', ruled Mr Justice Cross, 'but it assumes that any religion is at least likely to be better than none' (*Neville Estates v. Madden* (1962)). 'In 1972, we decided not to apply for reinstatement because it didn't seem worth the trouble, but following the experience of the South Place Ethical Society and the BHA we are obviously considering our position,' said Nicolas Walter of the Rationalist Press Association. He added, 'As you may expect, we feel rather bitter about the present situation' (Letter to the author, 17 August 1988).

In 1969, in the *Segerdal* case, Ashworth had used the seeming absence of a deity in Scientology to deny their 'chapel' registration. In the context of the time, it is difficult not to speculate that the main purpose of the bench was to deny privileges to an organisation which had been denounced in Parliament rather than to debate the precise importance of a deity to religion and charity.

However, one of the major drawbacks of case law, as was seen with the effects of the 1736 Mortmain Act, is that issues decided with a pragmatic purpose in mind – perhaps the exclusion of a cult – need to have reasons given and principles advanced. That rationalisation sets the precedent. So there is a suspicion that the eminently rational and moral RPA was excluded at least partly because of the decision in the Scientology case, that no deity meant no religion meant no charitable status. In 1980, the Inland Revenue continued the crusade against the infidel, in the form of the South Place Ethical Society. The society had started off as a Unitarian sect at a time when it was barely tolerated for not accepting the Trinity. The Unitarian deity shrank to the point of vanishing, and members admitted they had given up actual prayers a century ago, in 1869, when they became increasingly sure that no one was listening. The Inland Revenue advanced the argument that no God means no religion means no charitable tax concessions.

Mr Justice Dillon did not accept the society's objects as stated in Rule 2, 'the study and dissemination of ethical principles and the cultivation of a rational religious sentiment'. He said, 'Religion as I see it, is concerned with man's relations with God, and ethics are concerned with man's relations with man. The two are not the same, and are not made the same by sincere inquiry into the question, What is God?'

This is a logical and clear distinction. It also flies against the prevailing legal prejudice that ethics are an impossibility without divine inspiration. As a Commons Committee (1975) said, 'The traditional role of the Church in the field of charity, its guardianship of the moral order, and the historical fact that it was primarily due to religious teaching that society became increasingly conscious of the need to provide for human needs, requires no elaboration from us.'

Dillon concluded that the society, no matter how moral, could not be a religious trust, quoting Lord Parker on the National Secular Society (*Bowman v. SS* (1917)): 'It relegates religion to a region in which it is to have no influence on human conduct.' When the question of Buddhism was raised as a possibility of a non-theist form of conduct he admitted that 'it may be that the answer is to treat it as an exception'. He ruled that the South Place Ethical Society was for the advancement of education and the public benefit in that it contributed to the moral and spiritual welfare of society, adducing that, 'It is on the basis of mental or moral improvement of the community that animal welfare trusts have been accepted.'

Following the decision over the South Place Ethical Society, the RPA is unsure whether to try again and pay the huge legal cost of a challenge, despite the attraction of analogising from RPA to RSPCA. South Place spent £25,000 fighting its case, which explains why few decisions of the commissioners are challenged in the courts.

The irony of the crusade against the humanist societies, which led to their deregistration, became apparent in the 1989 White Paper (p. 8) where it was argued that the 'removal of religion as a head of charity would leave many existing trusts, some of which are of considerable antiquity, in an impossible legal limbo'.

Despite the ruling by Dillon, it would appear that actual anti-religious campaigning as such would not be charitable, as opposed to positive promotion of an ethical, albeit atheist viewpoint. So as the law stands, it is charitable, because conducive to public morality, for the Christian Mission to the Jews to seek to persuade members of another religion to apostasy, although that religion in itself is perfectly moral and charitable. It can do so even when another charity, the Council For Christians and Jews, is working hard on the equally charitable objective of building bridges between the two faiths!

Protestants can evangelise Catholics and vice versa, and the Hindus and Muslims can convert all – but anyone who wishes to persuade the world that all religions are superstitious (as opposed to all the *others*) is neither moral nor charitable. It is charitable for an imam to call for action against Salman Rushdie, or for an Anglican bishop to add his groatsworth with a call for the extension of the blasphemy laws to cover the author. But for the RPA to call a plague upon both their houses for intolerance and irrationality is not charitable.

Squaring the Circle

The 1989 White Paper responded to the deep concern of many over the activities of the cults: 'Anxieties have been expressed, in particular, about a number of organisations whose influence over their followers, especially the young, is seen as destructive of family life, and, in some cases, as tantamount to brainwashing charities,' 1989, (p. 8). However, it seems to have run into the logical impasse discussed earlier. How does one distinguish?

The Goodman Committee had wrestled with how to bring the humanists into the fold – while excluding the 'religions considered detrimental to the community's moral welfare'. Society 'must exclude from charitable status what it regards as evil' Goodman, 1976, (p. 24), it reported somewhat subjectively. Most religions, after all, define themselves by anathematising the beliefs and practices of others. Polygamy, arranged marriages, infant baptism, confession, ordination of women, subordination to priests or ritual slaughter of animals, are all practised by some religions and vehemently opposed by others.

After the purge against the humanists, a Charity Law Reform Committee had been set up which strongly advocated a new category of Non-Profit-Distributing Organisations, to remove the subjectively and biased tests on 'objects' of charities. Such an open house approach was not considered in the White Paper and implicitly rejected by the Goodman Committee, worried that a 'political party should not be permitted to masquerade under the cloak of an ethical or philosophical system and thus gain charitable status' (ibid.). The roots of that moral fear of political activity lay in the presumption that, first, the established church and, later, all religions were for the public benefit.

When the the Charity Commission hosted its seminar on Charity Law in October 1988, there was concern at what was called 'a rebuttable presumption in favour of religion'. Some were further concerned that the rebuttal set too high a test, letting in some organisations whose sincerity left much to be desired. Earlier,

Robin Guthrie, the Chief Charity Commissioner, had said, 'We must . . . apply vigorously the criterion of public benefit to religious cults, as well as to charities that owe their continuing existence to their ability to charge substantial fees' (CC Report, 1987).

In the case of the Scientologists, for example, the two heads coincide. But as we have shown, the cases of the Moonies and others are much more intractable. There are few criteria to isolate the examples of 'cults' from that of 'religions'. Robin Guthrie said:

Public benefit is to me the key, and one which has been used in the courts sometimes to test the other heads. One has to admit that there would have been concern about the early Christians, there were about the Quakers, and most certainly about Roman Catholics.

However, to strike out a religious body on the ground of its objectives would mean distinguishing between one religion and another. I think that is a task which no one would wish upon themselves. I certainly don't, and I don't think that anyone should wish it on parliament.

So if we accept that the public benefit head of charity is applicable, there are only two lines of approach open to us. Firstly and importantly, if in any sect the doctrines and the worship are not genuinely open to the public then that cannot be held to be for the public benefit. It is essentially a secret society for whatever religious intentions.

In that he has the support of the Hennings case of 1963, which debarred a Mormon Temple from rates relief because its services were only open to a select group of Mormons, 'The Recommends', in good standing and therefore were not open for public worship.

The other point – never tested – is the question of method and whether they are against the public interest. For example, if they lead to the break up of families, or the failure of individuals to fulfil their family responsibilities to their dependents, or if they disrupt personal and social life in a way which is against the public interest then one could challenge them on the basis of whether their *methods* were in the public interest. It is a very important distinction beween methods and objects.

But would this not apply to the twelve apostles, or to monks and nuns joining a monastery?

If someone joins a monastery, and deserts his family, of his
own volition and one can see no undue outside pressure then
that's simply what he chooses to do – it is, of course, very
much a matter of judgement. I quite agree that a lot of early
sects that are now respectable would have been caught up in
this way – nevertheless, I don't think you can get them on
objects – I do think you can get them on exclusiveness, or
secrecy and methods. I'm saying neither of those have been
tested in the court. The courts have ruled that Religion entails
belief in a supreme being – although they then allowed
Buddhism in, which doesn't quite fit. Personally, I think it
would be very difficult to distinguish between organisations
which are, or are not, in the public interest and that for the
ethical and humanist societies claiming charitable status is
perfectly understandable for their own interests – but an
extension would allow for an area of decision making that was
even more subjective. (Interview with author, October 1988)

The real problem is clearly the reconciliation of the ancient
privileges of the Established Church with public benefit. Intellect-
ually, the two are irreconcilable. It would, for all the reasons we
have discussed, be difficult to legislate the removal of cults from
charitable status without also removing the religions, and to do that
would pull down the whole edifice of 500 hundred years of charity
law.

But whatever historical reasons there are for continuing the
present rules, there are pressing needs for reform. In a society with
a majority which is not actively religious, and whose religious
minority is subdivided into mutually competing faiths, there is no
justification for continuing such privileges. That is even more the
case when they result in patent injustice to the humanists, and
indeed to secular political organisations.

Ben Whitaker's Minority Report to the Goodman Commission
mooted a break with tradition:

Although in the past charity often had religious origins, today
religion and charity are two distinct concepts which may or
may not necessarily coincide. There are clear practical
arguments in favour of concluding that religious bodies should
be granted charitable status only in so far as they carry out
otherwise charitable activities ... If charitable status is, however, to be granted also to religious bodies advocating beliefs

and propaganda, it obviously must in fairness equally be available to similar non religious bodies. The present position cannot be defended whereby churches and the Lord's Day Observance Society conduct propaganda and political campaigns with the help of the tax benefits of charitable status while, for example, the Humanist Trust or the National Secular Society is forbidden to do so. If the propagation of a religious philosophy is deemed charitable in equity so must also the advocacy of humanistic liberalism, Marxism, or other ethical and political philosophies.

The satisfactory test of a religion in this context poses superhuman problems; what law court or human agency empowered to demarcate charitable status is competent to judge the validity of a religion or the genuineness of a guru or claimant to be a new Messiah? What would have been the verdict of an early Charity Commission on Jesus Christ, or the first Christians or the Inquisition? Surely these are questions for a God rather than any earthly agency or Mammon; and therefore whereas the comparative study of different religions, ethics and philosophies is a part of education, religious proselytising cannot be termed charitable except in so far as other propaganda is allowed to be so. (Goodman, 1976, p. 146)

Whitaker's arguments were restated, unacknowledged, in the 1989 White Paper: 'While the advancement of religion might cease to be a charitable object, religious organisations would still remain free to propagate their doctrines, and if they wished, to promote and to administer trusts for such purposes as the relief of poverty which would remain charitable as before' (p. 8).

However, as we saw above, the government was not convinced, and the inclusion of this, the most radical solution, in the 'green' section of the paper, indicated that it was intended to provoke a storm of opposition – or of desperately creative thinking – by the churches.

The White Paper's own inclinations seemed to be towards Robin Guthrie's solution, of tightening the existing law and applying public benefit provisions. It suggests that the commissioners should remove offending charities from the register under the powers it has in the 1960 Charities Act, which would be made more explicit. It does not address itself to the backdoor method of registering as a place of worship, as tried by the Scientologists in *Re Segerdal* (1969).

In short, it is unlikely to produce a satisfactory result at all. Like the pubs which ban talk of religion or politics, the White Paper baulks at radical solutions to the confusion in charity law on just those heads. They are the ones in which the present law is mostly the product of prejudice and class interest in the past, and least amenable to rational examination now.

11

From Superstitious Uses to Subversive Activities: Part I

Previous chapters have shown how religious tolerance 'just growed', Topsy-like, beyond all original intentions. In this century, the gap between what was permissible to religions, but forbidden to lay charities, also grew. As the Charity Commissioners wrote: 'The pursuance of political activities relating to issues of morality and behaviour by religious charities would not in the normal way be objectionable because such issues are an essential concern of religious bodies and therefore it is not likely to be outside the powers of any charity having wide religious objectives' (CC Report, 1975). It was a point amplified by the inability to construct a case against the Unification Church, which, in the words of one sympathetic affidavit in the case, 'is heavily involved in political work in so far as its beliefs commit it to a struggle against communism; this element (which is more pronounced in America than in the United Kingdom) is reflected in the establishment of newspapers such as the *Washington Times*, a daily newspaper ... which has a definitely right wing character' (Affidavit of Eileen Barker to AG).

In contrast, in recent times, 'political activities' by lay charities have provoked a moral panic in some quarters. The 1989 White Paper summarised the all encompassing scope for sin. 'The powers and purposes of a charity should not include the power to bring pressure to bear on the government to *adopt, to alter, or to maintain* [author's italics] a particular line of action, although charities may present reasoned argument and information to Government.' This section examines the legal roots of the concept of 'Superstitious Uses' in the field of theological heresy, and the relatively recent application of it to political action. It will examine the applications of the current doctrine as a manifestation of the paternalist trend in British society.

141

The wide range of judges' rulings have left a surprising variety of charities open to political ambush. At various times, Action on Smoking and Health (ASH), the British Pregnancy Advisory Service, and the Family Planning Association, as well as more recently, War on Want, Christian Aid and Oxfam, have been the subject of complaints about 'political activities' (see Charity Commissioners' Reports). In addition, bodies like SHELTER and the Citizen's Advice Bureaux have been the subject of politically motivated smears about their political motivation. It is very rare for such complaints to originate as an abstract concern from the public, although the 1989 White Paper claimed 'some signs that the public is anxious that the behaviour of a few charities may stray beyond the bounds of what is permissible or desirable'. Such complaints as are made seem to be by political opponents. In the case of ASH, the complaints came from the tobacco industry; against BPAS, they came from anti-abortionists; and against the overseas aid agencies, they came from right-wing political groups.

It is strange that a democratic country should be so scared of political activity that this should be forbidden to voluntary organisations which need the protection of charitable status. It is even stranger that such a solid-looking doctrine, with an appearance of great antiquity, should have been erected on such flimsy and recent foundations.

From Superstition to Subversion

The evidence indicates that the doctrine against political activity by charities is a modern one, albeit reflecting ancient prejudices. In earlier times, politics were expressed in theological terms, and heresy and subversion walked together. In addition, before the Reform Acts, any political activity by the disenfranchised could be seen as suspect and subversive. When the majority of the population gained the right to participate in the political process, the prejudice against 'superstitious uses' and heresy seems to have transferred, with all its subversive connotations, to political activity.

The first case to touch upon what we would accept as political activities was in 1852 (*Russell v. Jackson*). It concerned a bequest to set up a school to educate children in socialist principles. Vice-Chancellor Turner ordered an examination of socialism to determine whether it was against public policy or subversive. He made it clear that if it were not, then the trust was indeed charitable. The issue was not resolved, allowing Tudor (1984, p. 43) to say that 'it is thought... it would not be followed today'.

Three decades later, in 1888, the doctrine against political activity appeared, unparented, in a legal textbook, Tyssen on *Charitable Bequests*. By a process of legal osmosis, 'political purposes' were vaguely recognised as a hoop to be jumped through by Stirling in the *Scowcroft* case in 1889. This is an amusing case, not least because it has been held to be wrong by most subsequent authorities. Stirling held that a gift of 'the building known as the Conservative Club and Village Reading-room... to be maintained for the furtherance of Conservative principles and religious and mental improvement and to be kept free from intoxicants and dancing' was charitable.

Stirling reasoned, or rather rationalised:

> Whether or not a gift for the furtherance of Conservative principles is a good charitable gift is a question upon which I do not think it necessary to express any opinion in this case, because it seems to me that the reading which is suggested is not the true one, but that this is a gift for the furtherance of Conservative principles and religious and mental improvement in combination. It is either a gift for the furtherance of Conservative principles in such a way as to advance religious and mental improvement at the same time, or a gift for the furtherance of religious and mental improvement in accordance with Conservative principles; and in either case the furtherance of religious and mental improvement is, in my judgment, an essential portion of the gift.

The modern doctrine against political purposes and activities can be traced back to 1917, when the Secular Society was refused charitable status, allowing Lord Parker to claim an ancient pedigree for the newly invented doctrine (see Chapter 9).

In effect he ruled that anti-religious activity was 'purely political', and that

> Equity has always refused to recognise such objects as charitable... A trust for the attainment of political objects has always been held invalid, not because it is illegal, for everyone is at liberty to advocate or promote by any lawful means a change in the law, but because the court has no means of judging whether a proposed change in the law will or will not be for the public benefit and therefore cannot say that a gift to secure the change is a charitable gift. (*Bowman v. Secular Society*)

The shaky foundation on which this monumental decision rested was the case of *De Themmines v. De Bonneval* which ruled in 1828 that a trust to distribute literature asserting papal supremacy was void because it was against public policy – in short, that the views were subversive to the existing order. In addition to claiming an ancient pedigree for his judgment, Parker disingenuously disclaimed the ability of the courts to judge whether a proposed change in the law would or would not be for the public benefit. Yet he and his colleagues had been, were, and are still, pronouncing on public benefits, and public policy. In the very case with which Parker was dealing, he was making an assessment of what was public policy – and that any disagreement with that would be bad. Indeed, the 1989 White Paper proposed that the Charity Commissioners and the courts should exercise their powers to examine religious charities to ascertain their public benefit.

Following Parker, in the twenties and thirties, the Bonar Law Memorial Trust and the Primrose League were deemed uncharitable because of their close ties to the Conservative Party. The doctrine became even more comprehensive after Lord Simonds vented his establishment feelings against the National Anti-Vivisection Society in 1947: 'Is it for a moment to be supposed that it is the function of the Attorney-General on behalf of the Crown to intervene and demand that a trust shall be established and administered by the court, the object of which is to alter the law in manner highly prejudicial, as he and His Majesty's Government may think, to the welfare of the state?'

In 1949, Judge Vaisey, doubtless totally uninfluenced by a Labour government being in power, made the decision which the Charity Commissioners were to cite in their guidelines on political activity in 1981. He ruled that to defend *existing* law was a political and therefore uncharitable purpose (*Re Hopkinson*).

In most democracies, constitutional political activity would be seen as of public benefit – particularly in a country where general political involvement is so low that frequently less than half the voters turn out in local elections, and where even general elections leave a quarter unmoved to exercise their franchise. But in Britain, active involvement is to be suspected rather than encouraged. The overall political ethos is in fact encapsulated in the traditional charitable nexus of bounty, as opposed to bargain.

The disapproval of political activity by charities reflects a deeper suspicion of any grassroots involvement in political life, as if the bulk of the population, subjects not citizens, should be grateful at being ruled by their bountiful betters.

The Growth of the Grassroots

The growth of voluntary, charitable activity in the post-war world reflected changing social conditions. The Welfare State accepted national responsibility for many areas previously left to charitable endeavour. For many charities, the means of relieving distress shifted from direct provision of aid to persuading national or local government to do so. The Nathan Commission of 1952 which paved the way for the 1960 Charities Act and the establishment of the Charity Commissioners, did not give any consideration to 'political activity' as such.

Indeed, Nathan seemed to approve of activities which were later to be stigmatised as political:

(55) Some of the most valuable activities of voluntary societies consist, however, in the fact that they are able to stand aside from and criticise state action, or inaction, in the interests of the inarticulate man-in-the-street. This may take the form of helping individuals to know and obtain their rights. It also consists in a more· general activity of collecting data about some point where the shoe seems to pinch or a need remains unmet. The general · machinery of democratic agitation, deputations, letters to the Press, questions in the House, conferences and the rest of it, may then be put into operation in order to convince a wider public that action is necessary.

(56) This is one of the fundamental arguments for interposing this wealth of voluntary associations between the citizen and public authority, however enlightened and benevolent this latter may be.

In 1966, C. P. Hill, who had prepared the 1960 Charities Act and was the first Chief Commissioner under its dispensation, wrote a comprehensive book, *A Guide for Charity Trustees*, in which political activities did not merit a heading of their own. But by 1969 the Charity Commissioners' Report included guidelines on political activity. What had happened to provoke it?

The 1969 report does not identify the specific activities which gave rise to concern, yet it was certainly the case that Harold Wilson's Cabinets had displayed signs of hypersensitivity to criticism and that organisations like SHELTER and the Child Poverty Action Group had been giving the Labour government a political mauling over its record. They had somewhat self-consciously set themselves up as radical reformers in the charity world as well, doubtless alienating more traditionalist organisations.

SHELTER's practice was 'a rejection of so much that had become out-dated in the thinking and working of institutionalised charity', said Des Wilson, even though many of its founders were 'representative of the middle class paternalism that had character-ised charity since Victorian Days' (Wilson, 1970, p. 113).

SHELTER reflected as much as it initiated the mood of the time. In 1968, 'The Haslemere Declaration' trumpeted, 'We cannot continue to merely be polite, respectable, and ineffective lobbyists for "more and better aid" when we have lost all faith in the ability of our governments to respond realistically to the desperate human need of the poor world... we therefore intend to become involved in a political campaign.'

Des Wilson himself wrote, reflecting upon SHELTER's approach, 'One had to question the nature of charity itself. In some instances, it could be a form of oppression. In others it tackled a symptom of the problem instead of the cause – economic or social powerless-ness. In most it only helped individuals, but only touched the fringes of mass need' (ibid., p. 114).

The campaigners were consciously at odds with traditional charity practice. They expressed a feeling that the voluntary sector could do things that the State could not, while using political leverage to force the State into new activities. In addition they showed a concern with enfranchising the poor which contrasted sharply with the ethos of 'bounty' permeating the welfare thinking of both State and older charitable sector alike.

'Charities used to be anxious to keep out of politics for fear that their fundraising may slacken or dry up. Many are still very careful. One of the four voluntary agencies in famine relief, Save the Children Fund, under world patronage and rather establishment minded, still tries to keep its nose clean,' wrote Ivan Yates at the time (*The Observer*, 11 January 1970). He did not mention any worries about the legal consequences of political involvement, possibly because the commissioners' report for 1969 was not then published. Instead of giving out alms, they were taking to arms, but still on behalf of, as a substitute for, their clients. 'It is when the homeless can identify with SHELTER as a campaign *for and of them*, that SHELTER will have finally changed the face of British Charity completely,' Wilson (1970, p. 125) said bravely.

He was remarkably blasé about the role of the Charity Commissioners: 'SHELTER may not like the word "charity" as it is commonly understood . . . In fact charity status is not the straitjacket that many people seem to assume, for the Charity Commissioners . . . appear to be more enlightened about the need for change in the concept of organised charity than many charities themselves' (ibid., p. 129).

While SHELTER combined direct relief work with political pressure, the Child Poverty Action Group had neither the intention nor the ability to undertake 'rescue work'. Its method of work was overtly political. Its first major campaign was based on a knowledge of how to pull strings in the Labour Party which was then in power. Frank Field, now a Labour MP, quoted Richard Crossman as the unwitting architect of the campaign strategy, when he 'had gone on to say that one way of applying maximum pressure to a party was to question its central myth in the crucial period prior to a General Election' (Field, 1982, p. 30). One of the Labour Party's central myths was the war against poverty, and by a fitting turn of fate, the Minister of Social Security was Crossman himself – who did not like having his own dicta used against him. Field admits that the title of the campaign, 'The Poor Get Poorer Under Labour' was designed to do just as Crossman said, rather than reflect the intellectual content of the CPAG campaign.

It was a piece of calculated political leverage based on the fact that industrial earnings had risen by 51 per cent during Labour's rule, while National Insurance benefits had only risen 48 per cent (ibid., p. 34). It was a campaign which could only work against a government with a soft spot – a replay based on that size of difference would have been unlikely to make an impression on more recent Cabinets.

Field rationalised afterwards

How well the charge 'the poor get poorer' stands up in examination is still an issue which surfaces sometimes in debate. More important now is what effect the campaign had on the Government's policy to the poor, and the development of the Group's standing and influence, which were to be important in a number of political battles throughout the seventies. (ibid., p. 37)

The organisation of a public campaign has been held usually as 'a sign that the group has failed to secure acceptance by the appropriate government department as an effective interest' (Birch, 1967). The role of campaigning charities like SHELTER and CPAG was not to be 'effective interests', power blocs like existing organisations, but as blocs of the powerless, using leverage on their behalf. The homeless, the jobless and the poor on supplementary benefit, even the old, were not powerful sections whose views could directly sway ministries. Their only negotiating power was in the political sphere, in embarrassment, since then, as now, 'active citizenship' and voluntary donations could not cope with the wholesale demands on finance made by such overwhelming social problems.

The approach required was completely different from the 'voluntary service' of the past when the NCSS could see the major role for the volunteer as sitting on adminstrative committees of the NHS (see Chapter 7).

Activity Unbecoming a Charity: The 1969 Guidelines

The Charity Commissioners' 1969 guidelines read like a gently indulgent admonition of the firebrands, perhaps inspired by a word over lunch with some peeved Cabinet minister who wanted 'something done' for dessert. The guidelines illustrate the tenacity of the concept of disinterested 'bounty' as a prerequisite for charity.

One contemporary development which has given us some concern has been the increasing desire of voluntary organisations for 'involvement' in the causes with which their work is connected. Many organisations now feel that it is not sufficient simply to alleviate distress arising from particular social conditions or even to go further and collect and disseminate information about the problems they encounter. They feel compelled also to draw attention as forcibly as possible to the needs which they think are not being met, to rouse the conscience of the public to demand action and to press for effective official provision to be made to meet those ends. As a result 'pressure groups', 'action groups', or 'lobbies' come into being. But when a voluntary organisation which is a charity seeks to develop such activities, it nearly always runs into difficulties through going beyond its declared purposes and powers. No charity should of course undertake any activity unless it is reasonably directed to achieving its purposes and is within the powers conferred by the charity's governing instrument.

It was a fair and temperate statement of the position as the law stood at the time. As one observer remarked: 'They place less emphasis than one would expect on the requirement that promoting a change in the law should be an ancillary purpose. What seems to matter more is whether the efforts of an organisation in this direction are sober and restrained ("watching and advising") or strident and outspoken. It is virtually a question of style' (Chesterman, 1979, p. 187).

The belligerent and outspoken style of people like Field and Wilson would very likely have provoked objections. But it was at least as likely that those who objected did so, not because of abstract qualms about political activities by charities, but because they disliked the particular political stance or consequences of the charities' activities. It was a continuation into the modern age of earlier prohibitions against superstitious uses; subversive causes decided by the bench to be against 'public policy'.

The 'style counsel' guidelines of 1969 were not to last long. In 1977, Amnesty International tested the legal doctrine by setting up a trust and applying for registration as a charity. The commissioners refused to register the trust in 1978, and the organisation had the resources and pugnacity to appeal. The purpose of Amnesty International was to secure implementation of the United Nations' Universal Declaration of Human Rights for prisoners of conscience, which includes people imprisoned for their sex, colour, language, ethnic origin, or their political, religious and conscientious belief.

This was, presumably, public policy since the government endorsed these aims on behalf of the nation. But Mr Justice Slade, in refusing Amnesty, accepted, in Eldon's words, 'monstrous propositions' in favour of the status quo. 'The elimination of injustice has not, as such, ever been held to be a trust purpose which qualifies for the privileges afforded to charities by English Law. I cannot hold it to be a charitable purpose now.'

He showed the modesty with which the bench occasionally cloaks its omniscience: 'The court will not have sufficient means of satisfactorily judging, as a matter of evidence, whether the proposed reversal [of policy] would be beneficial to the community, in its relevant sense, after all its consequences, local and international, had been taken into account.' One wishes that one could feel sure that the same decision would have been taken if Amnesty had restricted its attentions to Eastern bloc countries instead of exposing allies and opponents of the Western Powers with equal condemnatory zeal. Slade expanded the definition of political activity by concluding that it was now not a charitable purpose to secure legislation nor even a change in 'administrative policies' of *foreign* countries.

The monstrous blandness of a statement like 'administrative policies of foreign countries' has to be rolled around the palette to be appreciated. In the case of Amnesty, this euphemism may refer to arbitrary imprisonments, tortures and executions – often flouting the laws of the country involved. Slade's reasoning struck an especially ominous note:

> before subscribing charitable status to an English Trust of which a main object was to secure the alteration of a foreign law, the court would also, I conceive, be bound to consider the consequences for this country as a matter of public policy. In a number of such cases there would arise a substantial prima facie risk that such a trust, if enforced, could prejudice the relations of this country with the foreign country concerned.

As a US President is alleged to have said about a Central American colleague, 'He may be a bastard, but he's *our* bastard.'

Slade considered a point which seemed to have particular relevance in 1989, when author Salman Rushdie had been sentenced to death by the Ayatollah Khomeini:

> It appears from the Amnesty International Report 1978, p. 270, that Islamic law sanctions the death penalty for certain well defined offences, namely, murder, adultery, and brigandage. Let it be supposed that a trust were created of which the object was to secure the abolition of the death penalty for adultery in those countries where Islamic law applies, and to secure a reprieve for those persons who have been sentenced to death for this offence. The court when invited to enforce or reform such a trust, would either have to apply English standards as to public benefit, which would not necessarily be at all appropriate in the local conditions, or would have to apply local standards, of which it knew little or nothing.

So if we hypothesise that apostasy and blasphemy also carry the death penalty under Islamic law and further that the UK government would have liked for commercial and political reasons to maintain good relations with Ayatollah Khomeini's Iran, then clearly a trust to secure the reprieve of Salman Rushdie would not have been a good legal charity.

The work of the Anti-Slavery Society was and is not charitable by that definition, since it is a matter of the politics and administrative policies of the countries involved. Perhaps – by analogy – both Amnesty and the society could claim that their work was listed in the 1601 preamble as the 'redemption of captives'. However, the society has been continuing in its good work since 1839. It describes itself as 'the oldest human rights organisation in the world' and has among its aims, 'the elimination of slavery and the slave trade, the abolition of all forms of forced labour and the protection of Human Rights in accordance with the Universal Declaration of Human Rights, 1948'.

There are several 'administrative policies' and laws which seem to echo the Amnesty case – but the Anti-Slavery Society had the good fortune to be thriving, active and charitable before 1917, when the ancient tradition of non-political charities sprang like Athena fully formed from Lord Parker's brow. (And how like a goddess, since the new-born principle was to smite down the National Secular Society for advocating disestablishment of religion.)

The anomalous position of religion is brought into relief by the entirely charitable work of the Eastern European Bible Mission: 'We take quantities of Bibles behind the Iron Curtain to churches which otherwise would be without, translate and print requested Christian literature where allowed legally and support "underground" Bible printing projects in more difficult countries' (CAF, 1988–9). They do the latter, presumably, because the states involved as a matter of law or administrative policy do not want Christian missionary work. If there are enough converts they presumably would like to press upon the authorities the need to reconsider their position. But so long as it is old tribal customs, incorporated in Leviticus, rather than modern declarations on human rights which inspire the bench, the mission will get the support of the judiciary, even if it has repercussions on relations with Britain.

Similarly, the Greek Animal Welfare Fund, and the International Donkey Protection Trust, and SPANA, the Society for the Protection of Animals in North Africa, can devote their attentions to protection

of the brute creation, usually without fear of diplomatic repercussions. The Greek Animal Welfare Society was founded in 1959
and presumably carried on its good work through the years when
the Junta of Colonels governing the country was imprisoning and
torturing its opponents. Amnesty could not charitably look after
them, but 'The GAWF should be proud of the change it has brought
in Greece in the care of animals' (CAF, 1988–9).

Political Paranoia – The 1981 Guidelines

The Amnesty case gave the Charity Commissioners the opportunity,
in 1981, to summarise the 'basic principles' which they had found
possible to deduce. Their severity may be seen as the swan song of
the then Chief Commissioner, Terence FitzGerald, who encapsulated the bounty principle when he told the *Sunday Telegraph* (24
June 1979): 'The role of the charity is to bind up the wounds of
society. This is what they get their fiscal privileges for. To build a
new society is for someone else.'

In case of foreign operations, the commissioners summarised their
guidelines:

(54, vii) Charities, whether they operate in this country or
overseas, must avoid:
   (a) Seeking to influence or remedy those causes of poverty
       which lie in the social, economic and political structures of
       countries and communities.
   (b) Bringing pressure to bear on a government to procure a
       change in policies or administrative practices (for example,
       on land reform, the recognition of local trade unions,
       human rights, etc.).
   (c) Seeking to eliminate social economic political or other
       injustice. (1981)

It will be observed, that animal welfare is not on the list of bans
and prescriptions. Religion and animals seem to have run together
as a sort of golden calf – to be honoured above men and prophets.
However, the guidelines did not restrict themselves to absurdity
abroad. They were quite comprehensive in their domestic effects.

   (i) A trust for the attainment of a political object is not

charitable since the court has no way of judging whether a proposed change in the law will or will not be for the public benefit – *Bowman v. Secular Society Ltd* (1917).

(ii) To promote changes in the law, or maintenance of the existing law is a political purpose and not charitable – *Re Hopkinson* (1949).

(iii) To seek, not necessarily particular legislation, but a particular line of political administration or policy, is a political purpose and is not charitable – *Re Hopkinson*.

(iv) Political propaganda in the guise of education is not charitable – *Re Hopkinson*.

(v) The word 'political' is not necessarily confined to party politics. Any purpose of influencing legislation is a political purpose and is not charitable. – *IRC v. Temperance Council of Christian Churches of England and Wales*.

(vi) A trust for the education of the public in one particular set of political principles is not charitable (although education in political matters generally could be) – *Bonar Law Memorial Trust v. IRC* 1933.

(vii) Although an association for promoting some change in the law cannot itself be a charity (see (i) and (ii) above), an association would not necessarily lose its right to be considered a charity if, as a matter of construction the promotion of legislation were one among other lawful purposes ancillary to good charitable purposes: it is a question of degree – *National Anti-vivisection Society v. IRC*.

(viii) Research to be charitable must be directed to increasing the store of communicable knowledge in a public, as opposed to a private way. – *Re Hopkins' Will Trusts 1965*.

(52) In addition to removing doubts on the question of whether the constraints on domestic political activities extend to attempts to influence the politics and administrative policies of foreign countries, the Amnesty case has served to re-assert the validity of the principles set out above (CC. Report, 1981).

On the face of it, the clarification so helpfully set out by the commissioners is a complete prohibition of any form of active social and political involvement. The good news is that many of the major charities have ignored it. A retired official of one major overseas aid agency says that they considered splitting into a political and a charitable trust, but decided that it would be cowardly and inefficient and so decided to carry on as before.

Domestically, under those rules, one presumes that the great
Victorian campaigns, including the abolition of child labour, of
sending children up chimneys, would all have been deemed
uncharitable, while existing charities like the Howard League for
Penal Reform and the Anti-Slavery Society would not be successful
if they were to try to register now.

In section (vii) appears what looks like a saving grace, 'it is a
question of degree'. It is, of course, the opposite. Trustees would
not know until it was too late whether they had overstepped the
'degree'. This could be a very effective threat since the Report went
on to explain that trustees risked being 'In breach of trust . . .
personally liable to repay to the charity the funds spent on such
activity' and risked 'losing some tax relief'.

Hair Splitting in Action

As a result of the developing doctrine, absurdities grew along with
voluntary activism. Francis Gladstone records the case of the
Community Association which according to the commissioners had
'been concerned to act as a pressure group to secure, inter alia, a
crossing on —— Road . . . Seeking to bring pressure to bear to achieve
an objective is not a charitable purpose' (Gladstone, 1982, p. 101).

As was shown in cases like the Anti-Slavery Society, guidelines
are often not applied strictly to already established charities, and
not at all to the religions. They are at their strictest at the only point
at which the commissioners have had the resources and power to
regulate, at the time of registration, when applicants can be
squeezed through the eye of the judicial needle.

For example, in Liverpool, the Parent's Association of a Primary
School on the fringes of Toxteth applied for registration for the
group, which had as its object the promotion of the education of
the children attending the school. However, in the course of
expanding on ways to promote the partnership between parents
and teachers to support this end, the association pledged itself to
promote and support 'positive anti-racist and anti-sexist practices in
our children's education'. Although this was clearly in line with
existing legislation, it was too strident for the commissioners'
delicate sensibilities, who suggested its deletion.

Also on Merseyside, Open Eye was a group established to
educate and train people and community groups in the use of
visual techniques. Their registration was refused because their

political activities could not be proved to be for the public benefit. One of them was the making of a video for the Runcorn Playgroups Association which sought to persuade the local council of the need for more funding. The other was a video made for the Vauxhall Neighbourhood Council which sought to make the community's case against the planned Liverpool Inner Ring Road which would have demolished their community. Both deeply concerned the commissioners' staff who felt unable to weigh the public benefit of the retention of inner city homes against the benefits to passing commuters of speedier journeys to the suburbs. That application was abandoned.

Underneath the concern over political activities lurks a subtext of mistrust for ordinary people doing things for themselves, and refusing to rely upon their betters. In Tudor times, they would have been whipped for impertinence, more recently they were refused registration – and thereby access to financial support from many grant-making sources which insist on registration.

The suspicion that that is so is reinforced by the examination of the organisations which do not have trouble registering, and which do not excite Conservative backbench anger. The prohibitions do not seem to apply to the right-wing think tanks we examine later. Similarly, animal welfare charities conduct campaigns which, if fought on behalf of humans, would be regarded as clearly political, and would in another more subversive context have MPs baying after their blood. Indeed, the internal squabbles within the RSPCA breed constant correspondence with the Charity Commissioners from those pursuing their faction fights through what they consider to be the referee for charities. (There is even a body for members seeking 'justice' in the RSPCA, called – Watchdog.)

Happily, the commissioners, under a more enlightened regime, clarified the 1981 guidelines, tacitly extending them in a common-sense way. In September 1986, they re-issued the 1981 guidelines, translating legal wording and detachment into a more vernacular and permissive view.

It is right and natural that a charity concerned with a particular group such as the elderly, for example, should present the Government and others with reasoned arguments about the defects or virtues of the social security system in the sense that it affects the well-being of the elderly whose condition and problems the charity exists to improve or alleviate. Equally it is open to such a charity to inform public thinking and political debate by publishing material based on reasoned research and direct experience. But it would not be proper for such a charity to advocate a particular line of policy or legislative change unless this is justifiable as entirely subsidiary to the achievement of its charitable purpose, and the manner and content of that advocacy is appropriate to that end. And it would not be open to a charity for the relief of the elderly to campaign on some completely different cause like apartheid or defence policy.

They go on to say, 'Where there is clear public debate on an issue such as famine relief (even though there may not have been a White paper or Green paper from the Government of the day, or a manifesto from an opposition party which is a would-be Government) then the spirit of the annexed guidelines . . . justifies charities contributing to that debate by putting forward reasoned argument based on relevant experience.'

This liberal rewriting indicated to charities how they could continue political activity, while covering themselves legally. It diplomatically added, 'political activity – like the elephant – is difficult to describe but easy to recognise'. However, it is worth bearing in mind the poem about the

> Seven wise men of Hindustan,
> To learning much inclined,
> Who came to see the elephant,
> Though each of them were blind.

Perhaps the changing temper of the Charity Commission in the eighties was best demonstrated by its rectification of the long-standing absurdity over race relations (see Chapter 3).

Robin Guthrie, the new Charity Commissioner, epitomises the enlightened attitude which sees the present case law as flexible enough to include what most charities want to do. But at the same time he does not believe that outright political bodies should have charity's privileges. As he put it, 'But what about bodies like the National Front?'

His speech to the Charities Aid Foundation sums up his attitude, and therefore, one must presume, the current application of the law by the commission.

Political activity by charities is a matter of considerable public significance, but fortunately not one which makes inordinate claims on our resources. I take a robust view of this matter. Charity is part of the life of the nation. It cannot avoid influencing or being influenced by the politics of the day, whether it be 1601 or 1991... It is not intrinsically wrong for charities to engage in what others – particularly those who disagree with their objects or their interpretation – might feel to be political pressure. The extent of such activity must be judged by two factors; its relation to the objects of the charity; and the proportion of the charity's efforts and resources that are put to the task of persuasion, as against activity in direct pursuit of those objects. Charities have a responsibility to draw public attention either to factors which impede the fulfilment of their charitable objects or to knowledge, whether derived from research or from experience, that affects their objects and their beneficiaries. If they are working in circumstances adverse to their objects, they should seek to influence and encourage change in those circumstances if they can. But how far should they persist if the powers that be take no notice, and the circumstances remain the same? Not very far in my view. They must get on with the job, so far as they can; and while they may deliver a forceful message they should not assume the role of politician by committing major resources to political ends, let alone by engaging in a major campaign or public agitation. Although motive is an elusive criterion, I shall always be interested in the extent to which the charitable activities in question are driven by needs of the beneficiaries, or by commitment to some prior view or ideology about how the world should be ordered. (Guthrie, 1988)

Despite recent Charity Commissioners, the situation has an inherent instability. A change of commissioners, a definitive law suit, a paragraph in the next Charities Act, could upset the present smooth progress of the apple cart. Cliff edges may make wonderful views and picnic spots, but the sensible do not praise their suitability as house sites. Charities which camp close to the edge realise the vulnerability of their position.

Advice to Active Citizens – Toe the Line

The sensitivity of Wilson's government to criticism was more than matched by Thatcher's from 1979 onwards. Shooting the messenger with bad tidings seemed to become a political reflex. This is perhaps exemplified by the curious position of the Citizen's Advice Bureaux. On the face of it, it is the finest example of the voluntary principle, exemplifying 'Active Citizenship' as advertised by Cabinet ministers. Autonomous CABs across the country are staffed by thousands of volunteers who inform any enquirer about their rights and entitlements under law. NACAB, the National Association of Citizens' Advice Bureaux, is a support organisation funded by the Department of Trade and Industry, while the local offices are funded by donations and council grants.

It had never occurred to any Labour member to question the CABs just because, as the *Sunday Times* quoted a Tory backbencher (18 April 1983), 'Most of us know that the average citizen's advice bureau is dominated by good Tory ladies.' However, Gerard Vaughan, the Minister for Consumer Affairs, announced that he would withhold half of NACAB's grant until it had 'put its house in order'. Vaughan was MP for the Reading South Constituency in which Joan Ruddock worked part-time for the Citizen's Advice Bureau. She was also the Chairman of CND at a time when issues like Cruise bases were hot political issues. Part of ordering a good household at NACAB, it was implied, was removing Joan Ruddock. Vaughan had already complained to NACAB about her position, and was clearly not satisfied when the association's enquiries found no evidence to suggest that she carried out CND work while being paid by NACAB – indeed she had gone part-time precisely to avoid such a possibility.

While denying that his action was directly motivated by pique over Ruddock, Vaughan did little to allay the fears of opponents when he told *The Times* (11 April 1983): 'The job of the CAB is to provide information and advice, and I think the advice they give should be impartial and objective. I have been getting complaints from people who have said that the thing has become very left-wing and that they are constantly indulging in local pressure groups.'

He later raised another ghost, the spectre of financial mismanagement, which was soon exorcised when it was revealed that not only had he *not* raised this aspect previously with NACAB's officers, but the Department of Trade had observers on its governing bodies.

The seeming ineptitude of the minister's approach cost him his portfolio, but it may not have been his fault. A *Guardian* leader at the time (12 April 1983) suggested, 'Maybe the Prime Minister, upon learning that Mrs Ruddock was responsible for administering public funds, instructed her Minister to do something about it.' He would not be the only minister to pay a political price for loyalty to the Premier's whims, and he was knighted the following year.

This case illustrated the difficulties which voluntary organisations have in maintaining independence when they depend for cash on a government which rewrites political conventions as it goes along. It also illustrated, in a very crude way, the basis for the developing convention of political involvement. The government did not like the information and advice coming from the CABs – so this was labelled 'political'. It did not like some of the staff, and it particularly did not like the idea of those staff benefiting from funds in the government's bounty, therefore NACAB was political. Ian Waller in the *The Sunday Telegraph* (18 April 1983) summed up;

> I am inclined to acquit Dr Vaughan of personal bigotry but his attitude seems to me to reflect a streak of it apparent in some circles in the government and the Conservative Party today – that anyone not dedicated to it (and even to the true faith of Thatcherism within it) is suspect. It is a disturbing trend, alien to the traditions of British politics and Tuesday's reaction showed the Commons' distaste for it.

That episode ended with a review which was seen at the time as a victory, if anything, for the CABs. More recent events at the beginning of 1989 indicated that ministers have long memories. As a condition of their grant (£8.38 million in 1988/9) the DTI carried out a staff inspection of NACAB. As *Legal Action* (January 1989) pointed out, 'It has been carried out under Treasury Guidance and on Civil Service principles, which will undoubtedly lead to questions as to the suitability of this approach for a voluntary organisation.'

One late draft of the report had the DTI's inspectors making it clear that NACAB's democratic structure was 'hampering' the association's 'efficient and effective organisation'. They wanted the governing council to be restricted to consideration of advice on policy and membership issues while the Chief Executive would have power over 'physical and human resources'. The DTI would, of course, be not unimportant in the selection of the Chief Executive, whom they would expect to be more in tune with their thinking on the need for a 'more dispassionate judgement' of 'when and how to pursue sensitive policy issues'. These are the penalties attached to government money.

NACAB could easily fall into the group of whingeing charities, always complaining instead of doing – since its *raison d'être* was to advise citizens on their rights and entitlements, it is difficult for it to avoid being otherwise. Nigel Lawson had complained (Goodman Lecture, 2 June 1987), 'Too often, people who spot a problem in our society simply complain about it to the Government, or to their local authority, and then wait for something to happen.' John Moore picked up the theme (Speech to Conservative Political Centre, 26 September 1987); 'Even many voluntary organisations shifted their emphasis from small groups who actually gave help to pressure groups who simply pushed the government to give help.'

As *Legal Action* commented on the CAB affair, 'Do the larger voluntary organisations really need now to model themselves on quangos or local authorities, or will that stifle the very flexibility, responsiveness and commitment to service delivery which in the past has distinguished from such bodies?'

For the editors of *Legal Action* it was a rhetorical question, but to the mind which saw a volunteer as a premature conscript it was a real point, to be answered positively. The final report on NACAB omitted the references to the failings of democracy, but the managerial proposals were widely seen within the organisation as pursuing the same ends through managerial means. 'Implementation of the report would give NACAB the classic local authority management structure,' said *Legal Action* (March 1989) which quoted Glenn Sutherland, a NACAB staff union representative. 'The report represents an attack on NACAB and on its ability to provide a proper service for the bureaux. We are expected to become civil servants and not advice workers.'

The destabilising effect can be seen in the political campaign run by the Tories against SHELTER. Prepared by lobby leaks that it was in the PM's sights, it ran into flak in March 1989. The original cause of the row was simply that the charity had given an exclusive to *The Observer* rather than the *Sunday Times*.

SHELTER had asked young homeless people to keep a diary, and the results were harrowing tales of prostitution and life on the fringes (*The Observer*, 26 March 1989). The *Sunday Times* attacked the diaries as concocted for political reasons. While SHELTER put it down to pique at the *The Observer* getting the story, the *Sunday Times'* attack was along the well-worn path of political bias by charities. In a year when the government announced a White Paper on charities, and a scrutiny of the efficiency of government funding of them, it was a chilling weapon.

12

From Superstitious Uses to Subversive Activities: Part II

Going Overboard on Overseas Aid

Although the Charity Commissioners seem to have adopted a relaxedly civilised attitude to 'political activities', the government, as we saw, has not. The rigorous case law and the 1981 guidelines can be used to 'ambush' charities engaged in work opposed by political factions, and while the domestic charities upset the government, the overseas aid agencies upset many governments.

Oxfam, Christian Aid, and War on Want often work in areas of political controversy, particularly as the military expression of political disagreements frequently causes the famine and disease they seek to alleviate. In the Horn of Africa, in the frontline states of southern Africa and in Central America, military and political conflict accompany desperate need.

Even if an aid agency were to restrict itself to food aid rather than more long-term development, the problems of operating in such areas make it practically impossible to observe the Charity Commissioners' 1981 guidance. The government troops or the rebels confiscate the food, or requisition the transport of the agency. They retaliate because the agency is operating on the wrong side of the lines – how does one avoid political involvement in such cases? If the agency is shipping in food supplies paid for by charitably minded people, and the regime prefers to ship in whisky and weapons, then doesn't the charity owe it to its donors to point this out? If the hungry are so because they have been driven off their land by diktat, then is this 'an administrative policy' against which the charity must keep silent, or is it not a circumstance directly related to the work of the charity? Taking it further, if the hunger is a direct consequence of land ownership systems which dispossess peasants to make way for cash crops, then is that not a cause of legitimate concern for, and activity by, a charity?

The line between legitimate and illegitimate political activity is not so much a clear boundary as a wide freefire zone with mines and booby traps spreading between a few fixed points of judicial dicta. For those trustees bold enough to risk their personal wealth on venturing into the area, there are guerrilla bands marauding in the form of groups trying to score political points.

Even though the major agencies meet regularly to coordinate responses to such difficulties, no charity is going to be foolish enough to attack the 'political activity' doctrine in public. Many admit privately, '*Of course* we're political', but to do so publicly would have disastrous repercussions for their work, which is often assisted by government funding from the Overseas Development Administration. A public admission would force the Charity Commissioners to administer the full rigour of the law, because whatever their own inclinations, government pressure through the Attorney-General would force them to act. Indeed, one of the aspects of the pragmatism of the Charity Commissioners is that they are very reactive in their method of work. They rarely initiate action themselves but they do respond to public complaints. The major charities have in practice ignored the guidelines, and so have the commissioners, who have taken a much more liberal view in practice than appears in their theory. However, the problem of having silly law implemented by sensible people is that it leaves the latter open to pressure to implement it. In the case of the aid agencies, their particular bane is Western Goals.

Sources inside the Home Office have remarked upon the influence which right-wing organisations like Western Goals have with Number 10. Andrew Smith, one of the founders, was happy to confirm that they had indeed targeted agencies which they felt were operating against what they saw as Western interests in areas like southern Africa. 'We started by complaining to the charities themselves, then we complained to the Charity Commissioners, and now we complain to Government ministers,' he explained (interview with author). Western Goals was not a charity itself (although they had considered applying). As will be shown, many similar groups have been registered.

It was evident that Western Goals' objection was not to political activity *per se*, but to forms of it with which they disagreed. Their report of Summer 1985 said, 'Western Goals – UK is charged with the specific task of disarming the radical left in Britain with educational material designed specifically for consumption by the

British Public.' Among such material was a telegram of support from Lieutenant-Colonel Oliver North, then facing charges over his alleged diversion of the proceeds of arms sales to Iran to his Contra friends.

Western Goals' American parent was the eccentrically right-wing Heritage Foundation, established by Congressman Larry McDonald, whose claims to fame ranged from being a member of the John Birch society to being shot down in the Korean Airliner KAL 007 in 1983. He once nominated Rudolf Hess for the Nobel Peace Prize, which indicates partiality to Western values of a special kind. The UK branch has a parliamentary advisory board which has Neil Hamilton, Bill Walker, Martin Smyth, and as patron former MP Patrick Wall (a political line-up as wet as the Sahara in midsummer). Its Domestic Affairs Unit (Charities) claims to be carrying out 'A highly successful series of research and media operations against a number of Third World Relief Operations – most notably War on Want, Christian Aid, and Oxfam which have been subverted to leftist objectives and which have become increasingly noted for their anti-Western anti-Capitalist stance.'

Western Goals complained to the Charity Commission that the charities involved were guilty of political activities or of producing politically contentious materials. However, the commissioners replied:

> Charities by the very nature of their altruism and passion will be bound to be drawn into public debate on important issues of the day in which relevant charities have direct experi-ence ... It seems to us reasonable that a group of charities concerned with relieving distress throughout the world should wish to draw attention to the need for further effort in this direction on the part not only of voluntary agencies, but also of government (Letter from Charity Commission)

In fact the biggest success Western Goals claimed – against War on Want – was, according to the Charity Commissioners, nothing to do with them at all. 'They just jumped on the band wagon after we had already intervened,' said the Charity Commission. War on Want, the most overtly political of the aid agencies, was indeed having financial problems in early 1989 – but it is likely that this was less to do with donor disapproval of its ideological stance, and more with the continuing controversy over its previous General Secretary, George Galloway, and his way of life while in office. (At a press conference in 1987, he had admitted to adultery while officially on WOW business at a conference on a Greek island. Since many charitable donors resent any money going on salaries, it would hardly be surprising if there were financial problems following such revelations.)

Sexual peccadilloes apart, War on Want had been almost deliberately challenging with the 'style' of their campaigns as much as with their content, and had been rebuked by the commissioners for it. Whether or not this was wise, it perhaps demonstrated the foolishness of rules which depended so much on the comedian's adage, 'It's the way you tell 'em'.

As for Christian Aid, it noted that although none of Western Goals' complaints was upheld, 'time and effort was diverted from Christian Aid's charitable work to respond in detail to the Commission's investigation of the allegations and to respond to worried supporters who picked up garbled versions of the story in the press' (remarks to author).

Similarly, a disgruntled ex-employee of Christian Aid combed details of recent grants and objected to the Charity Commission about one which was made to a church human rights monitoring group in El Salvador, not long after Archbishop Romero was assassinated there. It was upheld because of the Amnesty case but Hugh Sampson, recently retired from Christian Aid, recalled, 'Western Goals put out press releases claiming it as one of their complaints – just to get publicity.'

Robin Guthrie has followed a line clearly at odds with the moral panic school of jurists: 'I have been tested on it by Oxfam and SHELTER, who have challenged me to say look at this instance, or look at that instance, would you say it was charitable? I have never found a case they raised which I could not to my satisfaction, and the apparent satisfaction of those listening, explain the difference in each case' (interview with author).

The case he used to illustrate the point was a Christian Aid Campaign which exhorted people to write to the South African Embassy to complain about RENAMO activities hindering the Charity's work in Mozambique. Ever punctilious about affairs of benevolence and charity, the South African Embassy wrote in to complain.

Guthrie advised Christian Aid that if they addressed their requests for protest letters to their regular subscribers it would be all right. 'If Christian Aid and its subscribers felt that another party was interfering with the achievement of their objects and contributing to the destruction of charitable property, they had a moral responsibility to draw attention to the facts in the relevant quarters, as far as they could be established' (Guthrié, 1988).

Perhaps indicative of the partiality of such complaints to the commissioners, the South African Ambassador did *not* complain about the Namibia Charitable Trust, nor did Western Goals. Formed to promote the 'advancement of education, the furtherance of health and the relief of poverty, distress and sickness in Namibia', its original head was former South African diplomat Sean Cleary (*The Guardian* 15 February 1989). The charity's secretary in 1989 was Patrick Watson who had set up a London foreign affairs bureau for the South African appointed 'transitional' government in Namibia. (In illustration of the Thatcher government's conception of non-political, one of the founding lights of the trust was Lord Chalfont, the Prime Minister's own appointee as deputy Chairman of the Independent Broadcasting Authority, whose special remit was to guarantee good taste, decency and 'due impartiality'.)

The Right Institutes

The Namibia Trust exemplifies a general principle, that while the voluntary sector is under sustained chastisement from Conservative supporters for its political activities, the right, and the Conservative Party itself, make extensive use of registered charities.

The Charity Commissioners have registered a whole series of right-wing think tanks, including Thatcher's own creation, the Centre for Policy Studies. Others include the Common Cause College, the Institute for Public Policy Research, the Institute for Economic Affairs, and its offshoot, the Social Affairs Unit, and last but far from least, the Adam Smith Institute. They all seem to fall under the heading of the 'Advancement of Learning'.

The IEA is for the 'promotion and advancement of learning by research into economic and political science and by educating the public therein'. Its charitable status secures it substantial privileges with covenants of £93,880 and donations of £550,674 in accounts available at the commissioners in 1989. Its income has risen steadily from £37,273 in 1978 (over a period when the Chancellor had claimed that charitable giving had risen). A donation would have been a shrewd investment for industrialists who approved of its arid advice, carefully listened-to advice to Downing Street.

The industrialists started early. The first accounts filed with the

Charity Commission, in 1964, show that the major donor was British United Industrialists, which handles company donations for the Conservative Party. The IEA has tried to live up to the high, but hardly apolitical, praise given it by Milton Friedman: 'The young in your country and mine are far more likely to be attracted by the free market doctrines the Institute of Economic Affairs presents so effectively, than they are by the standard socialist pap which still dominates university reading lists' (Hoover Lecture, 24 July 1978, quoted Labour Research Department, February 1984).

Still on the dry side, the Adam Smith Institute is registered for the 'advancement of learning by research into public policy options, economic and political science, and the publication of such research'. ASI President Madsen Pirie boasted to the *New Statesman* (29 June 1983) that its 'Omega Project will give the government a comprehensive range of policy objectives and the means to achieve them'. His colleague Michael Forsyth added, 'Our report goes beyond the Conservative Manifesto. We want privatisation to include all services, including professional ones such as architects and surveyors.' One of ASI's more influential documents was 'Revising the Rating System' in 1985. By 1989 this was being implemented as the Poll Tax. However, the institute could claim it was not vulgarly *campaigning* for a change in the law. It was merely producing research material which was music to the Prime Minister's ears.

Outlines of what appeared to be independent ideas were floated past the Prime Minister's Policy Unit before being made public. Since the government had dissolved the Central Policy Review Staff, Whitehall itself depended on such bodies to feed the government's ideological boilers. With her generally acute sense of the electorally possible, Margaret Thatcher could float ideas through the think tanks and adopt or deny them depending on public reaction.

The right has not gone unchallenged. In 1984, the Labour Research Department (not a charity) complained to the commissioners about the political activities of the IEA, the Social Affairs Unit, ASI and Common Cause. After examining their publications, the Charity Commission decided that there was 'no substance' to the complaint. A commission representative commented, 'They were research publications. The fact that they were right wing was incidental to the entertainment.' Private research, like private prayer, is not charitable, but their public form is.

Still, in 1982, a complaint was upheld against the British Atlantic Committee, which had been established to 'advance public education in the aims of the Atlantic Treaty and NATO, and the duties and responsibilities of the government and people under the treaty'. It had issued leaflets against CND but promised that it would not do it again (CC Report, 1982). What would the reaction be to a 'Urals Committee' with similar aims for the Warsaw Pact, one wonders?

In 1979, the Institute for European Defence and Strategic Studies was set up to 'assess the impact of political change in Europe and North America on defence and strategic issues. In particular, to study the the domestic political situation in NATO countries and how this affects the NATO posture.' To help it along, it received $427,809 from the US Heritage Foundation. Gerald Frost, the executive director of IEDSS was formerly secretary of Margaret Thatcher's own CPS.

In 1988, the commissioners accepted the Institute for the Study of Terrorism on the register. Its three directors were politically active on the right, but the commissioners decided that they could not take the political affiliation of trustees into account in making their decision (CC Report, 1988). This was in seeming contrast to their decision on WRP influence on 'Youth Training' in the 1982 Report where they accepted 'extrinsic evidence' as to the political intentions of the trust.

Showing balance, the commissioners in recent years also accepted the Institute For Public Policy Research, a left-wing think tank set up by Labour members. The preponderance of right-wing organisations probably reflects the greater resources available for their political bent rather than bias on the part of the commissioners. Although left-wing bodies are more likely to be complained about than right, complaints from both sides are fielded in a pragmatic way.

Robin Guthrie said:

> We get a lot of letters from organisations of one or other political wing who make representations about people on the opposite wing. We can deal with them. It shows a lively awareness of the state of affairs from members of the public, and as long as they don't take up too much time, I'm all for it. Sometimes they're right, and sometimes they're wrong. (Interview with author, 5 September 1988)

However, there is a definite bias in the law which is apparent even when refracted through the commissioners' recent liberality.

The Industrial Trust was registered in 1986 after surviving twenty years without charitable status. Its objects are, 'To promote the efficiency of industry, commerce, and the public services for the public benefit, by among other things, the improvement of industrial relations.' It is no surprise that its work has focused on ameliorating the intransigent attitudes of workers, rather than that of the employers who put up the money. As the *Independent* revealed (2 February 1989) the trust passed on the bulk of its money (£364,000 out of £423,000 between 1984 and 1987) to a right-wing organisation called IRIS, which used the money to fight political battles within the trade union movement. The money came from companies like Allied Lyons, Bass, Boots, BP, Glaxo, Guinness, P&O and Whitbread – which were, of course, each eligible for tax relief on their charitable donations.

A recent example should illustrate the point even more forcefully. In November 1988, a registered charity, the Centre for Policy Studies, produced a pamphlet advocating the end of the National Dock Labour Scheme. Its advice was followed by its very close friends in the Conservative Party, and in April 1989 legislation was rushed through to do just that.

The dockers' union, the T&GWU, was in a weak position. The dockers' only possible weapons were a political campaign, and a strike, the ballot for which was immediately subject to an injunction. The strike would be political, claimed the employers. The charitable Centre for Policy Studies produced great political results because it had the ear of the Establishment. Yet any charity which raised money on behalf of, or campaigned for public support for, the dockers would almost certainly be in breach of the 'political activity' doctrine. In the nature of such things, left-wing, reforming, movements are outsiders which need to influence large masses of people to secure their aims. They are not 'effective interests' like those with more conservative aims who only have to address their friends in power.

The doctrine of forbidden political activity has not been seriously opposed since the seventies when Ben Whitaker and the Charity Law Reform Committee proposed removing the illogical constraints on lay political activity. Much later, in 1989, Jack Straw, the Labour Education spokesman denounced the Grant Maintained Schools Trust for political involvement. The trust was set up to assist and encourage state schools to opt out, and as Straw pointed out, 'Its chairman is a Conservative MP and its director a Conservative Councillor.' In the best traditions of fostering independence for the

Nanny State, the government had given it a grant of £29,000 for 1989 with £150,000 to follow the next year. However, Straw's complaint missed the opportunity of highlighting the hypocrisy and absurdity of the whole doctrine of 'political activity'; it helped legitimise a dogma which has a very dubious parentage.

Away With All Tests

There is a pressing need to review, indeed to repeal, all the 'guidelines' and dogmas of political purposes and activities. Active charities are inhibited from actions which they may otherwise consider necessary. The lack of clear and explicit guidelines breeds a form of self-censorship which inhibits even action permissible within the guidelines.

Moreover, the commissioners' relaxed approach cannot be guaranteed against government pressure to implement the letter of the law. Indeed, while at the moment charity trustees can be held personally liable for expenditure on non-charitable political activities, the 'green' section of the 1989 White Paper opens up the possibility of more draconian action. It claims, on little evidence, that 'there are ... some signs that the public is anxious that the behaviour of a few charities may, on occasions, stray beyond the bounds of what is permissible or desirable. The Government have accordingly considered whether the law could with advantage be tightened' (Charities, 1989, p. 8).

It promises that 'the Charity Commissioners will take vigorous action with the support of the Attorney General'. It should be remembered that the White Paper envisages increased power for the commissioners to suspend trustees, to appoint a receiver or manager, and to transfer the charity's property to another charity. The Thatcher government has not been noted for its tolerance of alternative views, nor for moderation in its response to them.

Above all, there is a question of principle. The 'doctrine' of political activity was descended from the now defunct doctrine of superstitious uses. As this chapter has attempted to demonstrate, the prohibitions against political activity do not apply to religions; and they are not applied to 'think tanks' serving the recognised political élite. The doctrine is only applied to reforming or liberal causes, most especially those which seek to involve large numbers of people. It is perniciously élitist and anti-democratic, reeking of the bounty principle. It should be opposed in total rather than redefined.

13

Active Citizenship

While charities are enjoined to keep out of politics, there is no rule keeping politics and politicians out of charities. Beginning in 1987, the Conservative Party moved into the charitable sector, in what looked like a concerted drive to coopt charities and their benign connotations to serve Margaret Thatcher's radical transformation of British society. The key phrase urged upon the public was 'Active Citizenship', although, confusingly, each minister had a different meaning for it. But then, '"When I use a word," Humpty Dumpty said in a rather scornful tone, "it means just what I choose it to mean – no more nor less."' And as he explained, 'The question is, which is to be the master – that's all.'

'Active Citizenship' was a catch-phrase – like 'freedom' or 'choice' – in which favourable connotations are far more important than precision of thought. One observer aptly described the process as 'seizing control of the commanding heights of the political vocabulary'.

'Active Citizenship' was clearly a portmanteau policy of Good Things like family and individual self reliance, reduced state involvement and public expenditure, while locking out Bad Things, like local councils, social security scroungers and the feckless poor. The phrase itself was a recurrent theme throughout 1988, although it seemed to disappear during the first half of 1989. Whether this was the result of overexposure, or a rethink to harmonise party thinking on the matter is unclear. Whatever its fate, the penumbra of policies surrounding the phrase were unlikely to go away. This was quintessential Thatcherism with all its admonitory commandments and injunctions, as this chapter will show.

Populism – and the Unpopularity of Paupers

Perhaps the key element of Active Citizenship is a 'moral' concept of individual salvation. It considers that most of the poor are so because of their own individual failing. It is morally good for the rich to volunteer help, but it is morally degrading for the State to take resources compulsorily to achieve the same end. It is also morally degrading for the beneficíaries to be dependent on the State, but it is somehow more bearable if they are dependent on private largesse. And, finally, tax reductions will leave the philanthropic more resources to donate. Since at the same time Victorian values are often invoked, it is worthwhile repeating Dickens' parody of them the last time they were current. 'Lord Decimus Tite Barnacle had risen to the official heights on the wings of one indignant idea and that was "My Lords, I am yet to be told that it behoves a minister of this free country to set bounds to the philanthropy, to cramp the charity, to fetter the public spirit, to contract the enterprise, to damp the independent self-reliance, of its people"' (*Little Dorrit*). Or, as Margaret Thatcher modernised it, 'I came to office with one deliberate intent. To change Britain from a dependent to a self-reliant society – from a give-it-to-me to a do-it-yourself nation; to a get-up-and-go instead of a sit-back-and-wait-for-it Britain' (*The Times* 9 February 1984).

As Herman Melville wrote, 'Of all the preposterous presumptions of humanity over humanity, nothing exceeds most of the criticisms made on the habits of the poor by the well-housed, well-warmed and well-fed.' But however atavistic an attitude, it is still current. In 1976, 43 per cent of the public thought that 'people who live in need' did so because of 'laziness or lack of willpower' (Rentoul, 1989, p. 108). This archetypal Victorian attitude was the one harnessed by Thatcher's populist attacks.

Yet, as unemployment soared, it began to sink in that while the poor may always be with us, there were now a lot more of them about. By 1983, only 19 per cent saw laziness as the reason (ibid.). That need not have inhibited the electorate espousing Victorian values, since one of the pluses of being a populist politician is that the public are often no more consistent than you are. Thus the British Social Attitudes surveys over several years showed that between 64 per cent and 70 per cent of those questioned thought that large numbers of people falsely claimed benefits – yet between 79 per cent and 84 per cent thought that large numbers of people eligible for benefits did not claim them.

Rentoul adds, 'The researchers' main finding – that hostility towards welfare benefits is more closely related to authoritarian attitudes than to anti-egalitarian ones – may seem surprising, but it is logical. The belief in "large numbers" of scroungers is a moral, not an economic one' (ibid., p. 118). That belief was the cornerstone of Victorian organised charity, when city missions would count the money well spent even if it meant that the deserving got less so long as the undeserving got nothing.

However, the public showed a far less Victorian attitude to taxation. In 1987, according to a Gallup Poll, 66 per cent of people thought that they would prefer more taxes with better public services. The Chancellor gave them half of what they wanted: the proportion of national income taken in taxes was 45 per cent that year, 7 per cent higher than ever before. The following year he admitted that it would not 'be possible in this budget to reduce the burden of taxation – that is to say, to reduce taxation as a share of GDP'. That did not inhibit him from claiming that tax reductions had led to more charity. 'What I do think is important is that those who are well off should show a sense of social obligation, and I am very glad indeed that since we took office charitable giving has something like doubled in real terms' (*This Week Next Week*, 21 April 1988). We shall examine those figures in more detail later – but it is clear that the correlation between having 'loadsamoney' and being generous to charities is far from proven, even when given theological backing by Thatcher: 'No one would have remembered the Good Samaritan if he'd only had good intentions – he had money as well' (*Weekend World*, 6 January 1988).

However, the moral importance of giving voluntarily is consistently stressed. Chancellor Lawson said (2 June 1987), 'People who devote time to charitable work or give money to charity do so voluntarily. There is positive moral worth in this. But services provided by the state are funded by taxation and the moral worth in complying with the legal obligation to pay income tax is hardly in the same league' (Arnold Goodman Lecture).

Although Lawson's relaxed fiscal regime almost made tax paying as optional a matter as charitable giving for the rich, it is hardly likely that those most punctilious in avoiding one form of public responsibility will respond very enthusiastically to another. None the less, Douglas Hurd also claimed an 'immense increase in charitable activity' (5 February 1988).

Michael Brophy of the Charities' Aid Foundation, which tries to collect accurate statistics, countered the implied equation that making the rich richer also made them generous.

The people in the prosperous South give not only a lesser

percentage of their income to charity, but less in total than people elsewhere. Companies still give only about 0.2% of their pretax profits. The effect of the tax breaks to encourage giving have been marginal to date at least. Private giving is therefore still light years behind the rhetoric which encourages it. (*The Times*, 14 October 1988)

(Ironically, the reduction of 2 pence in the pound in income tax rates in 1988 reduced income to charities by £11 million because of the covenant system, while the Give As You Earn scheme inaugurating the Brave New World for charitable giving will, on the most optimistic evidence, net roughly the same amount – by 1990!)

In fact much of what 'immense increase' there was resulted from public response to the concept that charity does not begin at home. It was a huge response to overseas famines and disasters which led to an outburst of spontaneous giving. Perhaps the most egregious example of flexible philosophy was when the government gave the Telethon Appeal a 'charitable' donation of £1 million representing money which it had underpaid pensioners.

Relieving the State of Its Burden

Douglas Hurd made it clear that more was expected from people than widows' mites:

A social policy founded upon ideals of responsible and active citizenship is compatible with market economic policies. Private Property is the natural bulwark of liberty, because it ensures that economic power is not entirely concentrated in the hands of the state. It also buttresses personal responsibility by harnessing man's acquisitive instinct to the demands of stewardship (*New Statesman*, 29 April 1988)

More than his colleagues, Hurd tried to reconcile the scattered use of buzzwords into an ideological framework. In Tolstoyan vein he continued: 'The diffusion of power is a bulwark against despotism and corruption, and the key to active and responsible citizenship . . . the strongest loyalties are to family, neighbourhood and nation.' Of course, he never elaborates on how the neighbourhood minnows can face the Leviathan of the State on equal terms, and blithely skips on; 'Of course, some aspects of our policy, like the national curriculum, or the uniform business rate involve taking powers from local councils to the centre in order to prevent its abuse or atrophy.' Kenneth Baker, the architect of a centrally enforced national curriculum, was another unlikely convert to decentralisation: 'One thing we have learnt over the years is that the smaller unit is more personal, more identifiable, more human and more effective than the larger unit' (Bow Group Annual Dinner, 27 April 1988).

However, there is a limit to even theoretical decentralisation. It was consistently implied that ordinary people are not fully competent to administer their own affairs, not least the poor who are by definition morally flawed. So, in 1989, it was being mooted that some single women who became pregnant only did so to obtain decent housing. To avert this, a proposal was being considered which came straight out of the Victorian ethos. *All* such women would be offered 'deliberately unattractive hostels' (*The Observer*, 16 April 1989).

While traditional definitions of charity stressed its altruism, Hurd's definitions of active citizenship brought the ethos of the shadier end of the market. 'We must,' he told the London Rotary Club Lunch (28 October 1987), 'increasingly mobilise the interests of the individual active citizen in making such services more responsive to the needs of those they exist to serve.' The first example he gave of this was 'parent power as a lever to raise standards in schools'. He was not talking about concerned citizens overseeing *collective* educational needs, but a consumer lobby of parents looking after the interests of their children – by implication against an uncaring local authority. One might extrapolate that Andrew Carnegie would only fund libraries or universities which his children attended.

His second example was 'the power we want to give to council tenants to break away from those local authorities who manage council estates badly, or treat their tenants' needs and wishes with contempt'. Once again, this gave as little space in the self-interested universe for groups who were concerned about the homeless as it did for tenants of private landlords.

A recurring example of active self-interest was Neighbourhood Watch schemes which, once again, were hardly altruistic. There may indeed have been schemes where affluent citizens from the suburbs go to patrol inner city streets to protect pensioners there from burglaries and muggings – but if so, they were unpublicised.

It has to be said that there is something extremely unattractive about this self-motivated view of society. The old belief that people who were charitable would get their reward in Heaven is preferable to an expectation of quick returns in more cash and better services.

An active citizen is thus one who looks after himself in every sense. It is a status which can be achieved by simply *not* doing things. Lord Quinton summed up the official view in *The Times*, glossing the Hurd instincts, by writing that an active citizen 'must be someone who does more than the law requires of him and, perhaps, does not claim all from the state to which he is entitled by law, with deliberate intent and not by some mischance' (8 October 1988). This implied that a rich pensioner who eschewed the £10 Christmas bonus was an active citizen, while the one on FIS who helped run the tenants association was in some sense a client rather than a citizen. It implied that BUPA members and public school patrons are full citizens, while those who used the state services were somehow relegated to a lesser form. The whole moral burden of 'activity' is thus to relieve the state of its load of responsibility.

Making a Scapegoat of the Nanny State

Minister John Moore made this distaste for state services more explicit: 'Talk of "rights" came to dominate the public debate, but "rights" in this context simply meant welfare benefits handed out by the government'(8 June 1988). The disfavour with which such an approach was regarded became quickly evident. SHELTER's campaign for the homeless was shortly threatened with action in lobby leaks to *The Times* (11 July 1988).

Moore's view of collective welfare is a fine example of the Titus-Barnacle behoving machine in operation. 'The shape and pattern of the welfare measures enacted in those years too often had the effect of increasing people's dependence on the state and its attendant bureaucrats, and reducing the power and control they might have hoped to gain over their own lives. Dependence in the long run decreases human happiness and reduces human freedom' (Speech to the Conservative Political Centre, 26 September 1988). (More so, presumably, than independent hunger, homelessness and ill health).

Another fundamental characteristic of active citizenship appeared to be the firm idea that individualism is incompatible with collectivism. Modern charities are major collective enterprises, depending on the voluntary efforts of many socially concerned people, among whom there are probably activists of a kind not admired by the government. However, those forms of collective endeavour were *not* what the Active Citizen ideologues had in mind.

Margaret Thatcher herself said, 'There is no such thing as society. There are individual men and women, and their families. And no government can do anything except through people, and people must look after themselves' (*Woman's Own*, November 1987). Nigel Lawson phrased it less elegantly, 'A person's first duty is to look after his or her own family. As their income rises, they are better able to give to others' (2 June 1987).

Mrs Thatcher invoked scriptural backing for her views when she sermonised the General Assembly of the Church of Scotland, 'You recall that Timothy was warned by St Paul that anyone who neglects to provide for his own house (meaning his own family) has disowned the faith and is worse than an infidel.' Unfortunately, she did not read on to where the apostle says, 'For the love of money is the root of all evil.'

Kenneth Baker tried to rescue the Prime Minister's concept from its inherent primitivism, when he made an attempt to recycle the devalued coin of community by describing, 'Our nation as a community of individuals' (Bow Group Annual Dinner, 27 April 1988). But the concept appeared to allow no recognition or encouragement of any lesser group of individuals, be it civic, charitable or trade union.

Moreover, after the family had done its duty by itself, it had only a moral, not a legal, responsibility. 'When we have finished our duty as taxpayer, we have not finished our duty as citizens,' said Margaret Thatcher, in a statement which a poll showed was approved by 92 per cent of those questioned. Douglas Hurd echoed his leader, 'Many people have a substantially higher standard of living than they used to. I find that more and more people are prepared to set aside part of that, and time to help others' (*On the Record*, BBC, 18 September 1988). Lewis Carroll's Bellman said, 'What I tell you three times is true,' but no matter how often ministers repeated this incantation, it remained stubbornly disputable.

It was a clear example of how abideth faith and hope and charity – with charity being much the lesser of these things. The same poll which showed 92 per cent approval of the Prime Minister's general statement showed that only 3 per cent of those questioned were intending to give money theyy had received from tax cuts to charity, so we must presume that they were exercising *their* right to make words mean just what they wanted them to.

No one has polled the recipients of state welfare services on how they feel about the implied move from assured statutory benefits to reliance on the good will of those better off. People dependent on 'charity', in the sense of private bounty, would drop right through the bottom of the 'market' in the sense of their having any bargaining power. It would leave them in a form of command economy in which it is the whims and prejudices of the benefactor which control the provision of goods and services.

Active Citizenship in Practice

It is worth examining not just the Conservative government's statements, but also its actions. In one sense, the future is already here. Applicants to the Social Fund were, in 1987, being referred to lists of local charities which the social security clerks had to hand. The Charity Commission promptly issued a reminder to charities that trustees were not supposed to relieve the state of its functions and therefore should not consider applications unless the applicant had been refused by the Department of Social Security. Now, the clerks refuse the application – and *then* refer their clients to local charities!

Reinforcing the anti-statist message, Hurd said, 'We have been encouraging the growth of voluntary organisations which can offer far greater flexibility and enterprise than government schemes, which have perforce to comply with set patterns and find it difficult always to adapt to local needs' (*New Statesman*, 29 April 1988). The local charities who get these applications do not generally see themselves as being replacements for the Welfare State, but rather supplementing it. For example, in 1988, the centuries-old Thomas Coram Foundation originated an imaginative scheme to provide facilities and advice for homeless families with children, placed in bed and breakfast accommodation. They could only finance it with difficulty, despite a substantial old endowment and a recent fund-raising drive. But there is no way whatsoever that they could afford actually to *house* the people they are helping. Yet the government's withdrawal of housing benefit from young people meant that many charities have had to try to do just that.

There are some voluntary organisations which, for a variety of reasons, saw a window of opportunity in the rolling programme of voluntarisation inaugurated by the government, like those in the health service referred to above. As Usha Prashar of the NCVO said:

> Voluntary Organisations have themselves been critical of State provision and its capacity to meet changing needs. But their critique is quite different from that adopted by this government. They have sought to extend the opportunities for choice and the mixed economy *within* the welfare state and to develop partnership with private and public provision. Their response is exemplified by the wave of advocacy and community-based provision that began in the much maligned 60's and that is based in a collective sense of responsibility for dignity, health, security, freedom, and fair life chances for all people. (Speech to Conference of Northern Charities, Manchester, 14 November 1989).

That kind of organisation would be the least likely to get government funding. The successful tenders for welfare provision would come from organisations with Royal in the name, and an ex-army officer behind the desk, rather than those run by the client groups themselves. This would involve a reversal of the trend among even long established charities, which, as Usha Prashar said, 'are changing their own style of operation ... working *with* service users, rather than *for* them' (ibid.).

Prashar went on to offer a far more attractive – and coherent – vision of active citizenship as 'about much more than giving money to passive recipients. Who is the real active citizen – the person who puts a fiver in a charity collection box, or the single mother who gets involved in community action, sets up a childcare scheme, but also demands adequate services from the council or adequate benefits from the state.' Such a mother would fail to meet the government's criteria for citizenship on almost every count. As we have seen, this concept of enfranchising the beneficiaries is not to be found in the ministerial pronouncements.

But how much more of a nightmare for Mrs Thatcher would be Dr Brian Harrison's vision of the active citizen 'discussing, arguing, agitating, frequently bloody-minded, but also frequently creative and constructive. Such people, wielding as weapons the procession, the public meeting, the periodical, and the petition, inevitably pushed forward the boundaries of toleration, strengthened the priority given to free speech, and enhanced civil liberties by defending many victims from exploitation and oppression' (Sir

George Haynes lecture at 1987 AGM NCVO).

It cannot be coincidental that any citizens doing those things would not only draw upon themselves the obloquy of a government with strictly circumscribed concepts of citizenship; they would also, if organised into charitable bodies, run foul of two centuries of case law!

14

Who Pays and Do They Call the Tune?

After the establishment of the Welfare State, there was a consensus that if voluntary organisations had a role it was a supplementary one, identifying discrete areas of need not dealt with by the blanket responsibilities and bureaucratic slowness of the state agencies. Charities saw it as their role to secure more government spending, not to substitute for it.

As we have seen in the previous chapter, the implication of 'Active Citizenship' was to try to reverse that approach. Instead of being scouts and guerrillas working ahead of the frontiers of welfare, charity's new allotted role was to occupy and consolidate the territory left by the retreating forces of the Welfare State. However, most charities have neither the inclination nor the means for such a role, whether funded by public or private money.

The devolution of government-provided services to voluntary organisations also provides problems for the consumers. The beneficiaries have a degree of electoral control, no matter how exiguous, over the government-provided services. If the government moves to the US model, disbursing public funds through quasi-independent agencies, it deprives the beneficiaries of a direct approach and allows elected officials an extra barrier of defence against responsibility. It is likely to transform the goals of the agencies themselves from that of satisfying the consumers to keeping the politicians happy.

Many ministers have referred to the higher level of corporate and individual giving in the US culture. However, as one American observer wrote, 'In the human service field at least, government – particularly the federal government – does very little itself in the United States' (Salamon, 1985). But he added:

What it does, it does through other institutions – state governments, city governments, county governments, banks, manufacturing firms, hospitals, higher education institutions, research institutes, and many more. The result is an elaborate pattern of *third party government*, in which government provides the funds and sets the directions but other institutions deliver many of the services, often with a fair degree of discretion about who is served and how. (ibid.)

That is perhaps more accurately described as *third party administration*, since the agencies are under the effective control of their financiers, the Federal, State and local governments.

Salamon showed that in the USA, government funding accounted for 41 per cent of the revenue of non-profit organisations (exclusive of hospitals and higher education) while fees accounted for another 28 per cent. Non-profit activity in sixteen communities in the USA accounted for the majority of welfare activities in every sector but housing. He also showed that state backing had fallen steadily over the years of Reaganism. UK moves for schools, hospitals and other services to be 'opted out', dealt with above, implied a shift, conscious or otherwise, to the American 'agency' model.

However, the US model has itself been changing. Salamon summarised: 'By cutting back on government spending, therefore, the Reagan Administration has significantly reduced the revenues of the non-profit sector while calling on this sector to do more. Although non-profits as a group have overcome the resulting cutbacks, they have done so chiefly by increasing their income from service charges rather than their private charitable support.' It is that changed model which appeared closer to the implied plans of the UK's Conservative government.

Public Funding

In the UK, despite all the talk of how active the affluent citizenry was, there was a coy reticence in the Cabinet about exactly how the voluntary sector was financed. Michael Brophy of the Charities Aid Foundation called for 'the current debate about citizenship and generosity to take place on a basis of fact rather than rhetoric'. He added, 'And as yet, Government shows little sign of collecting its own figures' (McQuillan, 1988, p. 3).

The government seemed to ignore what figures were available in its enthusiasm for the moral worth of private giving. Ministers understated the contribution of fees and government finance, while emphasising the role of private and corporate sector donors. In fact the UK pattern is already close to that of the US in terms of sources of income.

Dr John Posnett found that in 1985 fees and charges represented 60.7 per cent of charities' income. The largest part of that was public school fees, which netted £3.167 billion, while arts organisations charged their users £2.687 billion. Housing rents and charges formed most of the rest with £1.536 billion (McQuillan, 1986 pp. 6–8). In 1988, £157 million was charged in fees by the private charitable hospitals (source, Independent Hospitals Association).

Sums represented by ticket purchases at the Royal Opera, BUPA pay-outs, and the payment of school fees in Harrow, were being called in evidence as 'increased charitable activity'. For example, Nigel Lawson, in his 1987 Arnold Goodman lecture, referred to the turnover of the charitable sector as 'now around £10 billion a year'. He went on to conclude: 'The upsurge of charitable activity over the past few years is thus very striking.' He then gave figures of government 'grants and payments to voluntary bodies for 1985/6 as totalling £268 million.' Later, Thatcher announced that government support for voluntary bodies had risen. 'In the period between 1979/80 and 1986/87, the level of Government support to voluntary bodies has risen by about 221% (in real terms 92.4%)' (Hansard, 14 April 1988). Like many such answers, it contrived to be true – and misleading.

In fact total central government support came to £3,600 billion in 1986–7, if the £600 million tax rebates are included. Indeed the 'indirect subsidy', the total fiscal gain to charities from exemption from rates, corporation tax, VAT, inheritance tax, etc., has been estimated to be as high as £2.5 billion. In direct spending, the MSC alone was responsible for £613,250,000 worth of grants under the Community programme, Youth Training Scheme and Voluntary Projects Programme. Under the Urban Programme, the Department of the Environment gave another £76 million, and the DoE itself gave £33,294,000 (Hansard, 14 March 88).

Lawson similarly overlooked grants ranging from the £1.46 billion which went to Housing Associations, to the Arts Council's £135 million parliamentary grant in aid for 1987. The size of the government input is further enhanced by its contribution to the fees and charges which make up over 60 per cent of the income. They include fees paid by the NHS to independent hospitals, and school fees. For example, in January 1988, 52,764 pupils at fee paying schools were assisted by the local authority, or on the Assisted Places Scheme, or were children of Service men and women. Almost 10 per cent of the fees paid to public schools were paid either in part or in full by the public sector (ISIS, 1988).

Since Housing Association tenants are, almost by definition, disadvantaged, a large proportion of their rents would be met by the Department of Social Security, as would the charges for the many 'voluntary' homes for old people, children, and mentally and physically handicapped.

The government's reticence to advertise all this implies that the private input to the voluntary sector was being exaggerated to put truth in political rumours; that the sector could deal with society's problems and in doing so reduce government expenditure. The drift of Conservative policies, under cover of active citizenship, was towards the post-Reagan American model: a voluntary sector dependent on charges and non-governmental provision which would cut public expenditure, and boost the sink-or-swim enterprise culture espoused so vigorously by Downing Street.

The Price of Independence?

In some ways, a reduced dependence on Whitehall funding may not be an entirely bad thing. As NACAB's problems showed, an overweening paymaster brings difficulties as well as money. A major strength of the voluntary sector has been its independence, which is precisely why there have been occasional 'political activity' panics to keep them in line. In a country where political power is being increasingly centralised, the existence of independent agencies in the field of social welfare is welcomed. They provide services and information which have been increasingly useful as political control of the statistical services has made UK official figures as reliable as Airstrip One's chocolate ration weight. However, independence has its price.

How can independent organisations fund themselves in the face of an interfering government? The first call for local charities would normally be the town halls, which, despite a fall, still gave £546 million to charities in grants, fees and rate relief in 1986–7 (McQuillan, 1988). Nevertheless, reliance on local council funding can be precarious. In many urban areas where social problems were greatest, Metropolitan County Councils like Greater London,

Merseyside, South Yorkshire, and Greater Manchester played a significant role in funding and encouraging voluntary initiative. They were abolished in 1986.

When the Conservative government began its big push for political hegemony over local government, it made the GLC the number one target. By analogy, the executioner's axe also fell on the regional metropolitans, so that the dawn of the new age of active citizenship coincided with the ripping out of the drip which kept many of the much-lauded efforts alive. Judith Unell estimated a 20 per cent decline in funding in the metropolitan areas over 1985–6 (ibid.).

There had been something of a hothouse atmosphere in the years between the government's pronouncement of their death sentence and the actual execution. Since they saw no reason to leave large surpluses for the government-appointed residuary bodies to inherit, some authorities' funding displayed a generosity which exacerbated the problems when they disappeared.

Merseyside showed both the financial and the political dangers of dependency on the town hall. The County's abolition produced three significant casualties, The Equal Opportunities Project, which worked to improve women's access to education and employment, The Merseyside Association for Racial Equality in Employment, and the post of development worker for the Credit Unions. None of them was likely to match government conceptions of the active citizen – especially the last, which was a classic self-help organisation designed to rescue the poor from the credit slavery imposed by the financial institutions.

At the core of Merseyside is Liverpool, for four years under the effective control of the Trotskyist Militant Tendency, which dominated the council Labour group and seemed determined to prove that the left could be every bit as vindictive as the right. Here, the local voluntary organisations suffered for reasons both ideological and financial. On the financial side, all payments were delayed until the last possible moment – or later. The council was indeed being squeezed by central government, but its own policies of increasing the municipal payroll and financing the Urban Regeneration Strategy, the council house building programme, swallowed all available resources. The pressure from central government was common to many local authorities which frequently transferred their problems on to the voluntary sector. It was easier to make somebody redundant by proxy than it was to sack one's own employees, not least when their unions had political influence through the local Labour Party.

In Liverpool, the degree of political motivation in decision-making easily matched that of central government, and against remarkably similar targets. As Edward Murphy of the Liverpool Council For Voluntary Service said, 'The peculiar reductionism of the Militant Tendency's politics makes them uniquely hostile, as a matter of ideological principle, to voluntary organisations and voluntarism as an ethos.' He identified three types of organisations which suffered 'catastrophically' from this philosophy: Black organisations, housing cooperatives and associations, and neighbourhood groups. The black organisations paid the penalty for disagreeing with a Trotskyist analysis of race which saw it as a distraction from the unity of the working class. For the purposes of this thesis, the working class tended to be represented by the overwhelmingly white council workforce (see *Liverpool Black Caucus*, 1986).

LCVS reported, 'Seven housing cooperatives did not develop, and a thousand new cooperative and housing association dwellings were lost in 1983–5.' In addition, some cooperatives were 'municipalised' while 'real and lasting damage was done on the ground to the network of neighbourhood groups, of tenants and residents associations, and to the infrastructure, particularly the Community Relations Council, the Community Liaison Section, and the Community Councils which supported them'.

The changes forced charities into self-reliant policies – which in the long term may have done some good. The LCVS itself developed its financial services income so that it was 90 per cent self-supporting, while Age Concern Liverpool made practical charity pay by developing a special range of discounted insurance policies for the elderly, thus generating income to substitute for municipal funding. The Housing Associations broadened their geographical base to build up income from work outside the city.

Most of these organisations did not see their role as supplanting or opposing the city council, but rather as supplementing their services on behalf of the citizenry. As at the national level, voluntary organisations want creative tension rather than confrontation, to temper the excesses of bureaucracy and complacency.

Often responsible 'bureaucrats' welcome such tension, not just because it provides information and a sounding board for policies, but because of the nature of hierarchical organisations in which it is useful to cite an *external* reason for initiating activity.

Sheer doggedness was the hallmark of voluntary associations

formed by citizens who were tired of being spoken for, whether by old style charities or equally condescending councillors. In the case of the Housing Cooperatives, Prince Charles quoted Thomas Jefferson approvingly, having forgiven him for the misunderstanding of 1776: 'I know of no safe depository of the ultimate powers of society but the people themselves, and if we think them not enlightened enough to exercise their control with a wholesome discretion, the remedy is not to take it from them, but to inform their discretion' (McDonald, 1986, p. 10). It is an eloquent denial of the 'we know best' attitude of old charities and of government at local and national levels.

Privatisation – or Deprivation?

While downplaying the role of fees and public money, the government has been stressing the role of the private donor. However, the CAF estimated that overall, private giving in 1987 had increased by a mere 2 per cent in real terms. That this was not a biased estimate can be judged from the fact that their figures for household giving are consistently higher than those collected by the government's Family Expenditure Survey. FES showed donations of £33 per household per annum in 1986, while CAF's Charity Household Survey showed £70. The CHS produced a more detailed checklist in 1987, which produced a figure of £103. The FES figures give a total individual giving figure of between £650 million and £800 million pounds, the CHS figure produces a total of between £1,800 million and £2,700 million.

The discrepancies are partly explained by the different viewpoints of the surveys. The FES takes a moral stand and only counts actual donations, while the CHS survey counts purchases from jumble sales and charity shops, and even the buying of raffle tickets, as charitable income.

Apart from the supply side method of reducing taxes to boost income and generosity, the other means the government deployed to channel private funds into charity was Payroll Giving. Advocated by the Goodman Committee in 1976, it was not introduced until the 1986 budget. Payroll Giving allowed employees or pensioners to have regular donations taken from their pay or pension to be set against tax. It was supposed to herald a brave new world for the charitable sector, but if the government saw it as a means of allowing the private conscience to replace the public purse in the

war on want, it was quickly disabused. Lawson budgeted for a cost
in tax relief of £20 million per year when he introduced the
scheme, implying an anticipated revenue of around £100 million a
year (Goodman Lecture, 1987).

The biggest agency for the scheme, with almost 2,000 employers
and over 70,000 employees subscribing, was the CAF, which, by
December 1988, was passing on the money to 2,160 nominated
charities out of the 8,000 hopeful good causes which had registered
with them. But David Wickert, director of the scheme, admitted that
it had had a faltering start. The employers registered with CAF have
7 million workers, so the take-up of 70,000 left a long way to go.
Wickert was confident that that would soon be doubled, and hoped
to have an 'annualised rate' of around £10 million donations by
April 1989 (interview with author, December 1988).

The scheme is useful for many charities, especially because of its
regularity, but it has not produced enough money to finance the
social counter-revolution implied by 'Active Citizenship'. Even the
doubling of the tax deductible limit of donations to £240 per
annum in the 1989 budget was unlikely to increase it significantly.
To put it in perspective, the annual target would have been less
than a day's spending by the Department of Social Security. By the
end of 1988, donations were coming in at an annual rate of £3
million a year which was equivalent to half an hour's DSS spending.

Jolly Good Companies

Next to the charitable individual donor in government iconology,
was the concerned company. After a decade in which taxes for
companies, their shareholders and managers had fallen considerably, the 10,000 companies which gave to charity were far from
making significant inroads into the state's welfare budget. According to the Directory for Social Change's *A Guide to Company
Giving, 1987–88*, they donated £135 million in 1987. The State
whose withdrawal they were supposed to be covering gave over £4
billion to the voluntary sector (the health and social security budget
was, of course, considerably higher at £68 billion).

Although the government was discreetly prodding companies to
put their money where the ministers' mouths were, the effect was
difficult to gauge. For example, Littlewoods, which had financed
and organised one payroll giving agency, had done so as the result
of fairly heavy government pressure – and had been far from

overwhelmed with the response. The company expected to carry the loss for many years before the agency's throughput allowed it to support itself.

As ever, the statistics show a range of inexactitude. 'We can be 95% certain that the annual level of charitable contributions by the population of small companies as a whole lies somewhere in the region between £474 million and £964 million in 1987–88,' said the Charities Aid Foundation (McQuillan, 1988).

In cash, the top 200 companies gave over £63 million in 1987–8 which was an increase of 12 per cent in a year when tax had fallen as fast as profits had risen. The Directory for Social Change suggested that this is increased considerably by gifts and aid in kind, which pushed it up to £250 million. However, this included sponsorship and similar 'giving' which could just as well be on the advertising and PR budget. Some donations, like Distillers' £560,000 to the Thalidomide Children's Trust and Gallaghers' donation of £687,500 to the Health Promotion Research Trust – could be looked on more as reparations than as generosity. Other companies' donations to right-wing front organisations like the Industrial Trust were hardly a manifestation of charitable spirit.

Perhaps one of the more telling epitaphs for the concept of corporate concern was the Staffordshire Community Trust which was 'a fund raising and grant giving charity aimed to increase the effectiveness of company giving to the voluntary sector by directing resources to the most appropriate needs and redirecting as needs change'. The needs stayed the same – unmet, according to the *Guardian*, which reported that the trust had had a £30,000 government grant in 1986 – and had spent it all while only giving £588 to the poor. The costs included £7,703 for a champagne launch party – but for all the effort it only raised £5,538. The chairman of the trust told the *Guardian*, 'The patient isn't dead yet' (11 November 1988).

Sir Hector Laing, Chairman of United Biscuits also gave the *Guardian* the official line:

> The charitable giving which was once done by families and the wealthy, which might have devolved onto wealth creating industry, passed instead, in the early 1950's, to government. I think everybody said 'They' will do it. In 1979 a government came in with a wholly different attitude, and took a big step back from industry. It took some time for people to realise that, as the government stood back, we, the wealth creators, had to step forward' (8 December 1988).

The government may have stepped back, but many industrialists were more than a little peeved with how forward it was in asking companies to come forward. Sir Hector was founder of the Percent Club which had been founded with Prime Minister Thatcher's blessing, and quite possibly at her instigation. The unkind might have regarded its title as a half truth, since its 170 members were only pledged to give a half of a per cent of pretax profits to charity – and that includes secondment of staff and donations in kind. Sir Hector played up the role of enlightened self-interest in the campaign, which hoped to increase the percentage. 'A decaying society means decaying profits. What's in it for us is a better society, more people in jobs, more entrepreneurial flair in communities, and therefore more chance of making worthwhile profits' (ibid.).

None the less, the suspicions of many were expressed by Sir Mark Weinberg, Chairman of Allied Dunbar which has consistently earmarked 1.25 per cent of its profits in 'community giving'. 'The fear is that once you start being efficient yourselves, government will say it's reducing its commitment' (ibid.).

Perhaps it was a fear shared by the 400 major donor companies which collectively gave only 0.2 per cent of their profits to charity in 1987 (MacQuillan, 1988), or maybe British business ethos remained closer to the government's spiritual mentors than the government itself. After all, Milton Friedman had said, 'Few trends could so thoroughly undermine the very foundations of our free society as the acceptance by corporate officials of a responsibility other than to make as much money for their shareholders as possible' (quoted *The Observer* 5 June 1988).

And What Hath the Righteous Done?' – the Foundations

The government does not talk much about the work of the foundations, as if ministers were worried that an outbreak of corporate altruism on this scale would undermine the ideological foundations of the enterprise culture. But it has passed on to them the burden of research in the UK. 'It is clear above all that the foundations would need reassurance that Government was not looking to them to assume responsibility for meeting basic research needs and was not seeking to entice the foundations into the formal governmental funding mechanisms for such research. We respect the determination of the foundations to retain their independence, flexibility and diversity,' said the Advisory Board of

Research Councils (quoted, Wellcome Trust, 1986). It was not a respect shared by the government which saw the natural role of the foundations as the reduction of public expenditure. Indeed, charities could find themselves privatised in ways hardly conducive to an active voluntary sector. In 1987, the government sold the National Seed Development Organisation and part of the Plant Breeding Institute to Unilever for £66 million – in the teeth, it might be said, of protests from the scientific community. Later it discovered that the Plant Breeding Institute, of which it had sold part, was in fact a registered charity. The Treasury was forced to hand over £38.5 million plus interest to the institute. The Charity Commissioners thwarted a last desperate attempt to keep the money under government control, and forced it to hand over the money to the charity (*New Scientist* 4 February 1989).

The foundations are the big money in the alms business, with expenditure of £286 million in 1988 (FitzHerbert, 1989). What they spend it on is not always as public as it should be, since the accounts lodged with the Charity Commissioners sometimes have so little detail that they could easily have been written on the back of the proverbial Woodbine packet. (A Charity Commission investigator gave it as a rule of thumb that those which detail their grants are above board – but that his interest would quicken if all that was written was a global sum for grants and donations.)

The TV and radio appeals, despite all the publicity, raised only £43 million, in comparison with £150 million from dividends, interest, rents and endowments. It was spent on all four heads of charity; health and welfare took 40 per cent, £114 million; research took 29 per cent, £82 million, with medicine taking the lion's share at £57 million; religion took £26 million with Christians taking £14 million and Jews £12 million. Overseas work accounted for a mere £3 million – the Overseas Aid charities tend to spend quickly what they get rather than store it in endowments.

Much of the work of foundations has been made possible because some companies were completely or substantially handed over to charities. Insulated from the vagaries of fund raising, some foundations are financiers to some of the most radical and politically sensitive work of other charities. Others have more than a whiff of private interest about them. They have caused deep concern in the USA where they come under fire from both sides:

On the left they have always been unpopular as cosmetics that soften public attitudes towards the unacceptable face of private wealth . . . The simultaneous cross-fire criticism from populist and conservatives – that such trusts escape public scrutiny and accountability in their dispersal of patronage and funds that are arguably the taxpayers', or alleging they are subsidising subversion while evading any elected responsibility. (Whitaker, 1979, p. 13).

For the British foundations, Robin Guthrie warned: 'What is often not recognised, particularly by the founders of a trust, is that once it is set up, it has an independent existence of its own. It is no longer their pet under their control. They have transferred some of their resources to the public domain (not the public sector) – a charity has an independent existence of its own' (personal interview).

Breaking Loose from the Founders

The motives for founders vary, but few have ever recorded gratitude for government economies as their motive. Only eccentrics and Conservative chancellors see the reduction of the National Debt as a significant act of benevolence. Some were the modern equivalent of chantries, intended to perpetuate the memory of the founder down the ages, while others hoped to use the perpetuity of charitable trusts to perpetuate dynastic control of businesses. In fact the better foundations do demonstrate a tendency to slip away from the founder's will and control. The Wellcome Foundation plc is the pharmaceutical company itself. Until 1986 the rapidly growing company was completely owned by the Wellcome Trust. It must gall new right theoreticians that one of Britain's most successful companies contrived to become so without profit-hungry shareholders to spur it on, even as it pleases them with the reduction in public expenditure. 'They make the money – and we spend it' was how trust director Briget Ogilvie described the relationship between trust and plc, asserting that none of their medical research grants impinged upon the company's R & D programme. In 1986, the trustees divested themselves of 25 per cent of the shares because they felt that the 1961 Trustee Investments Act required them to. Section 6 of the Act 1961 reminds trustees that they must consider 'the need for diversification of investments of the trust in so far as is appropriate to the circumstances of the trust'.

The advice is both legal and sensible. Loyalty can exact a heavy price – The Nuffield Foundation lost over £400 million because the trustees were overscrupulous in their respect for what they thought the wishes of its founder would have been.

Nuffield's original endowment was entirely of Morris Motors shares and was probably intended to ensure corporate continuity in addition to benefiting the public. Morris Motors merged with Austin, in 1952, and Leyland, in 1968, and what is left ended up with British Aerospace. The foundation's percentage holding fell steadily with each merger. Nuffield's trust deed restricted the sale of the shares while he was alive, requiring his consent for any such sale, and after his death they could only be sold to meet death duties.

In 1955, the Charity Commissioners removed the restrictions – but they could not remove the mental mortmain over the Ordinary Trustees who were reluctant to go against the founder's will, even though circumstances had changed considerably over the decades. Even after Nuffield himself died in 1963, they hung on out of loyalty to the founder. In 1970, the Charity Commissioners urged the trustees to consider sale and diversification, but it was only in 1971, when dividends dropped, that they took the advice. They sold one-third of their holding, realising £6 million. In 1975, the government bought out the remaining two-thirds – for £2.5 million. By the end of 1975, even with reserves the foundation was worth only £16 million. By 1989, it had built back up to a healthy £90 million – and had no connection whatsoever with Morris's original industrial empire and its descendants.

The trustees of the Baring Foundation would doubtless consider such divestment entirely inappropriate to their particular circumstances. The foundation is the sole owner of Barings Bank, one of the historical pillars of the City. In 1985, at a time when social concern did not perhaps have the highest profile in the square mile, Barings plc became wholly owned by the charity, completing a process begun in 1969 when it had first been given 75 per cent of the business.

Barings had been a partnership since the 1890s. Partners had neither brought capital when they were invited to join, nor taken any out when they eventually retired. However, while they *were* partners, they shared the not inconsiderable profits of the business. But modern mores did not recognise such gentlemanly traditions. 'In the sixties there were several risks. There was the threat of a wealth tax, and the death of a partner in office could have exposed us to heavy death duties,' Nicholas Baring explained (personal interview, December 1988). The primary motive was, therefore, corporate continuity in the face of the possibility of confiscatory tax rates on wealth of the kind which the Labour Party was considering.

'The Council of the Foundation does not interfere in the running of the bank, but is the passive recipient of the dividends,' Baring commented. In 1988, the foundation distributed over £3.5 million from its current dividends. The directors of Barings received profits-related payments, 'drawn up with the need to give the Foundation a reasonable return on its capital'. In 1987, the directors' emoluments totalled £2,011,000 while the income of the foundation was £2,831,972 which was a considerable rise from the £25,000 given in 1970.

In the light of the bank's £55,000 donation to the Conservative Party, there may be some irony that in 1986 the foundation decided to alter its field of operation from London and national causes to allow attention to be paid to the North East and Merseyside. 'They were areas with which Barings had a traditional connection – over a century in the cotton trade in Liverpool – and both areas of considerable need,' said Nicholas Baring. (They were also areas which tended to blame the Conservative Party for their problems.)

Although it generally targets 'unpopular causes' like the mentally handicapped and drug abusers, some of its grants would be arguably charitable in political if not legal terms. A 'substantial' donation to Westminster School for a new science complex, where substantial is glossed at around £20,000, is not everybody's idea of a good cause, for example. However, although the Baring Foundation was clearly set up for fiscal rather than philanthropic motives, as a result charity gets more money than the directors – and may end up getting more still. It may well move even further from its original intent under pressure from trustees' legal responsibilities.

Similar dynastic considerations must be in the minds of the trustees of the three Ronson Trusts which also indicate a close relationship with their founder. Two of them have perhaps the most valuable but unremunerative investments of any trusts. The three between them would appear to have a controlling interest in Heron International through their massive shareholdings, although Ronson himself puts their holding at 45 per cent (*Jewish Chronicle*, 10 February 1989). In the same article, the Ronson Foundation is attributed with 60 per cent of the group's shares. Heron's ultimate holding company is now Heron International NV which is based in the Netherlands Antilles and estimated to be worth £1 billion, and which made a profit of £55 million in 1988.

The trusts' share holdings keep growing through rights issues, but Heron International has not made a practice of issuing dividends and its shares are not quoted. As *Private Eye* said, 'the charities, purely incidentally, would appear to guarantee Ronson control of Heron International plc under all circumstances short of World War III or a militant takeover of the Conservative Party' (29 November 1987).

The Gerard Ronson Foundation was founded in 1983 to pay the 'income of the trust fund to the Society of Friends of Jewish Refugees in perpetuity'. So far its 28,148,940 common, and 94,251,061 deferred, shares have yet to yield any income, and are valued in the accounts as worth 'NIL'. The Ronson Second Foundation, after some years of inactivity, 'has become active in the last year and has paid out £11,909 in charitable donations' said the stark report for the year ending 1987. To do so, it had to borrow £9,102 since its holdings of 91,800,000 deferred 25p shares in Heron were not productive of income. Indeed the charity *owed* loan repayments of £193,477 that year.

It has to be said that the Ronson Foundation itself did make donations of £507,662 in the year ending March 1987, but they were financed by covenants of £305,883 and loans of £440,000. Income tax recoverable was given as £270,088. Once again, the 61,200,000 deferred Heron International shares did not raise much in the way of income.

'If you are fortunate in life to have the ability to acquire substantial wealth, your responsibility is to put it back into society,' Ronson told the *Jewish Chronicle* (10 February 1989). The accounts filed with the Charity Commissioners do not detail the donations made by the Ronson Foundation, although a stray letter on the file gives a breakdown for 1975 of £152,500 to the Jewish National Fund, £5,000 to the Lubavitch Foundation, £7,000 to the Joint Philanthropic Association for Israel and the Middle East, and £1,000 to Stepney Jewish Clubs.

There has been nothing to stop Heron International making such large donations under covenant and thus securing all due fiscal relief. If posterity is the problem, then there is nothing to stop Mr Ronson leaving large shareholdings to charity after his death. But as it stands, one can but wonder what charitable purpose is served by having several hundred million allegedly worthless shares donated into the public domain.

When approached informally on the principle, two charity commissioners had diametrically opposed views on what could be

done about trusts with disproportionately small charitable activity
in relation to their assets. 'Nothing,' said one, who thought that if
the trust had powers to build up reserves, then no action could be
taken. The other thought that there was indeed possible action, in
that the trustees, albeit in a negative way, were breaching their
trust. The question of charitable ends becomes more acute when
one considers foundations which engage in financial activity
without ever producing charitable donations. The Inland Revenue
can, and does, insist on further and better particulars from charities
which it suspects, but it has its own rules of confidentiality. The
Revenue very rarely prosecutes but comes to arrangements with
what it considers to be lax taxpayers. The fact that an arrangement
is made at all, let alone the details of it, is not a matter which would
normally be publicised.

However, while little action seems to be possible against trusts
guilty of lack of active charity, there are prompt measures available
against those which allow their bleeding hearts to interfere with
money-making. The Attorney-General, in 1988, reminded the
Rowntree Memorial Trust's trustees that holding on to shares in
their founding company was actionable in face of the Nestlé take-
over bid. As it happened, the trust doubled its money to £88
million when it reluctantly sold its stake. It was not loyalty to the
company but to the locality and the workforce which had fuelled
the reluctance to sell. Indeed, the Rowntree Trusts had been at
loggerheads with the company for some years over its southern
African connections.

The reluctance to sell was based upon the effect the trustees
feared on the economy of York. However, if justice is blind, charity
law is blinkered. The trustees could only have regard to the
increased cash, not to the potential social consequences of their
accepting the offer.

The incident epitomised the practice of Rowntree's Trusts which
are a convincing demonstration that charity can be warm and
altruistic. Joseph Rowntree's memorandum to his trustees was a
remarkable document which broke out of the penny-pinching
mould of Victorian philanthropy. He gave over half his holdings
while still alive, which allowed him a degree of experimentation
which would have been denied in a will. The trusts had a
controlling interest in the Rowntree chocolate company, but it was
not intended to be a 'dynastic' trust. The shares were divided
equally between trustees to vote with as they wished, which meant
that only total unanimity among them gave control. He even

specifically asked that fitness rather than consanguinity should be the criterion for appointment of trustees.

Rowntree provided that

> The Charitable Trust is established for purposes which are 'charitable' in the legal sense of the word; the Social Service Trust for purposes which though to my mind at least of equal importance to the well-being of the community, are, as I am advised, mostly outside the limits within which the law at present confines the operations of charitable foundations, and would if included in the former Trust, impair its legal validity. I hope that in future those limits may be considerably widened and that it may be permissible to include among charitable objects those which can only be attained by alterations in the law of the land. (quoted Waddilove, 1983)

The establishment of the Social Service Trust was remarkably prescient. Realising that much of its work would be politically controversial, it avoided harassment by not being a charity. It pays tax on its income but still has half a million pounds a year to distribute. (In fact, in 1988, it paid the Inland Revenue £160,221 (Letter from the JRSST, 3 April 1989).)

The Village Trust was much more in the traditional mode of charity – providing homes – but how un-Victorian and indeed 'un-Enterprise' in its attitudes. The Peabody Trust had forbidden its tenants to have pictures on the wall and required politely servile behaviour from its tenants, but Joseph Rowntree was

> especially desirous that nothing may be done under the powers hereby conferred which may prevent the growth of civic interest and the sense of civic responsibility amongst those who may live in any community existing on the property of the Trust. I should regret if there were anything in the organisation of these village communities that should interfere with the growth of the right spirit of citizenship, or be such that independent and right-minded men and women might resent. I do not want to establish communities bearing the stamp of charity, but rather of rightly ordered and self-governing communities – self governing that is within the broad limits laid down by the Trust.

It is a statement of purpose which contrasts sharply with the cruelty and absurdity of several centuries of case law and of social practice. It is now dangerously radical again because of official reversion to older norms of charity. As Hood had it, 'Alas for the Rarity/Of Christian Charity'.

Conclusion: A Return to Alms

To sum up, there have been two consistently opposing principles in the development of institutional charity from Tudor to Thatcher times. The first is what one could call the Samaritan approach, characterised by empathy for fellow humans. When the Good Samaritan saw the man lying by the wayside, he did not conduct a Means Test nor did he interview the beneficiary to check upon his moral probity. He certainly did not consider the possibility that, by lending a hand, he was crippling his beneficiary's self-reliance. He saw the need, and he acted. (It may be added that Margaret Thatcher's implication that he had 'loadsamoney', and her consequent inference that he would have been unable or unwilling to act unless he had it, must be based on some very obscure apocryphal gospel from Grantham. It is not to be found in the Authorised Version.)

Opposed to Samaritanism is what one could call the Pharisaical approach, characterised by cold sociological motivation, devoid of empathy. Their good intentions pave the road to Hell, down which they have no intention of marching themselves; it is invariably a road built by the powerful and rich for the poor and weak. The Victorian Poor Law Commissioners who stopped funeral knells for paupers, and the modern politicians who want less eligible accommodation for pregnant single mothers show that the Pharisees survived the sack of Jerusalem, and continue to flourish.

Pharisees, whatever their denomination, cannot believe that people could be good without external force; they must be made to be good, whether by government regulation or by economic forces. Of course, Pharisees need not be religious, nor even right wing. The hard, centralising left shows exactly the same determinism, the same lack of faith in individuals' ability to be good unless goaded.

This schism in social attitudes is reflected in the contradictory connotations of charity. On the one hand, it denotes spontaneous altruism; on the other, it includes practices which are barbarously

cruel, no matter how kind the intentions. An outstanding example
was the recent revelation that until the 1960s charities shipped
thousands of children out to Canada and Australia to people the
empire. The children were lied to about their destinations, some
had their identities hidden – none was consulted about his or her
exile. Like many acts perpetrated in the name of charity, it would
not have been possible if the organisers had identified with the
'recipients'. Just as Tawney said of British civil servants, charity
organisers have often lacked 'personal experience of the conditions
of life and habits of thought of those for whose requirements in the
matter of health, housing, education, and economic well-being, they
are engaged in providing' (see p. 69 above).

Charity in its Pharisaical incarnation has at once reflected and
exacerbated some of the worst features of British society. In
education and health, it divided the population into those who
receive because they pay, and those who receive because their
lords and masters deign to give. That whiff of the Poor Law
pervades our public services, our schools and hospitals, in whose
running we have less and less influence. In addition, the public
schools have exercised their own baneful influence under the
broad façade of charity.

But charities have not always been unthinking supporters of the
status quo. Their most effective work has been achieved when they
have sought to goad the conscience of society rather than to
remould the souls of their beneficiaries. Charities have brought the
evils of slavery, homelessness and child poverty to the attention of a
complacent and uncaring establishment. They have forced action
on reluctant governments, and interposed independent voluntary
organisations between the powerless and the powerful.

In doing so charities have in the past, and are likely again in the
future, to press against the limits set them by charity law. However,
there has been little pressure exerted to reform charity law. For
many years those who wished to better the lot of the poor and
dispossessed saw the state as the appropriate means. Charities and
the poor were not 'an effective interest' in the corridors of power.

Now, with the experience of a decade of Thatcherite control to
set against the post-war 'Butskellite' consensus, many socialists are
much less enamoured than they were with the concept of a
powerful, state-reforming society. There is a growing feeling that
Britain, with no constitution, and with a strong tendency to
centralisation, needs alternative centres of power to counterbalance
those of the State. There is also a realisation that public sector

professionals, backed by the authority of the State, have often disenfranchised those they nominally serve. As Raymond Plant (1988, p. 13) said, 'Providing a base of entitlement and empowerment in the welfare field means challenging many of the professional producer interest groups in the public sector. Clearly the empowerment of the citizen as consumer will involve a limitation of the power and scope of professional groups such as social workers, doctors, teachers and social security officials.'

Like a growing number of socialists, Plant sees the citizen's ability to choose between service providers as a means of exercising power – and the voluntary sector as an important agent in that 'empowerment'. Indeed, there is a role beyond that of service provision: independent voluntary organisations, backed by an involved and active citizenry, can have direct political and social influence to counter an overweening state. What is more, unlike most other interest groups – unions, professional associations, or employers' organisations – voluntary groups can represent the people who are normally disenfranchised in the power-broking which fuels social processes. Better still, they may motivate ordinary people to take responsibility for their own lives – often from bureaucrats and elected officials who have been loath to let it go.

Margaret Simey, who wrote about the charities of Victorian Liverpool and their effect on the dispossessed, discovered a degree of alienation during the Toxteth Riots of 1981 which surprised even her, who had lived in the area for over half a century. She concluded, 'The imperative of the future lies in finding some other means of ensuring the universal right of the individual to be a responsible member of the society in which we find ourselves. It is our common deprivation of that right which results in the social disintegration of today' (1988, p. 8).

Echoing Melville, she wrote that the people of Toxteth had 'survived circumstances of life far beyond the comprehension of those who sit in judgement on them'. But her leap beyond the Victorian conception is clear, 'the nineteenth-century tradition of voluntary service as a perquisite of the leisured must be drastically redefined and enlarged so that it becomes a universal right of citizenship' (ibid., p. 123). That desirable end is inhibited by the existing charity laws, whose basic premises are in complete antithesis to that degree of social enfranchisement.

The Status Quo – or Raising the Ante?

In considering solutions, the first question is how to reconcile the independence of the voluntary sector, which is its most positive aspect, with sufficient regulation to stop social and fiscal abuse. The second question is much more difficult: namely, what is an abuse? In the trade-off between regulation and independence, the social and political questions are the most problematic. The opening of accounts to more detailed public scrutiny, and increased powers for the Charity Commission to deal with financial abuse are both elementary and unexceptionable measures proposed in the 1989 White Paper. Yet what of the customs and practices which have crept in over the centuries which many regard as moral abuses, even if they are legal. The most obvious examples are those charities which effectively exclude the poor, such as the public schools and private charitable hospitals, and which reflect an in-built social bias in charity law apparent even to those who administer it (see p. 93 above).

Less apparent, however, is the social bias in the law which comes from treating beneficiaries as passive recipients, and seeing their active participation in organisations as not charitable. The dim view of 'self-help' organisations, taken together with the doctrine against political activity, reinforces the passive role of the poor and underprivileged.

The denial of the privileges and protection of charitable status to organisations seeking to help the poor in ways which involve organisation or political campaigning stands in sharp contrast to the law's leniency in fields with goals more acceptable to the status quo. In this context, the definition of charity has more than just a semantic significance, as the considerable efforts of the public schools to retain charitable status indicate.

Yet all attempts to reform charity law, to extend or restrict its privileges, run into a barrier of legal stone-walling. In an elective dictatorship without basic law, a convenient convention has developed that charity law is as unalterable as the laws of the Medes and Persians. The most frequently voiced objection to change is that redefinition would involve the withdrawal of the status from existing charities. But, as we have seen, this was done with equanimity in the case of the Humanists and the Anti-Vivisection League. Indeed, the Humanist societies had their status withdrawn despite a promise that existing registrations would not be affected after the 1960 Charities Act.

Therefore, giving the Charity Commission more powers under the present rules and definitions of charity could lead to serious restrictions on organisations which are in any way 'anti-establishment', such as those activist bodies responsible for most of the social advances which charities have achieved. However, the law governing, and circumscribing, their activities was mostly made with the wills of the dead rather than with the welfare of the living in the mind of the judiciary. The law's assumptions were made in entirely different social circumstances, and as previous chapters sought to prove, those assumptions are élitist and stifle popular initiative.

The law's distaste of political activity by ordinary people contrasts sharply with its indulgence for religions, animals, and think tanks The principle that charity must be of benefit to the poor, restated throughout the precedents, loses its practical application when the public schools and private hospitals are considered. The result is that the only consistent principle discernible in the definitions over the centuries is the preservation of the status quo ante. Indeed, charity law has yet to reconcile itself with the universal franchise.

The complexities of the law preclude any attempt to lay down a blueprint, but some conclusions follow naturally from earlier chapters. The disestablishment of the Church is naturally desirable (and even likely, for the wrong reasons, if bishops wilfully continue to sermonise against the government. A prime minister undeterred by the barrister's wig is unlikely to quail before the bishop's mitre).

More specifically, the first anomaly to be addressed is why bodies peddling philosophical convictions derived from supernatural premises can remain charities, while bodies wanting to promulgate philosophical and political doctrines derived from lay principles cannot. As Ben Whitaker concluded, charitable status should be accorded to both or neither. If both, then the privileges should, of course, be conditional upon the production of detailed and satisfactory accounts. (It would be interesting to see whether the Conservative Party would prefer financial confidentiality to the tax relief available to charities if charitable status were available to it.)

The recognition of a category of 'Non-Profit Distributing Organisations', as advocated by the Charity Law Reform Committee, would be a clean sword sweep through the tangled Gordian knot of definitions. Combined with provisions ensuring public accessibility, this would allow most, if not all, of the existing charities to continue in their privileges. More importantly, it offers prospects to boost popular involvement in civic life. However, even these partial solutions need the sector to be liberated from the restraints imposed by judges over the centuries in their attempts to legitimise existing privilege, which is why this book has spent so much time on the legal and institutional details.

The purpose of this book has not been to draw up blueprints for a new edifice. First, it is intended to look at charity from an outsider's point of view and thus to puncture some of the official Panglossianism which surrounds the sector. Secondly, it is intended to provoke socialists to look at a sector which exemplifies so many of the problems, past and present, of society, yet also offers solutions to some of the dilemmas socialists face as the twentieth century draws to a close in which raw capitalism seems to be triumphant: how to offer the choice of the market and the security of the Welfare State; how to achieve economic justice without creating dependency; and how to promote social and political equality without state coercion. All these are problems to which the voluntary sector offers both some solutions and many negative examples. If this book provokes further exploration of the sector, then it will have achieved its purpose. If it hastens the types of reform considered, then it will have overfulfilled its plan!

Bibliography

Adam Smith Institute (1989) *Wiser Counsels: The Reform of Local Government*, ASI, London.
Adam Smith Institute (1989) *Needs Reform: The Overhaul of Social Security*, ASI, London.
Allen C. K. (1964) *Law in the Making*, Oxford University Press, Oxford.
Atack, John (1989) *A Piece of Blue Sky*, Lyle Stuart, New York.
Birch, A. H. (1967) *The British System of Government*, Allen & Unwin, London.
Boyle, W. R. A. (1837) *A Practical Treatise on the Law of Charities*, Saunders & Benning, London.
British Parliamentary Papers, Nineteenth Century, House of Commons, London.
Buzzacott & Co. (1989) *Charities and Business*, Buzzacott, London.
Charities (1989) *A Framework for the Future* (White Paper), HMSO, London.
Charities Aid Foundation (1988) *The Give as You Earn Directory of Charities*, CAF, Tonbridge.
Charity Commissioners (CC) (1968–88) *Annual Reports of the Charity Commissioners for England and Wales*, HMSO, London.
Chesterman, Michael (1979) *Charities, Trusts, and Social Welfare*, Weidenfield & Nicolson, London.
Cobbet, William (1811) *Parliamentary Histories*, vol. IX.
Cook, Robin (1988) *Life Begins at 40 – In Defence of the NHS*, Fabian Society, London.
Dictionary of National Biography (1896) Oxford University Press, Oxford.
Eckstein, F. (1959) *The English Health Service*, Oxford University Press, Oxford.
Field, Frank (1982) *Poverty and Politics*, Heinemann, London.
FitzHerbert, Luke and Eastwood, Michael (1989) *A Guide to the Major Trusts*, Directory of Social Change, London.
Fleming, Lord (1944) *The Public Schools (Fleming Report)*, HMSO, London.
Gallagher, J. P. (1975) *The Price of Charity*, Robert Hale, London.
Garratt, G. T. (1935) *Lord Brougham*, Macmillan, London.
Gathorne-Hardy, Jonathan (1977) *The Public School Phenomenon 597–1977*, Hodder & Stoughton, London.
Gillard, Michael (1987) *In the Name of Charity*, Chatto & Windus, London.
Gladstone, Francis (1979) *Voluntary Action in a Changing World*, Bedford Square Press, London.

Gladstone, Francis (1982) *Charity, Law, and Social Justice*, Bedford Square Press, London.

Goodman, Lord (1976) *Charity Law and Voluntary Organisations (Goodman Committee Report)*, Bedford Square Press, London.

Griggs, Clive (1985) *Private Education in Britain*, Falmer Press, London.

Guthrie, Robin (1988) *Charity and the Nation*, Fifth Arnold Goodman Lecture, CAF, London.

Halsbury's Laws of England (1974) Butterworth, London.

Hay, D., Linebaugh, P., Rule, J., Thompson E. P. and Winslow C. (1977) *Albion's Fatal Tree*, Penguin Books, Harmondsworth.

Hill, Christopher (1968) *Puritanism and Revolution*, Panther, London.

Hill, Christopher (1969) *Reformation to Industrial Revolution*, Penguin Books, Harmondsworth.

Hill, Christopher (1972) *Intellectual Origins of the English Revolution*, Granada, London.

Hill, Christopher (1975) *The World Turned Upside Down*, Penguin Books, Harmondsworth.

Hill, C. P. (1966) *A Guide for Charity Trustees*, Faber, London.

Hounam, Peter and Hogg, Andrew (1985) *The Secret Cult* Lion, Tring.

House of Commons Expenditure Committee (1975) *Tenth Report*, HMSO, London.

Inglis, Brian (1972) *Poverty and the Industrial Revolution*, Granada, London.

ISIS (1987) *Fact Pack*, Independent Schools Information Service, London.

ISIS (1988) *Annual Census, 1988. Statistical Survey of Independent Schools*, Independent Schools Information Service, London.

Jones, Gareth (1969) *History of the Law of Charity, 1532–1827*, Cambridge University Press, Cambridge.

Jordan, W. K. (1959) *Philanthropy in England, 1480–1660*, Allen & Unwin, London.

Kamen, Henry (1976) *The Iron Century*, Sphere Books, London.

Keeton, George W. (1949) 'The Charity Muddle', *Current-Legal Problems*.

Keeton, George W. (1962) *The Modern Law of Charities*, Pitman, London.

Labour Party, (1980) *Private Schools*, Labour Party, London.

Lamont, Stewart (1986) *Religion Inc.: The Church of Scientology*, Harrap, London.

Lane, Tony (1987) *Liverpool, Gateway of Empire*, Lawrence & Wishart, London.

Lehn, Walter and Davies, Uri (1988) *The Jewish National Fund*, Kegan Paul International, London.

Lester, A. and Pannick, D. (1987) *Independent Schools: The Legal Case*, ISIS, London.

Lester, Joan and Ward, David (1987) *Beyond Band Aid*, Fabian Society, London.

Liverpool Black Caucus (1986) *The Racial Politics of Militant in Liverpool*, Runnymede Trust, London.

Liverpool Central Relief and Charity Organisation Society (1864) *Annual Report, 1863–4*, LCRCOS, Liverpool.

Liverpool Domestic Mission (1838, 1855) *Annual Reports*, LDM, Liverpool.

McDonald, Alan (1986) *The Weller Way*, Faber, London.

McQuillan, Judith (1986) *Charity Statistics, 1985–86*, 9th annual edn, Charities Aid Foundation, Tonbridge.
McQuillan, Judith (ed.) (1988) *Charity Trends*, 11th edn, Charities Aid Foundation, Tonbridge.
Miller, Russell (1987) *Bare-faced Messiah*, Michael Joseph, London.
Nathan, Lord (1952) *Report of the Committee on the Law and Practice Relating to Charitable Trusts, (Nathan Committee)*, HMSO, London.
Nightingale, Benedict (1973) *Charities*, Allen Lane, London.
Norman, Lady (1952) *Voluntary Service and the State*, National Council for Social Service, London.
Norton, Michael (ed.) *Company Charitable Giving: 1987 Statistics*, Directory of Social Change, London.
Norton, Michael (1986) *A Guide to Company Giving 1986–87*, Directory of Social Change, London.
Picarda, H. (1977) *The Law and Practice Relating to Charities*, Butterworth, London.
Plant, Raymond (1988) *Citizenship, Rights and Socialism*, Fabian Society, 1988.
Prochaska, Frank (1988) *The Voluntary Impulse*, Faber, London.
Rentoul, John (1987) *The Rich Get Richer*, Pluto, London.
Rentoul, John (1989) *Me & Mine*, Unwin Hyman, London.
Ross, James Stirling (1952) *The National Health Service in Great Britain*, Oxford University Press, Oxford.
Salamon, Lester (1985) 'Government and the Voluntary Sector in an Era of Retrenchment, *Journal of Public Policy*, vol. no. 6, pp. I, 1–20.
Salamon, Lester (1987) 'Of Market Failure: Voluntary Failure and Third-Party Government', *Journal of Voluntary Action Research*, vol. 16, nos. 1, 2 (January, June).
Salter, Brian and Tapper, Ted (1985) *Power and Policy in Education*, Falmer Press, London.
Sheridan, L. A. and Keeton, George (1983) *The Modern Law of Charities* University College Cardiff Press, Cardiff.
Simey, Margaret (1951) *Charitable Effort in Liverpool in the Nineteenth Century*, Liverpool University Press, Liverpool.
Simey, Margaret (1985) *Government by Consent*, Bedford Square Press, London.
Simey, Margaret (1988) *Democracy Rediscovered*, Pluto, London.
Swainson, Anthony with Zeff, Linda (1987) *Please Give Generously*, David & Charles, Newton Abbot.
Tarbet, E. M. (1956) *An Account of Some of the Legal Recommendations of the Committee on the Law and Practice Relating to Charitable Trusts*, May, unpublished thesis, Liverpool University.
Tawney, R. H. (1966) *The Radical Tradition*, Penguin Books, Harmondsworth.
Thompson, E. P. (1968) *The Making of the English Working Class*, Penguin Books, Harmondsworth.
Tudor, O.D. (1984) *Tudor on Charities*, 7th edn, Sweet & Maxwell, London.
Tutt, Nigel (1985) *The Tax Raiders*, Financial Training Publications, London.
Waddilove, Lewis E. (1983) *Private Philanthropy and Public Welfare*, Allen & Unwin, London.

Webb, Beatrice (1938) *My Apprenticeship*, Penguin, Harmondsworth.
The Wellcome Trust (1986) *50 Years of the Wellcome Trust, 1936–1986*, Wellcome, London.
Whitaker, Ben (1979) *The Foundations*, Pelican, Harmondsworth.
Wilson, Des (1970) *I Know It Was the Place's Fault*, Oliphants, London.
Woodfield, Sir Philip (1987) *Efficiency Scrutiny of the Supervision of Charities*, HMSO, London.
Working for Patients (1989) (Health White Paper), HMSO, London.
Young, Hugo (1989) *One of Us*, Macmillan, London.

Index